Of All That Is, Seen and Unseen

Seen and Unseen

Life-Saving Answers to Life-Size Questions

By
Dr. Gerard M. Verschuuren

Queenship

PUBLISHING COMPANY
P.O. Box 220 • Goleta, CA 93116
(800) 647-9882 • (805) 692-0043 • Fax: (805) 967-5133
www.queenship.org

NIHIL OBSTAT
Rev. Thomas Hoisington
Censor Librorum, Diocese of Wichita

IMPRIMATUR
Michael O. Jackels
Bishop of Wichita

Scripture quotations have been taken from the Revised Standard Version of the Holy Bible, Second Catholic Edition, © 2006
Quotations from the Catechism of the Catholic Church can be found on http://www.vatican.va/archive/

Library of Congress Number # 2012938578

Published by:

Queenship Publishing
P.O. Box 220 • Goleta, CA 93116
(800) 647-9882 • (805) 692-0043 • Fax: (805) 967-5133
www.queenship.org

Printed in the United States of America

ISBN: 978-1-57918-414-8

Dedicated to
Blessed Pope John Paul II,
staunch defender of faith and reason,
and to all those in search of the truth

Table of Contents

Preface

In his January 24, 2012 letter, entitled *Silence and Word: Path of Evangelization*, Pope Benedict XVI expressed his deep concern for the new evangelization efforts of the Catholic Church. He wrote: "faith is in danger of being put out, as a flame that finds no more fuel. We find ourselves before a profound crisis of faith, before a loss of the religious sense, that is the greatest challenge for today's Church."

It is my intense hope that this book may provide some fuel for the dwindling flame of our faith. It was specifically written for Catholics – fallen-away Catholics, lukewarm Catholics, struggling Catholics, would-be Catholics – for all those in search of the truth, as it gives life-saving answers to life-size questions. In this book I want to promote religious and Catholic literacy, which is dwindling more than ever in our society, in our culture, and even in our Church. It belongs basically to the genre of apologetics, evangelization, and catechization, thoroughly rooted in the Catholic tradition, with a mild philosophical touch based on the tradition of St. Thomas Aquinas.

This book is about our Maker, who is the Creator of all that is, seen and unseen, of all that is, visible and invisible. There is so much more in God's creation than what can be seen and captured by our senses. It is through the eyes of faith that we can discern much more than what we can touch, sense, hear, see, taste, or smell – in short, much more than what can be counted, measured, or quantified. Our Catholic faith reminds us that in fact more important than what can be seen is what is un-seen. There is a whole world that eludes our senses. The invisible is actually the cornerstone of all that is visible. And God is part of that unseen world, for no one has ever seen God (1 Jn 4:12), except in His Son Jesus.

In the chapters to come, we will see what this entails for our Catholic faith. Each chapter can be used as a guideline for discussions and seminars; each chapter can be read independently (that is why there are some repetitions). This makes the book also a perfect tool for the new evangelization. Because it has basically a format of question-and-answer, the text tries to engage its readers and users even more. Call it a form of catechization if you will – teaching us the principles of Catholic dogma, discipline, and ethics by means of questions and answers.

1. In chapter one, we will discuss the scary phenomenon that many of us are living in a society that has lost sight of what is unseen. If God cannot be seen, then there cannot be a God – such is the core message of atheism. Lately, our society and culture have been inundated with atheism. It comes in many disguises and through various messengers. As a matter of fact, there are some very vocal atheists who use mass media such as books, the internet, television, etc. to spread their new "religion." They seem to feel empowered from "on high" to declare to the whole world that there is no God, and that they are His prophets. Atheists like to take God's seat on the very throne that they had declared vacant. How can we heal ourselves from this highly contagious disease? The first rule is: Know your enemies!

2. Partly as a result of this modern mind-set, we get constantly bombarded with slogans telling us that what can be seen is all there is, that we are only what is visible in us and around us – that we are nothing more than a collection of atoms, molecules, genes, cells, neurons, and what have you. That is the issue to be discussed in chapter two of this book: Is there still space in our lives for what cannot be seen?

3. That takes us to the problem that science seems to have prepared all of the above by pushing religion into a fading territory. In chapter three, we will find out whether there is any space left for religion in an increasingly scientific world. Perhaps to your surprise, it turns out that the Catholic Church has a long history of dealing with science, and of actually promoting scientific investigation and exploration. Therefore, science and religion are not – or at least should not – be in competition with each other. Could the science of what is visible ever live in harmony with the faith in what is invisible? The answer is a definite yes:

Catholicism has this unique blend of faith-and-reason, religion-and-science, which allows the two of them to live together in harmony. Science should never silence religion, or vice-versa. Let's teach science, but not preach it – that is the message of this chapter.

4. Once science comes into the picture, we can no longer avoid the question as to whether the science of evolution is compatible with the Catholic belief that we were created by God. That is the main issue of chapter four in this book – evolution. I know this a very contentious issue in religion, but I do not want to leave it out, for there is hardly any school or college left where they do not teach evolutionary theory and some kind of Darwinism. How do Catholics deal with this? Is there a conflict between evolution and creation? If one is true, does that mean the other is false? Or are both perhaps possible? The answer may surprise you. Creation explains *why* evolution happens, whereas evolution explains *how* creation happens. We may have come here through evolution, and yet we came here from God – in the same way as our children come through us but not from us. In other words, don't loose your faith over evolution.

5. This chapter is about the human mind and soul. For those who do believe in evolution, humanity seems to have lost its dignity as a result. Some say we received our brains from the animal world, so we are nothing more than glorified animals. Catholics, for their part, will counter that a human being also has a soul with a mind. So the question is whether there is still space left for an invisible soul in a visible body. Is there really an invisible mind behind a visible brain? Chapter five will show us that the brain may be a product of evolution, but the mind and soul are gifts of creation. The human mind, including its rational intellect, does not come from our anatomy or physiology. We will even discover that, without God, we have no longer any reason to trust our intellect.

6. And yet, the visible world seems to have a strong grip on our lives. We seem to be under the control of genes, in the iron grip of DNA – which calls into question whether the freedom God

has given us, according to our Catholic faith, still has a foot to stand on. In chapter six, we will see how pre-determined we really are and where our God-given freedom comes in. The bottom-line is: Our (role) model is in Heaven, not on earth. So it shouldn't surprise us that atheists have been trying very hard to destroy the human image – since it is made in God's image. To those who say that the brain creates God, I would counter that it is God who created the brain.

7. Not only our rationality but also our morality has come under attack from various sides. How do we as Catholics respond? Do we retract to our new catacombs, the church pews? Or do we speak up and remind everyone how much Christianity, and more in particular the Catholic Church with her strong moral values, has contributed to our civilization? In chapter seven, we will discuss the contentious issue of morality. As it turns out, not only does our society have deep Judeo-Christian roots, but also do we owe most of our achievements – education, healthcare, science and technology – to the teachings of Jesus and His Catholic Church. However, we are not moral by nature; morality has to be taught and nurtured, above all by the teaching authority of the Church. Without God, we have no right to claim any rights. If rights really came from men, and not God, men could take them away anytime – and they certainly have tried many times.

8. The main pillars of Judeo-Christian morality are the Ten Commandments. Chapter eight shows us how these Commandments keep us on a straight path, from which so many people tend to deviate. They are vital for our society, although the Supreme Court has ruled that it is illegal to display them in public schools. Yet, the Ten Commandments are chiseled into the facade of the Supreme Court building, at the very place where this ruling was made! Well, not only did those vital Ten Commandments lose their prominent position on the walls of our court houses (your tax dollars at work), but even – what is much worse – "on the walls" of our conscience. What is at stake here? The answer is short and snappy: our eternal salvation!

9. Then there is at least one more topic that needs to be addressed in a book like this – because it touches the core of our Catholic faith – and that is the problem of evil, including suffering and death. Evil has been one of the strongest obstacles for Judeo-Christian faith. To put it in a nutshell: How does an all-powerful God get away with the evil in the world? If God is not able to take evil away, God cannot be all-powerful. And if God is really all-powerful, there shouldn't be any evil. Or should there? Chapter nine will try to deal with this haunting mystery.

You might think there is too much about science in this book. If you find that the case, the reason for this is quite simple: Science seems to take our sense of reality down several notches. If human life has lost significance for many of us, science – or rather the way we perceive science – is to be blamed for a large part. If abortion has become of no great concern or if embryonic stem cell research has gained unquestioned support, that is because science tends to look at embryos as a mere cluster of cells or a bunch of molecules. Although science has given us many blessings, if overstated, it can be misconstrued as an alternative for religion. In other words, we cannot talk about religion without dealing with the seemingly rising power of science that tends to obscure most of what matters in life.

You probably also think that all these issues together are quite a bit for such a simple book to contend with. It is up to you to decide whether it actually succeeds in its purpose, but I hope and pray that this book may give you back the strong foundation Catholicism has to offer. St. Ambrose once compared the Church with the Moon: When she is waning, she will be waxing again. Jesus Christ, our Savior, spoke of the rock on which He would build His Church, and He promised that the gates of Hell would not overcome it (Mt. 16:18). My advice to you would be this: Let no acid eat away the foundation that is underneath *your* life, for only God has life-saving answers for your life-size questions.

Acknowledgements

I wish to express my gratitude to those nameless who steered and corrected me in the long process of preparation for this book. In particular, I want to mention Bishop Carlos A. Sevilla, S.J., of the diocese of Yakima, WA, Francisco Ayala of the University of California at Irvine, Fr. Marcel Chappin, S.J., of the Pontifical Gregorian University in Rome, Peter Kreeft of Boston College, the late Fr. Marius Jeuken, S.J., of Leyden University in the Netherlands, and last but not least David Schaefer from Queenship Publishing. Obviously, they are not responsible for the outcome or for the parts they helped me with; if I erred, it is entirely my doing. They and many others make me realize that originality only consists in the capacity of forgetting about your sources.

And – as with all my books – I could not have written this book without the unwavering, prayerful, and loving support of my wife, Trudy. And then I pray there has been one more actor behind the façade of this book – the Holy Spirit.

1

The Avalanche of Atheism

A Cancerous Cult

Atheism comes in many disguises.

1. I do not *know* if God exists.
2. I find any God-talk *non-sense*.
3. I know there is *no* God.
4. I cannot *prove* there is a God.
5. I never *see* or experience God.
6. I do not *dare* to believe in God.
7. I declare God to be *beyond* my reach.
8. I do not *need* to believe in God.
9. I do not *trust* any belief in God.
10. I cannot believe there is a *just* God.
11. I just never *think* of God.
12. I *hate* any belief in God.

A reply (R) to various forms of atheism (A).

A: I do not *know* if God exists.

R: This version is called agnosticism – a word that Thomas H. Huxley invented; he described it as "not a creed but a method." Sounds harmless, doesn't it? Agnosticism asserts that we just do not know whether God does exist or not, and what is worse, we have no way of ever knowing one way or the other (but perhaps after we die). So this version is not really atheism in the strict sense, for it also says that we have no knowledge that God does *not* exist. It just keeps us in limbo, and therefore refuses to give God the honor and worship He deserves as our Maker.

How come there are so many agnostics, especially in science? Agnostics swear by logic, and they claim that logic cannot demonstrate the *falsity* of a belief in God (it is said to be an unbeatable, unverifiable hypothesis), but neither can it demonstrate the *truth* of a belief in God (it is said to be a daring, undecided hypothesis). The latter part explains why the French astronomer Pierre-Simon Laplace is often quoted in this context. When given a copy of his latest book, Napoleon Bonaparte received it with the remark, "They tell me you have written this large book on the system of the universe, and have never even mentioned its Creator." Laplace answered bluntly, "I had no need of that hypothesis."

What to make of Laplace's remark? First of all, I hate to ever call God a hypothesis that we stumbled upon or needed in our scientific endeavors. Second, I do agree that logic may not be the best tool to prove that God does or does not exist. G.K. Chesterton once said, "Atheism is the most daring of all dogmas, for it is the assertion of a universal negative." Chesterton is right; it is much easier to establish that there is a black swan somewhere on the earth than to prove that there isn't one at all. We may perhaps validly conclude that God is unknown (as agnosticism asserts), but it is very hard, if not logically impossible, to conclude that God is in fact absent (as atheism claims). It is just impossible to close a search for God with the conclusion that there is *no* God. No searches ever conclusively reveal the *absence* of their object. (Likewise, it is impossible to prove that some accident has *no* cause at all; the real cause may still be eluding us – and so may God.) On the other hand, I do think that we may be able to reveal the very *presence* of God, although probably never in a conclusive way. We will go into this debate later when we discuss other forms of atheism.

Agnosticism may appear to be pretty harmless, but very often agnostics do have a rather negative selective attitude towards religion and religious people in particular – they just declare them "stupid." Agnostics think that their own logic is so compelling that everyone who disagrees with their agnostic conclusions must be misinformed or just brainless. To be fair, I must point out that there are also agnostics who say they do not *know* of the existence of any deity, but still *believe* in God's existence. I wouldn't call those people atheists, though, in the strict sense.

Is it really "not a creed but a method," as Huxley pretended? True, as a method, it boils down to a "philosophy of the Unknowable," but very often it excludes only *religious* truth from the domain of knowledge. In contrast, the Catholic Church declares that "God, the beginning and end of all, can, by the natural light of human reason, be known with certainty from the works of creation" (Vatican I, *Const. De Fide, II, De Rev.*). The Bible testifies that "The heavens are telling the glory of God" (Ps. 19:1) and that God "did not leave himself without witness" as Saint Paul worded it (Acts 14:17), and that "since the creation of the world his invisible nature, namely, his eternal power and deity, has been clearly perceived in the things that have been made" (Rom 1:20).

Whatever way you want to define agnosticism, it should be criticized as a limitation of the mind's capacity to know reality. First of all, we do have plentiful evidence of God's existence that He has placed in His creation, as we will demonstrate in the chapters to come. Catholic philosophers such as Peter Kreeft from Boston College point out, though, that agnosticism's demand for scientific evidence through laboratory testing is in effect asking God, the Supreme Being, to become our servant. Such philosophers argue that the question of God should be treated differently from other knowable objects in that this question regards not that which is *below* us, but that which is *above* us.

Second, Pope Benedict XVI accuses agnosticism of limiting itself in claiming the power of reason to know *scientific* truth only, at the exclusion of religious or philosophical truths; besides, it is contradictory as agnosticism in itself is not a scientific truth either. Therefore, he considers agnosticism a choice of comfort, pride, dominion, and utility over truth, over self-criticism, humble listening to the whole of existence, a readiness to be purified by the truth.

Third, each day in a person's life is an unavoidable step towards death – and therefore, *not* to decide for or against God, who is the all-encompassing foundation, purpose, and meaning of life, is essentially a decision in favor of atheism. The nearest atheists ever get to a spiritual experience is their own death.

The *Catechism of the Catholic Church* (CCC) summarizes all of this as follows: "Agnosticism can sometimes include a certain search for God, but it can equally express indifferentism, a flight from the ultimate question of existence, and a sluggish moral conscience. Agnosticism is all too often equivalent to practical atheism" (CCC 2128). Agnosticism tends to stifle the religious sense engraved in the depths of our nature.

During the 2011 Assisi gathering with some 300 religious representatives, Pope Benedict XVI gave an unexpected twist to agnosticism by acknowledging that agnostics are still engaged in a quest for God. He said that the inability of agnostics to find God is "partly the responsibility of believers with a limited or even falsified image of God. So all their struggling and questioning is in part an appeal to believers to purify their faith, so that God, the true God, becomes accessible." Let's try to do so in the rest of this book.

A: I find any God-talk *non-sense*.

R: This viewpoint has been taken by some philosophers who consider any talk about God a violation of the use of common language. Whereas agnosticism regards God-talk unverifiable but nonetheless meaningful, this form of atheism maintains that, if unverifiable, God-talk is *ipso facto* meaningless. Language is supposed to be either empirical (dealing with facts, like in science) or logical (adhering to rules, like in logic and mathematics), otherwise it is considered a nonsensical abuse of language.

In this view, religious talk about God would be neither empirical nor logical. One can say that the *root* of a plant absorbs nutrients (an empirical statement), or that the *root* of four is two (a logical statement), but the statement that the root of a plant is two amounts to non-sense, as it violates the rules of language by mixing up two different kinds of using language. And the same presumably holds for God-talk – it is neither true nor false, but simply meaningless. As a consequence, we should, in the words of the Austrian philosopher Ludwig Wittgenstein, be silent about that which we cannot say – or in his own words, "Whereof one cannot speak, thereof one must be silent." The limits of language are supposed to be the limits of thought. Period!

I do not think this is a serious form of atheism nowadays, but it used to be rather popular among members of philosophical schools that are called positivism, logical-positivism, and language-analysis – and they had quite some impact in scientific circles. The fundamental problem with approaches like these is that they determine ahead of time the outcome they like to see. They define what is legitimate by making sure they exclude what they do not *wish* to be legitimate. And besides, you wonder whether this claim in itself is either logical or empirical – or just meaningless... Some people just have this contemptuous habit of dismissing as meaningless those concepts whose meanings elude them.

Currently, many have come to realize that religious discourse cannot be mere nonsensical babble. How could religious people ever disagree about what is considered non-sense? Isn't religion constantly dealing with disputes, dogmas, creeds, schisms, and heresies? How would disagreements on such issues ever be possible if religious talk were mere non-sense? There must be some mutual understanding here; otherwise religious people would have no idea as to where they disagree.

This fact has some important and perhaps unexpected consequences, though. When religious people talk to each other, they should always say what they mean and mean what they say. If they do not, there could never be any sensible communication in religion. Saint Paul puts it very bluntly, "I will pray with the spirit and I will pray with the mind also; I will sing with the spirit and I will sing with the mind also. Otherwise, if you bless with the spirit, how can any one in the position of an outsider say the 'Amen' to your thanksgiving when he does not know what you are saying?" (1 Cor. 14:15-16). Even "speaking in the spirit" should never convey non-sense according to St. Paul.

Well, the story doesn't end here, as it got an unexpected twist. The very Wittgenstein I mentioned earlier came to realize the narrow-mindedness of his original views and broadened them considerably later on in life. In addition, he said once he hoped his Catholic friends would pray for him. Well, they did at his death bed; he died shortly afterwards and was given a Catholic burial at St. Giles's Church of Cambridge in England. You never know what you are in for when you are an atheist.

A: I know there is *no* God.

R: And then we have those atheists who are very definite and sure there is no God. Where on earth do they get this profound knowledge and certainty from, I always wonder.

Somehow, they are "positively" sure that God does *not* exist because they adhere faithfully to the doctrines of positivism, empiricism, and scientism. You will find this kind of atheism especially in books of scientists such as Richard Dawkins, Daniel Dennett, E.O. Wilson, Peter Higgs, Carl Sagan, Peter Atkins, Francis Crick, Peter Singer, and Sam Harris, who have declared a jihad against religion by abusing science for their own ideological agenda. The list of names could go on and on.

What do they have in common? They are "devout atheists." I consider them the "missionaries" of atheism, who want you to *believe* that believing in God is just impossible because science has shown us so! The declaration *"I know there is no God"* has become their new creed. These atheists like to sit on God's throne that they had declared vacant and then publicize their own absolute decrees.

I think their view is best summarized by the title of one of Dawkins' popular books – *The God Delusion*. That is what God is in accordance with their view – no longer non-sense, but a delusion instead. How did they come to the conclusion of a delusion? As I stressed already, they are mainly scientists, or at least people who have full and exclusive confidence in science. How does science make them think this way?

These atheists have actually taken on the ideology of *scientism* – which is a dogmatic "creed" stating that science provides the only valid way of finding truth, thus eliminating everything that cannot be counted and measured. They claim that "the real world" is a world of quantified entities. Their trust is entirely in science, without any trust in God. Curiously enough, they maintain that science is the only way of achieving valid knowledge, but they seem to be unaware of the fact that scientism itself does not follow its own rule. How could science ever prove on its own that science is the only way of finding truth? There is no experiment that could do the trick! Scientism is therefore a baseless, unscientific claim that can only be made from *outside* the scientific realm, thus grossly overstepping the boundaries of science. It steps outside science to claim that there is nothing outside science. Scientism declares everything outside science as a despicable form of metaphysics, without realizing that anyone who rejects metaphysics can only do so on metaphysical grounds. So what is this claim based on then? Quicksand – or some form of "faith" at the best – I would say.

Nonetheless, these atheists keep promoting their dogma of scientism, which includes the dogma that there are no dogmas. As a consequence, they acknowledge only one territory – the territory of science. Whatever it is that science gains must therefore be at the cost of religion. In their view, scientific expansion means religious withdrawal – so religion must be on its way out whenever science advances.

But that is exactly where the misconception lies. Science doesn't gain territory at all, but it just learns more and more details about its own fixed territory – which is the domain of all that can be counted and measured. The rest is not part of its territory but was given away for other "authorities" to handle. Sorry, scientists, keep your scientific hands off of the religious domain! I do agree with these atheists, though, that if science doesn't go to its limits, it is a failure, but I must add: As soon as science *oversteps* its limits, it becomes arrogant – a know-it-all. Science should never forget that it is "blind" for many other aspects of life. In chapter three, we will discuss this issue more in depth.

Therefore, I go back to the question as to what entitles these atheists to declare God a delusion. I do not see any valid reason whatsoever, because science cannot possibly reach God. God is outside its scope, just as everything else that is unseen and cannot be counted or measured is outside its scope. What an arrogance these atheists show when they claim universal validity for local successes in science – in defiance of the fact that the astonishing successes of science have not been gained by answering every kind of question, but precisely by refusing to do so. That is why there's no reason for megalomania in science. Always keep asking for "the rest of the story," that science is "blind" for.

In other words, I find the arguments pleading in favor of this kind of atheism so poor that they actually give atheism a bad name (please take this as a yoke!). Yet, these atheists have gathered huge crowds of "faithful" followers – partly because of their very influential books that have sold millions of copies all over the world. They abuse their scientific expertise to make you think they are experts in everything else too. They are like plumbers trying to also fix your electricity. I think they are asking a lot of "faith" from their followers. Too much unwarranted faith for me...

A: I cannot *prove* there is a God.

R: The form of atheism we are discussing next demands full-proof certainty. We found out earlier that it is hard, if not impossible, to prove that there is *no* God, but it is equally hard to prove the opposite – that there *is* a God. So atheists seem to have found a safe strategy for victory. Do they?

Some philosophers believe one can prove things beyond any doubt in a way that is either empirical or logical. I will discuss these two approaches separately. Let's start with the *empirical* side.

Atheists in this category would declare that empirical proofs are impossible in religion, because God is certainly not measurable, quantifiable, or touchable. I would say they have a point here. Does this mean, though, that religion is based on a phantom world floating like a castle in mid-air, vanishing into thin air? I do not think so; there might be other strong arguments for God's existence that are still based on empirical data, but at the same time surpass empirical evidence. I am thinking of the following philosophical questions. How could nature be intelligible if it were not created by an intelligent Creator? How could there be order in this world if there were no orderly Creator? How could there be scientific laws in nature if there were no rational Lawgiver? How could there be design in nature, if there were no intelligent Designer? How could there be human minds, if the universe were mindless?

We have a choice here when answering these questions: We either accept that there is *no* explanation at all for these observations in nature (which is basically irrational) – or we look for a *rational* explanation of all of this. The only rational explanation would be that there is an intelligent, rational, orderly, and lawgiving Creator God who made this universe the way it is. Is this manner of reasoning compelling? Perhaps not, but I believe it is a very forceful line of reasoning. We do need some beliefs so that we may understand. Imagine this turn of events: It is faith that makes us understand.

Besides, we shouldn't forget that even in science, there is so much that we cannot prove in an empirical way but must just assume to be true. How do scientists know that this universe is comprehensible, that there is some underlying order connecting causes and effects, that there is a "law" stating that every event depends on some law of nature, and so on? If scientists couldn't *assume* all of this, they would have to give up on all their scientific endeavors. Even the principle of falsification depends on the fact (or belief) that like causes do produce like effects, which is based on the assumption of some kind of cosmic order operating in the "background." In addition, there is never certainty in science. Francis Crick, one of the two scientists who discovered DNA, couldn't have said it better: "A theory that fits all the facts is bound to be wrong, as some of the facts will be wrong."

What can we learn from this? As far as science is concerned, there is much more believing in what we know than many want to believe. And, vice-versa, in religion, there may be much more knowing in what we believe than many seem to know. Faith is certainly not blind but tries to make the best sense of everything there is on the basis of the limited evidence available.

Yet, the atheists we are referring to here remain suspicious of whatever religion comes up with. If there is anything "empirical" about religion, they would declare it a product of the mind, a form of wishful thinking, so they say. Hence, religion ends up being an illusion or delusion. When religion tells us that we were made in God's image, these atheists would point out that God was actually made in our own image. Sigmund Freud, for instance, believes that the adoption of religion is a reversion to childish patterns of thought in response to feelings of helplessness and guilt. We feel a need for security and forgiveness, and so invent a source of security and forgiveness: GOD. Religion is thus seen as a childish delusion, whereas atheism is taken as a form of grown-up realism.

Did atheists such as Freud refute religion? First of all, if Freud claims that basic beliefs are the rationalization of our deepest wishes, wouldn't this also entail that his own atheistic beliefs could also be the rationalization of his own wishes? Don't we often think what we wish? Don't some people, like ostriches, choose to deny what they fear? Second, even if belief in God were wishful thinking, one could never prove that it is nothing more than wishful thinking. The God one would like to exist may actually exist, even if the fact one wishes it encourages suspicion. Third, some religions admonish us to adjust our lives to the brute fact that things are *not* the way we would wish them to be in our dreams. A prophet's message may not be what we like it to be in our wishful thinking; how often did people beg the prophet Isaiah, "Prophesy not to us what is right; speak to us smooth things, prophesy illusions" (30:10). Instead, Jeremiah's response is, "How long shall there be lies in the heart of the prophets who prophesy lies, and who prophesy the deceit of their own heart?" (23:26). Fourth, the Bible does not project a human being onto heaven, but shows us from heaven what we as human beings can and should be like.

Let's move on to the *logical* side of the debate. The history of Catholic philosophy gives us many examples of what are called "proofs of the existence of God." These "logical proofs" have often been under heavy attack, but I must mention that they are having a come-back among some contemporary philosophers and logicians – and surprisingly, they came out still alive and kicking. I won't go into any details here, but I have to confess I am not so certain that these "proofs" really give us a definitive proof of God's existence in a logical sense. One of my reasons for doubting their decisive power is St. Thomas Aquinas himself – known for his *Five Ways* or "proofs of God's existence." So what does Aquinas say about them?

Let's begin with the question as to why our universe is the way it is, or why it even exists at all. As a matter of fact, our universe need not be the way it is, and it need not even exist. In other words, our universe is neither necessary nor absolute, but finite and dependent instead; a more philosophical term would be *contingent* – our universe is contingent. However, if there is no inherent necessity for the universe to exist, then the universe is not self-explaining and therefore must find an explanation outside itself. Obviously, it cannot be grounded in something else that is also finite and not self-explaining (that would lead to infinite regress), so it can only derive from an unconditioned, infinite and ultimate ground, which is a Creator God.

The so-called *Five Ways* (or "arguments" of God's existence) that Saint Thomas Aquinas mentions are essentially variations of this one way, the way from contingency. If there are contingent beings, there "must" be a necessary Being. "Contingent" means that they do not have to exist; but since they do exist, there must be a *necessary* Being that causes them to exist. This Being is not a super-being among other beings, but an *absolute* Being. Well, this Being is what we call God, according to St. Thomas.

I stress again these arguments are "ways," not conclusive "proofs" of God's existence in a logical or mathematical sense. Yet, these "ways" certainly are compelling in a *rational* sense, working like powerful "pointers" to a Creator God. Essentially, they are philosophical clarifications of what we mean when we speak of God. But let me underscore that even Saint Thomas did not have the presumption of logically proving God's existence; his reasoning is not concluded by the sentence "Therefore, God exists or must exist," but by the less overreaching statement, "And this all think of as God." He is more or less clarifying what we mean when we speak of God, and what this entails. Let's not forget that in the society Thomas lived in, there were no real atheists, so he didn't have to prove anything for doubters. Besides, faith is not a conclusion to a logical syllogism, but is ultimately a divine gift instead.

Does this mean that we have challenged the claim of atheists that there is no full-proof argument for God's existence? I would say the answer is yes and no. It is not a proof with mathematical or logical certainty, but it surely is a very powerful rational argument in favor of God's existence.

Besides, I would like to mention someone who came into this discussion from an entirely different angle. The famous mathematician Kurt Gödel from Princeton University rigorously and mathematically proved in his so-called *incompleteness theorem* that no coherent system – not even the system of science – can be completely closed; any coherent system is essentially incomplete and needs additional "help" from outside the system. Gödel even went as far as believing that we cannot give a credible account of reality itself without invoking GOD. Gödel was said to be very cautious to mention this belief in scientific circles, because he considered it potential dynamite. But what he did tell us is that our capacity to know truth transcends mere formal logic; in other words, there are truths that we cannot "prove."

Perhaps we could already have learned all of this from Shakespeare's Hamlet: "There are more things in heaven and earth [...] than are dreamt of in your philosophy."

A: I never see or *experience* God.

R: And then there are those atheists who no longer feel any need to protest or even deny God's existence, because they only believe in what they can see, feel, hear, and touch in a physical sense. As far as God is concerned: out of sight, out of mind. In a world of what can be seen, there is no space for the unseen.

This is a very common viewpoint in our modern society. We have been brought up with cameras, videos, TV-sets, iPods, and what have you – and these seem to determine what is "real" in life. However, instruments like these can only capture what is *physical* and "rock-solid" – entities such as X-rays, EKG's, brain scans, and so on. So we have in fact been brain-washed: What instruments cannot capture cannot and does not exist. Period! Our universe has been significantly reduced to what can be touched, measured, or counted. We even need ultrasounds to see that abortion is wrong.

My response would be: Wait a minute! Not only has science been masterful in discovering things we never thought existed, but science has also come up with entities that cannot be "touched" (gravity, entropy, electricity, etc). Besides, there is so much in life that thermometers and Geiger-tellers can never capture – things such as emotions, thoughts, hopes, dreams, beliefs... Are these perhaps not real? They may not be physical, yet they are definitely based on "facts" and have shaped human history to the core; they have even enabled research, technology, and most of what is surrounding us.

Consequently, there is so much more to life than what "meets the eye." Not being able to see or hold some specific things does not necessarily negate that they exist; just think of "things" like gravity, entropy, or reason and thought. Once applied to religion, we open up a wide domain of "invisible things" that are so vital to Christianity. It is called the *spiritual* realm! The supernatural world behind the natural world! God is the Creator of "what is seen and unseen," of "what is visible and invisible," in the words of our Creed. We need to look beyond the natural to see the supernatural, beyond the present to see the eternal.

Let me get some help from three scientists – experts in the

field of "touchable" entities. The first one is the German physicist Robert Pohl (the inventor of the solid-state amplifier). After each demonstration and explanation of some physical experiment in the class room, he used to conclude his experiments with the words "And that gives us all the more cause for wonder." He had a profound message for his students: There is more than what the eye can capture and the ear can register.

The second one is the nuclear physicist and Nobel Laureate Werner Heisenberg who once said: "The first drink from the cup of natural science makes atheistic… But at the bottom of the cup, GOD is waiting." Interestingly enough, Pope Pius XII had said already in 1951 that "true science discovers God in an ever-increasing degree – as though God were waiting behind every door opened by science."

And last but not least there is Max Planck, who revolutionized physics with his quantum theory. It was his observation that "the greatest naturalists of all times, men like Kepler, Newton, Leibniz, were inspired by profound religiosity." And then he goes on "For the believer, God is the *beginning*, for the scientist He is the *end* of all reflections."

It is needless to say that atheists have never gotten yet to the bottom of the cup, to the end of all reflections, to the invisible world behind the visible world, to the supernatural realm behind the natural realm. But they may someday… Because God is omnipresent, He seems to be "nowhere," yet He is only seemingly absent. They say about fish the last thing a fish would discover is water; well, atheists are in a similar predicament as far as GOD is concerned.

A: I do not *dare* to believe in God.

R: Some atheists do not want to be on the bandwagon of any faith, and certainly not of faith in God. Faith is a scary, forbidden word in their vocabulary. In their view, religion requires too much faith - which scares them away…

I must admit there is no belief in God without faith – religion always requires a final step of faith, a final surrender. But isn't that true of many other things in life? We found out earlier that scientists *must* believe in order and design, in rationality and comprehensibility – without that mental leap they cannot function the way they should. Whether they like it or not, whether they realize it or not, scientists actually harbor quite some faith – faith that the universe is orderly and comprehensible, for instance. So, in a logical or empirical sense, atheists have no more or no less power of "absolute proof" than religious believers.

In general, the power of strict proof grows to be weaker when the field of reference becomes wider. Let me explain this. Logic and math, for example, have a strong power of proof but happen to be about very little (their reference is narrow; some say even zero). Religion, on the other hand, has the reversed "problem": It has a much wider reference but consequently looses some power of proof. That is why I said before that, as far as science is concerned, there is much more believing in what we know than many want to believe, whereas in religion, there may be much more knowing in what we believe than many seem to know. It is as hard to prove what you believe as it is to prove what you doubt.

In other words, just take the risk of believing that the universe is orderly and comprehensible; otherwise you loose out on most scientific progress. In the same vein, just take the risk of believing that God exists, and this faith will change your life dramatically forever. It always startles me how some atheists devote their entire career to the very purpose of proving that life has no purpose whatsoever. Don't they see that is a pretty purpose-less enterprise? They are so sure that nothing is sure!

The Catechism speaks of two different kinds of doubt – voluntary and involuntary doubt (2088). *Involuntary* doubt is something we all experience. It is the kind of doubt St. Thomas had when others told him they had seen the Lord. He had his doubts in the face of what seems to be too good to be true. It is the kind of doubt we all experience time and again when surrounded by unanswerable questions – aroused by the great mysteries of life. This kind of doubt may lead to anxiety. In contrast, the form of atheism we are discussing here is a *voluntary* kind of doubt, rooted in a deliberate refusal to let God enter into our lives. It leads to what the Catechism calls "spiritual blindness" (2088).

A: I declare God to be *beyond* my reach.

R: When I said earlier that religion requires faith, I didn't mean "*blind* faith." Some atheists, however, maintain that religious faith, if they allow for such a thing, is necessarily "blind," since God is entirely beyond our reach. They have probably heard of terms like "God's transcendence" and "God's infinity," which seem to make the infinite, transcendent God completely inaccessible to the finite human mind – that is, if we take them the wrong way.

In other words, these atheists do not really deny God's existence, but they consider it so far beyond their reach that they rather remain entirely silent about God. Otherwise they would have only two options left. The first one is that our talk about God would be considered so open-ended that it becomes completely empty. I would say such a kind of faith comes very close to "blind" faith, and I would point out that blind *belief* is worth as much or as little as blind *unbelief*. The other option is that we can only speak about God in purely negative terms – "God is *not* this... and God is *not* that..." The problem with this latter approach is that one cannot merely say that God is not this and not that, without saying anything positive. A negative definition of God proceeds by elimination – it can begin, it can go on indefinitely, but it can never do its job.

This latter solution reminds me of Hinduism. At least, Hinduism does accept the full consequences of the (erroneous) idea of an unknown and unknowable God. Since religious truth is said to transcend all verbal definition, the core of Hinduism does not depend on the existence or non-existence of God, or not even on whether there is one God or many gods. If you cannot say anything right about God, you cannot say anything wrong either. So anything allegedly goes in religion! If one religion is true, then all of them are true! All religions supposedly share a "common ground" of being in search of the ground of all being. As a consequence, all religions are said to be the same manifestations of faith in an unknowable and ineffable god. Some hail this as "one faith... but many beliefs."

But how different is faith as it features in Christianity! On the one hand, Christians realize that God does transcend all our verbal definitions. Saint Augustine would say: "If you have understood, then what you have understood is not God." God always surpasses our human knowledge and understanding of Him. That is why any analogy has its limitations: "Our human words always fall short of the mystery of God" (CCC 42). Pope Benedict XVI speaks of the humble admission of ignorance that may be true knowledge.

However, this doesn't mean that our religious concepts and conceptions are empty and useless. If they were, we should immediately stop talking about God. Even when we say, "God is beyond our conceptions," we say something meaningful about God. But we should also add that, as human beings, we do need such conceptions. The same Saint Augustine once said of the Holy Trinity that we speak of such things because it is better to speak than to be totally silent.

But once we begin speaking about God, we realize that our understandings of the divine can be very divergent – and that is why religions can be so different. As a consequence, religions may share a "common ground" but not necessarily an equally valid path to that common ground, the living God. Truth is truth, even if you don't accept it; and untruth is untruth, even if you claim it. In other words, some religious conceptions may be wrong! Because God's transcendence is a true reality, we cannot just say about God whatever we choose. That's why we have a Creed!

Therefore, never take God's transcendence the wrong way. Some soon-to-be atheists stretch God's transcendence so far that they make God completely inaccessible to human knowledge; so they claim we cannot possibly know anything about Him or Her or It. When the apostle Paul tuned in to the philosophical mind of his Greek audience in Athens, he did refer to the idea of an unknown God: "I found also an altar with this inscription, 'To an unknown god.' What therefore you worship as unknown, this I proclaim to you." (Acts 17:23). But Paul certainly didn't imply that this unknown God is also unknowable, for he was quick to add, "Now what you worship as something unknown I am going to proclaim to you."

If God were transcendent in the sense of unknowable, we should stop right then and there, as there is no way to speak about the unknown, not to mention the unknowable. How could we possibly speak about the unspeakable? We cannot meaningfully say, "Oh God, if there is a God, save my soul, if I have one." In contrast, there is no longer a problem for us to get in touch with God, because God Himself tries to get in touch with us. He is a God of Love and wants us to feel and experience His presence in our lives – otherwise we wouldn't have the faintest chance of knowing anything about Him. The unknown God has made Himself known in Judaism and Christianity.

Why do some people still have a problem then? I think it is the philosophy of the famous German philosopher Immanuel Kant that is to blame for this perceived stalemate. Kant – a man who never left his hometown by the way – drew heaven and earth completely apart from each other by driving a wedge between God and the world. In human experience, so Kant states, there can be no space for God; if there were, God wouldn't be God anymore. So if God is really God, God cannot possible fit into our human experience. In Kant's view, heaven on the "other side" is totally separated from earth "on this side." Not only is God considered "other" than the world but even "totally other." We could never cross that infinite gap…

However, the statement that God is "other" than the world does not entail that God is "outside" the world. Apart from God's *transcendence*, Judaism and Christianity have learned to invoke another religious concept, called God's *immanence*, which states that God is "in" the world, in spite of God's "otherness." The way Jews and Christians know about God is through the world, not without the world. God is "part" of everything in this world, yet He is not a physical "part" of this world. That is where we need the concept of immanence, to counterbalance the other pole of transcendence. God is the Infinite Majesty, and yet He is intimately involved with everything and everyone. In his book *Jesus of Nazareth* (Part I, 55), Pope Benedict XVI speaks of "God, who is as much in this world as he is beyond it – who infinitely transcends our world, but is also totally interior to it."

"Immanence" adds a new dimension to "transcendence." Although God is invisible, we can *see* God working in this world; although God is inaudible, we can *hear* God speaking in this world. The concept of immanence stresses the fact that God is God throughout the world, not without the world. In what is going on in the world, we *see* God's presence (sometimes called "God's hand") and we *hear* God's presence (often called "God's Word"). In the midst of what is visible we see what is invisible. In this sense, God is not entirely beyond our reach. Since we were created in His image, we also share "in the light of the divine mind," in the words of Vatican II. When we call ourselves "only human," we are actually comparing ourselves with our "Model in Heaven," with Someone who does not have the limitations we experience. In some mysterious way, we are reaching out into the realm of the Absolute, far beyond ourselves, where God makes Himself known. In doing so, the "finite" catches a glimpse of the Infinite – which takes us far beyond atheism... (more on this in chapter five).

A: I do not *need* to believe in God.

R: This is the voice of atheists whom I like to identify with humanists. Humanism declares human beings as fully sufficient in themselves, fully self-made. Humanism declares humanity as the measure of all things. It pretends that all our problems – personal, social, technological, and what have you – can be entirely solved by using the right human knowledge, technology, reasoning, and judgment. We are supposed to be in full control of ourselves and should free ourselves through economic, technological, and social liberation. Not Heaven, but the sky is the limit.

Humanism usually bathes in practical materialism, "which restricts its needs and aspirations to space and time" (CCC 2124). So it shouldn't surprise us that even the weakest version of atheism, agnosticism, was called by Lenin a "fig-leaf" for materialism. The Man of humanism is setting out on his own to know and master his cosmos – all of it. Humanism "falsely considers man to be 'an end to himself, and the sole maker, with supreme control, of his own history'" (CCC 2124). It considers man as the "measure of all things."

In contrast, in Christianity it is Christ who is the measure of all things – not the old Adam but the new Adam. That is why I always like to ask humanists what we should do when disaster strikes us, when things do not go the way we had planned, when we become victims of injustice – in short, when self-made people reach their own limits? Don't we all know that life doesn't owe us a living? In addition, I would ask them: Isn't it striking that Christianity actually has the Cross at center stage in its religion; it claims there is some mysterious salvation for us in carrying our crosses in life. No wonder the Cross is a touchstone for Christians, but a stumbling block for non-Christians and humanists at the same time. As Saint Rosa of Lima said so pointedly, "Apart from the cross, there is no other ladder by which we may get to Heaven."

And besides, since the existence of our world is contingent, not a necessity, our world would be nothing, literally, if there were no God. Without God, there is a permanent vacuum in our lives; but because it is a vacuum, it may easily go unnoticed. In the words of Pope Benedict XVI, "Again and again man falls behind the faith and wants to be just himself again; he becomes a heathen in the most profound sense of the word" (*Light of the World*, 2010).

These heathens (of the humanist type) just have no *need* to believe in God because they think they are completely self-sufficient. They do not need God, they do not even want God, because such a God would undermine humanism – the power of Man, the power of "Me, I, and myself." The Catechism considers this "a false conception of human autonomy, exaggerated to the point of refusing any dependence on God" (2126). When people try to build their own tower of Babel into Heaven, they become divided from each other and lose their common language; it calls for Pentecost to unite them again.

There is this gravestone of an atheist in the town of Thurmont, MD that I think could not express things better: "Here lies an Atheist. All dressed up and no place to go." Indeed, atheists miss much more than just some great holidays; they also miss out on a destination in life, on a power that far surpasses what humans can attain on their own.

A: I do not *trust* any belief in God.

R: Then we have those atheists who do not have the guts to place their entire lives in God's hands, not even when the end nears. They just do not have enough trust! This made the Catholic philosopher and physicist Blaise Pascal contend that it might be the wisest logical decision to "bet" that God exists, since "If you gain, you gain everything; if you lose, you lose nothing," meaning you can gain eternal life if God exists, but if not, you will be no worse off in death than had you not believed (*Pensées* #233). Needless to say that such a decision is less based on faith and trust than on fear.

However, Pascal adds that there are three kinds of people: those who have sought God and found Him, those who are seeking and have not yet found, and those who neither seek nor find. The first are reasonable and happy, the second are reasonable and unhappy, and the third are both unreasonable and unhappy. If the Wager stimulates us at least to seek, then it will also stimulate us to be reasonable.

I would line up these matter-of-fact atheists with skeptics, who deny the validity of nearly all aspects of knowledge, because we are not supposed to know any truth with certainty. Skeptics find a flaw in every truth claimed. They just do not have enough trust to believe in anything.

Skepticism makes for a very restrained view on the world – actually so restrained that absolute skeptics cannot even know whether they have a mind to doubt with. Skeptics turn things the wrong way. We often do need to eliminate errors to get to the truth; yet, our ultimate goal is not to avoid *errors* but to gain *truth*. We want to know, not to know what we do *not* know. Skeptics, on the other hand, make it their final goal to avoid errors, in denial of the fact that eliminating errors is only a means to gaining truth – so they end up with an empty shell of complete mistrust.

Ultimately, skepticism leads us to the edge of an abyss; it leads to nihilism, claiming that there is no law, no authority, no rationality, no morality, and no purpose to life. Nihilism denies the very existence of all these fundamental aspects of life, and arrogantly declares them non-existent. I always wonder how one can be so certain that nothing is certain. But one thing is certain: Once we lose God, we can no longer fight the meaninglessness that the universe now threatens to become.

Skeptics have this persistent doubt as to how far they can go in trusting the world around them. Most of them may reluctantly accept the domain of causality, as it is about what is tangible, measurable, countable, and quantifiable – physical stuff, that is. But many would hesitate to include human thoughts and intentions in their outlook on life. By denying these, they neglect how much Hitler's intentions and his bigoted reasoning did shape human history. Were those less real than his gas chambers and his Zyklon B? Or I would ask them if they would consider winking to be less real than blinking your eyes.

Would skeptics dare to go any farther? Would they accept moral values in life as well? I wonder what the world would be like without moral values, as it is hard to deny that these values have had a real, and mostly positive, impact on human history (just think of our medical and charitable institutions). Without moral values, there wouldn't be good and evil; yet, we all know somehow – just look around – that evil is something to watch out for.

And then we have those origins and destinations that religion speaks of. Who would want to dismiss all issues about meaning and destination – a destination in this life, even beyond death? Skeptics would! Many medical doctors can tell you, though, that this may lead to ulcers, cancers, depression, and suicide. As a matter of fact, atheism ultimately offers no hope in life; atheism actually undermines all the pillars our lives are based on. The Hollywood actor Anthony Hopkins put it very clearly: "Being an atheist must be like living in a closed cell with no windows."

Someone who was very aware of the consequences of atheism was Friedrich Nietzsche of all philosophers. He understood how enormous the impact of the decline of Christianity would be. If we are only the fortuitous effects of physical causes, we have no other rational and moral measures but ourselves. That is why Nietzsche could say that humanism and other "moral" ideologies shelter themselves in caves and venerate shadows of the God they once believed in; they are holding on to something they cannot provide themselves – mere shadows of the past. I actually consider these atheists parasites, because they benefit from what our society has gained from religion, but have nothing to contribute themselves.

It always strikes me how many former atheists ultimately did change their minds when they got confronted with death... Woody Allen once said he wasn't afraid of death but didn't want to be around when it happens. Indeed, life is short, so I would suggest to not waste your time in the "windowless cell" of atheism. Have some trust! Surrender yourself!

A: I cannot believe there is a *just* God.

R: Some atheists have a completely different "style" of atheism. They have encountered so many problems in life that they cannot believe anymore there is a loving God who takes care of His people. The main obstacle for these atheists is often the problem of evil. I must admit it surely is a complex problem!

Interestingly enough, it was the then-atheist C.S. Lewis who once tried to prove that God did not exist, because the universe seemed so cruel and unjust to him. But then he realized, "in the very act of trying to prove that God did not exist – in other words, that the whole of reality was senseless – I found I was forced to assume that one part of reality – namely my idea of justice – was full of sense. […] If the whole universe has no meaning, we should never have found out that it has no meaning: just as, if there were no light in the universe and therefore no creatures with eyes, we should never know it was dark. Dark would be without meaning." Thus atheism turned out to be too simplistic for the turned-around atheist C.S. Lewis. He realized that by asserting "evil exists," he used an ethical standard in order to define good and evil – and such an absolute standard implies the existence of God.

Yet, many atheists keep struggling with this problem. Their reasoning goes along the following lines: How does an all-powerful God get away with the evil in the world? If God is not able to take evil away, God cannot be all-powerful. And how does an all-powerful God deal with human freedom? If God is almighty, human beings must be powerless... The French atheist and philosopher Jean-Paul Sartre worded this dilemma accurately: An almighty God doesn't leave room for free human beings, whereas free human beings do not leave room for an almighty God. God and Man seem to be in a power battle. Sartre opted in favor of human freedom over divine omnipotence and thus became an atheist.

Christianity tells us differently. The Catechism declares, in contrast, that "to acknowledge God is in no way to oppose the dignity of man, since such dignity is grounded and brought to perfection in God" (2126). In everything that happens, we can discern God's "hand" – not a hand that *causes* all the good and bad things that we hear about on TV, but a hand that *holds* all these things together by saving them for a better purpose and destination. God is not only an all-powerful God but also an all-loving God.

Let me use the following analogy. A sovereign king can pass a law that makes him no longer sovereign – which is somehow what our God did out of love for the world. He set limits to his own omnipotence by setting no bounds to human freedom. For our salvation, we are certainly at *God*'s mercy, but He has also chosen to be at *our* mercy. God could perhaps have chosen to eliminate the possibility of evil and evil-doing, but then God would have also taken away the possibility of good and doing-good. "In gathering the weeds you root up the wheat along with them. Let both grow together until the harvest" (Mt. 13:29).

Astonishingly, God lets the actors on the world stage be free actors, who may not act the way the Author of the play would like them to act. And it is for that very reason – because not all that happens on earth is God's will – that we must pray daily, "Your will be done on earth as it is in heaven." God *wills* perfection but *allows* imperfection. We may not know what the future holds, but we do know that God holds the future.

At those moments when life does *not* seem to make sense, especially when death, sickness, loss, and suffering strike us – at those moments, we experience our own powerlessness and ultimate limitation to the fullest. We either become bitter or better. These are the moments when we could easily turn angry or disappointed in life, even to the point of being "depressed" or "paralyzed." That is when some people end up losing all their faith and hope. They just cannot deal with this latest loss, this latest disaster, this latest disease. They may always have considered God as an intervening God – that is, intervening on their request. However, a religion that promises immediate answers to prayer and instant awards for good behavior is merely a commercialized version of religion. God is not a cosmic vending machine! Don't expect God to bail us out of situations we caused ourselves. In prayer, we always get what we need – not what we *think* we need but what we *do* need.

A: I just never *think* of God.

R: Here we encounter a completely different form of atheism. It is the kind that no longer feels any need to protest or deny God's existence, because atheists of this type no longer perceive anything spiritual or religious in their lives. The Catechism speaks of "spiritual blindness" (2088). These people can no longer hear God because they live in a very noisy world, filled with radio and TV, loudspeakers and earphones. They are a breed of their own, entirely engulfed by a secular world. When agnostics protest "I do not know if God exists" or other atheists declare "I do not believe that God exists," they may not realize it but both their protest and their assertion imply GOD; they imply that there is now a vacuum that was once filled by faith in God. It has left a "God-shaped hole" inside each one of us that only God can fill – and nothing else. As St. Augustine put it in his *Confessions*, "What place is there in me to which my God can come, what place that can receive the God who made heaven and earth? Does this mean, O Lord my God, that there is in me something fit to contain you?" Unfortunately, this very place seems to have quietly become empty and vacant.

This new "brand" of atheism has actually forgotten about being surrounded by a culture steeped in Christianity, because that culture has become highly secular in habits and practices. How could anyone forget? Our freedom, our democracy, our health care system, our scientific achievements, our educational system, our charitable institutions, and many other blessings wouldn't be what they are or they might not even exist if they didn't have Christian roots. So you wonder how some people can live in complete ignorance of such an obvious fact...

Let's keep in mind that, for centuries, it was unthinkable in the Western world to even deny God's existence. Although atheists are still a very tiny, yet very vocal minority in the Western World (± 4% in the USA), our society is changing fast. More and more people are no longer aware of this growing vacuum, as they have no memory of the way life used to be; they live obliviously in complete religious ignorance. The bottom has been taken out of their lives; they have lost their "sixth sense" and their "fourth dimension." They are spiritually illiterate. They never give God or religion a thought.

Here we have atheism in its simplest form: I just never think of God. This version of atheism has become very prevalent in our modern society. Pope Benedict XVI calls it "secularism," which leads to a lifestyle marred with complete unawareness of God. He also calls it "paganism," turning us into complete heathens. It doesn't deny God, doesn't fight God, it just ignores and neglects God. Its only commandment is "You shall never invoke the name of God, *unless* you do so in vain." A thoroughly secularized world is a world without windows or skylights – a prison cell.

When such a thing happens, when we lose sight of God and lead a life as if there is no God, we may also lose the foundation of morality, because we no longer know *why* certain things are not permissible. And without moral values, we could even lose our judicial laws, which have been protecting us so far to the extent they were derived from moral laws. All of this will ultimately lead us to the edge of an abyss – which is *nihilism*, claiming that there is no law, no authority, no rationality, no morality, and no purpose to life. The only thing left is the "rock-solid" reality of food, money, sex, and material possessions – all of which will collapse for us when we die.

When Aleksandr Solzhenitsyn, in his 1983 Templeton Prize lecture, tried to locate the root of the evils of the 20th century – two world wars, three totalitarian regimes with death camps, and a Cold War – he discerned a profound truth: "Men have forgotten God." What does this lead to? The writer Fyodor Dostoyevsky had already given us the answer when he said that, without God, all things are permissible.

Do we really want to go that way? I would say it is not too late to turn around, for we are headed for a dead-end. This is probably the scariest kind of atheism so far, because it doesn't raise its voice in protest or denial; it just lives and grows like a mushroom in complete silence and ignorance until its season is over. It quietly lives in a world of materialism and relativism, where people are possessed by their possessions – and they seem to be happy there, because they no longer know any better. They are quietly leading a life of religious amnesia – aimless and clueless. Pope Benedict XVI recently mentioned how the air we breathe in our societies is often polluted by a non-Christian, even a non-human mentality, concerned only with worldly things and lacking a spiritual dimension.

A: I *hate* any belief in God.

R: There is at least one more kind of atheism left; it is by its very nature a belligerent form that wants to spread far and wide by propagating itself through books, TV, and other media. It is becoming a real "cult" – a cult of people who vehemently *refuse* to believe in God and want you to *believe* that believing in God is "evil" (if I may say so) and needs to be attacked or even eradicated. These people consider spreading their message of God-hatred to be their "holy war," their "sacred mission."

There is something very peculiar about this form of atheism: It tries to constantly remind us of God while maintaining He does not exist! How could you hate something that is not there? Why would you persistently prove to people the non-existence of a being not really there? Cardinal Wyszynski, the late Primate of Poland, who dealt most of his life with the aggressive atheism of Communism, has an astounding answer to these questions: In order to hate God, you must first have faith that there is a God, for only when you firmly believe in God will you be able to hate Him. That was his explanation for the fact that the Communist media in his country used to persistently mention God in their atheist propaganda.

Why is this form of atheism so aggressive? Why on earth would one want to fight religion, which doesn't hurt anyone in any way? We have nothing to fear from Christianity; it doesn't endanger the common good but makes the deepest contribution to it; it actually gave a push to respect human rights and establish democracy, and it has been playing a main role in education and health care from its very beginning. If I were an atheist, I would say let religion just die quietly! (But I must admit religion keeps burying its undertakers.)

On the other hand, if people were fighting a certain dictator, I could see why they would do so, because dictators take our freedom away. Yet, that is not the case with religion. So why would one want to fight Christianity and its beliefs? I, for myself, would feel no need to fight Islam, for instance; but I would fight Islam tooth and nail if it were trying to impose its Sharia law on me. But Christianity has no intention of taking over society life, for it gives to Caesar what is Caesar's.

Some might counter that Christianity has its missionaries – so atheism should be allowed to have its own "missionaries" as well, even its own "army chaplains." My response would be that Christianity has "Good News" to spread, with the goal of helping people in their daily lives and saving them from eternal damnation, whereas atheism has only "bad news" to bring – their message being that, at the end of life, "there is no place to go." I wonder why anyone would want such a message to spread or to help it spread. In addition, we discovered that atheism has no foot to stand on – so you wonder why anyone would wish to propagate something that is impossible to even defend or establish.

I see only one possible answer to all the questions I posed in the previous paragraphs: There must be much more going on behind the scenes. The pivotal question is this: What is behind the deep-seated hatred that these atheists nurse against religion and against God? Let's face it, there is only one force that hates God's creation more than anything else – and that is Satan. Satan knows that God exists but wants no part of Him. It is Satan's ultimate goal to demolish all Christian elements in society and to damage the human image that was made in God's image. Could Satan be the real instigator of this aggressive form of atheism?

My answer would be a definite yes! Destructive atheism, in my view and in the view of the Church, is part of a much larger picture – a cosmic warfare, that is, between Good and Evil, between God and Satan. It is God's aim for each one of us to attain Heaven after death, whereas Satan's aim is to ensure that as many people as possible miss that eternal goal. Do not take these as two eternal principles locked in permanent conflict (like in Dualism and Manichaeism, CCC 285), for Satan and other demons are fallen Angels who were originally created good by God (CCC 391). But Satan is a reality; evil is something to watch out for. Prayer is the best weapon in this battle.

It is only the religious "eye" that sees all of history as a cosmic and constant war between God and Satan, waged everywhere and daily – "24/7." It "sees" how the power of evil, the light of Satan enabled men such as Hitler, Stalin, and Mao to spellbind and enslave the minds and spirits of millions, creating hell ahead of time, right here on earth. This explains how such people have sold their souls by following "orders" that stem from sources far beyond their own resources. Only religious people are able to see this dimension in history that historians usually miss. They see what is unseen behind all that is seen. Our history is also His-story.

And now we see again how the power of evil, the "light" of Satan is enabling *atheists* to spellbind and enslave the minds and spirits of millions, creating havoc on earth with religious erosion and mudslides. That is why I call atheism a new, dangerous, and cancerous "cult," for its followers were happy to sell their souls again to their new "master." No wonder the reality of evil goes far beyond material and physical powers; it goes even far beyond what human beings can do on their own. After all, could Hitler have ever done what he did relying on human power alone? I know the answer is no!

Do I have any indication that this analysis is correct? I realize it is hard to prove its truth to people who do not have a "religious eye," but I am going to mention some confirmation from an unexpected source – exorcism. Exorcists always need to distinguish demonic possessions from mental or psychiatric disorders, and they use at least three symptoms to identify people as possessed. First, those people have the ability to see *hidden* sacred objects, which they always want to be removed. Second, they have an extraordinary physical *strength*. And third, they show an aversion to the *sacred* (e.g. they begin to curse, remove holy pictures from their houses, stop going to church, etc.)

I am not saying that all atheists are possessed, but they seem to be at least "under the influence" of evil forces – and this is definitely true of those who follow the aggressive kind of atheism. If there is a cosmic warfare going on between God and Satan – and in the Catholic view, there is – atheists are definitely on the wrong side in this battle. They show a clear aversion to anything *sacred* and try to remove it with all the *strength* they have. Unfortunately, they get tremendous help from the satanic realm of evil, which gives them the power to do even more than they could ever do on their own. This explains how such people can follow "orders" stemming from sources far beyond their own resources. The fuel behind all of their convictions is some satanic force engaged in a battle against God's creation – which is the role of Satan, the "father" of all lies, the great divider who knows how to remain hidden behind the scene. This reality reminds me of Adolf Hitler again: Could Hitler have ever done all he did by just relying on human power alone? Satan is happy to lend such people some "spiritual" help from "beyond." That is why these atheists seem to feel empowered from "on high" to declare to the whole world that there is no God, and that they are His prophets. But you know whose prophets they really are...

Conclusion

I tried to show you that atheism is as much a *belief* as the religious beliefs that it is trying to wipe out from the face of the earth. Nevertheless, atheism is a very powerful force in our secular culture that has gathered a growing number of "converts" into its ranks. Atheism begins with eroding all Christian elements in society, layer by layer, and then sets off a mudslide that has the destructive capabilities of an avalanche, wiping out everything on its way. So we all end up in the mud. Where God is absent, nothing can be good.

But instead of the mud of atheism, I prefer the firm ground of religion to stand on. Sartre was right: If atheism is true, there can be no absolute or objective standard of right and wrong, for there is no eternal heaven that would make values objective and universal. This chapter was written as a counterattack, in an attempt to stop the mudslide by giving us back faith and hope in our Creator – our Heaven.

I think no one could do this better, though, than those "life-size" atheists who have gone through it all and, at last, came to see the Divine Light. There are many of them who finally discovered how they were deceived and had sold their souls. You will find their life stories everywhere – on the internet, in books, in articles. The list of former atheists and agnostics is quite impressive: Francis Collins (former leader of the Human Genome Project), Cardinal Avery

Dulles SJ, Peter Hitchens (a brother of the atheist who recently died), C. S. Lewis, Gabriel Marcel, Malcolm Muggeridge, Joseph Pearce, Charles Péguy, Aleksandr Solzhenitsyn, St. Edith Stein, Allen Tate, Evelyn Waugh, Simone Weil, Dr. Bernard Nathanson (the abortionist who became a Catholic pro-life advocate) – and this list could go on for quite a while.

Let me mention one of them more in particular, the French philosopher and renowned atheist Jean-Paul Sartre. Toward the end of his life, by then blind, in poor health, but still in full possession of his faculties, the man whom most people know as an uncompromising atheist had a profound conversion. In the early spring of 1980, he shared much of his time with an ex-Maoist, Benny Lévy (writing under the pseudonym Pierre Victor), and the two had a dialogue in the ultra-leftist *Le Nouvel Observateur*. It is sufficient to quote a single sentence from what Sartre said during this dialogue: "I do not feel that I am the product of chance, a speck of dust in the universe, but someone who was expected, prepared, prefigured. In short, a being that only a Creator could put here; and this idea of a creating hand refers to God." (*National Review*, 6-11-82).

Doesn't this sound like a profession of faith – actually much to the consternation of his life-long girlfriend Simone De Beauvoir, who spoke of the "senile act of a turncoat"? It seems to me that, at last, the blind and old man had been cured from his "mental myopia."

I hope and pray that you had a similar conversion yourself, if needed, when you made your way through this chapter, and that you feel better equipped now to face those atheists you will come in contact with (and we will encounter them in all the chapters to come). Atheism is a poison that requires an antidote. Just join Sartre who had finally seen a glimpse of the Light that Pope Benedict has been speaking off so unrelentingly. Isn't it better late than never? In Christianity, it is never too late in life. May this Light be our light as well, so we can live our lives by being drawn to God's Divine Light.

2

You Are Nothing But...

Really?

Don't you have the feeling, like I do, that we are under steady attack of decrees like these:

- You are only a speck of dust
- You are only an automated machine
- You are only a bag of genes
- You are only a string of DNA
- You are only a blob of cells
- You are only a pack of neurons
- You are only a bundle of instincts
- You are only a termite in a colony
- You are only a 3-dimensional being

Each one is basically a form of atheism – more in particular reductionism, which reduces the complexity of the universe to the simplicity of its parts. Their shared message is this: You're only dirt. Each one tries to distort your human image and strips you of your human dignity which you received from your Maker.

Don't you feel ripped off? I do! Perhaps a Catholic philosophy can show us why these attempts fail and how we can defuse them. But still, we also need *divine* help to restore our human dignity and our morality. May this chapter help us find our dignity back, so we realize again we are made after God's image.

Here is a reply (R) to these various
disguised forms of atheism (A).

A: You are *only* a speck of dust

This is the message: You have no soul, no Maker, no significance. All you are is a speck of dust. The astrophysicist Carl Sagan is known to have coined this expression; he calls our planet a speck of dust in the universe – "all that is, or was, or ever will be." You heard it right. It's this speck of dust that we call home. Look at that tiny dot. That's here! That's home! That's us! On it is everyone you love, everyone you know. No matter whether this saying refers to our little planet, or to the ones living on it, ultimately this line refers to you and me: We too are considered mere particles of dust. We become tinier by the minute and end up as star dust.

The idea is basically very old – it is the ancient pagan philosophy of *materialism*. It holds that the only thing that exists is matter; that all things are composed of matter and dust, and all phenomena, including the human mind, are the result of material interactions. In other words, matter is the only substance in this universe; physical matter has become the only or fundamental reality. In antiquity, the atomic theory of Greek philosophers had this notorious aura of claiming, not only that atoms are *everywhere*, but also that they are *all there is*. Ultimately, the visible world is all there is. That is how materialism started, and it has never really left us since. For some enigmatic reason, materialism has quite a spiritual appeal to it. However, the curious thing is that, if you deny the existence of anything immaterial, you also deny the existence of your very own denial which is certainly immaterial as well.

I must admit materialism is not *only* bad: Arguably, it inspired scientists to search for material explanations in their scientific research. And the marvelous results of their work are everywhere for us to enjoy. That is, for instance, how we discovered that infections are caused by "particles" and "germs." On the other hand, materialism is *also* bad: We still find it as a popular, but often hidden ideology among scientists who inflate their sound methodology of searching for material explanations into the baseless doctrine that there *are* no other explanations than material explanations. Carl Sagan is one of them.

It is in this latter sense that materialism shows its true colors. It inflates a sound scientific methodology into a flawed philosophical ideology. It bombards a partial truth into the full truth. It is, in essence, a world view or doctrine that declares and explains *everything* in material terms. So what is wrong with it then?

R: We are *more* than specks of dust

Is what materialism tells us really all there is? Or is there another side to the story? I would say so. Materialism is a form of what is called *reductionism* – or in the words of C.S. Lewis "nothing-buttery": The whole is *nothing but* the sum of its parts (atoms or so). All forms of reductionism reduce the complexity of the *whole* to the simplicity of its physical *parts*, and then claim there is nothing else but those parts, those specks of dust. But we all know intuitively that love is more than a chemical reaction. Reductionism tells us only one side of the story, but do not forget to fill in the blanks. We have gotten so used to this reductionistic mindset that your typical American mother doesn't tell her children to eat their vegetables but to eat their vitamins.

Interestingly enough, even science itself has come to question materialism. Quantum physics, for instance, has revealed to us that matter has far less "substance" than we might believe. And then there is philosophy. If you turn a certain rule into an *all-inclusive* rule, you run the risk of refuting yourself. The very *idea* that "nothing exists except matter" is self-refuting because, if it were true, neither it nor any other mental idea would exist; so it would deny its own existence. No wonder there are not many strict materialists left, other than some dedicated Marxists of the so-called dialectical materialistic school.

But there is a much more serious philosophical problem with materialism: How can matter ever explain itself, its own existence? All philosophers are expected to walk a road to understanding, so they are supposed to explain why things are the way they are, asking themselves what the ultimate "root" is of all that exists. As a matter of fact, there is no ground for this to be found in the world itself, for the universe cannot provide its own ground. Hence, from a rational point of view, there must be some power transcending this world, some infinite, absolute, and uncaused power – typically called God or Creator.

In this context, we should definitely mention Saint Thomas Aquinas, a famous *Doctor of the Church*. Aquinas calls God the "First Cause," the first "uncaused cause" of existence, on Whom the universe depends perpetually and permanently for its very existence. This Primary Cause is *un*-caused, not self-caused, but the Source of all being; not some super-being among other beings but an *Absolute* Being; not a super-power among other powers, but the source of all powers; not a cause prior to and larger than other causes, but a *Primary* Cause that all other causes depend on.

I should probably clarify a bit more what St. Thomas is actually asserting here, for his statements may raise many questions for some. You might ask: If the universe needs a cause or ground outside itself, why doesn't God need a cause or ground as well? The usual answer to this question is that the reason for God's existence is contained within itself – God is Absolute. But this may lead to the question why then the universe cannot contain the reason for its existence within. And the answer to this question is that things that have a beginning need a cause or ground outside themselves. God is eternal and absolute, and therefore doesn't have a beginning; He actually created time itself so that things can and do have a beginning. Consequently, the universe cannot be self-caused, because that would mean that the universe existed before it came into existence – which is a logical absurdity.

But there is another reason why the ultimate cause of being and the ultimate source of intelligibility of nature cannot be yet another natural thing. It must be something *beyond* nature, something that has the power to produce the totality of nature and does not itself require a cause. Both the existence and intelligible order of the natural universe, therefore, show that everything in it exists because of an ultimate, Primary Cause: GOD. So, for now, I would conclude there must be more to this universe than specks of dust.

A: You are *only* an automated machine

Here we have another form of reductionism: You have no soul, no mind, no free will, for all you do is in fact controlled by the machinary of your body. This idea is probably best known from the French physician and philosopher de La Mettrie, who wrote a book entitled *Man a Machine* (1748). His ideas became part of another ideology called *mechanicism*.

The doctrine of mechanicism is originally a theory about the nature of the universe, closely linked with the previously discussed version of materialism. Both are based on the extreme simplification of all reality into matter and its material motions. Its original version holds that the universe is best understood as a completely mechanical system – that is, a system composed entirely of matter in motion under an all-inclusive system of laws of nature.

As a consequence, mechanicism usually denies there is any freedom in this universe, for everything is determined by its past history, holding everything in the iron grip of determinism by working with clockwork precision. Applied more in particular to human beings, mechanicism became an important philosophical doctrine to declare that even all *living* objects, including human beings, are only and merely machine-like automata, which just follow all the physical laws of the universe. In this line of thought, Marvin Minsky, a pioneer in the field of artificial intelligence, described human beings as mere "machines made of meat." No wonder, Archie Bunker felt entitled to call his son-in-law "meat head."

According to this form of reductionism, everything about human beings can be completely explained in mechanical terms, with as much certainty as can everything about clockwork or gasoline engines. Needless to say that human freedom has become a farce.

R: We are *more* than automated machines

Viewing human beings as merely automated machines leads us into lots of trouble. First of all, when we make truth claims – as we do when claiming that humans are machines – we need freedom of will to do so. How can this be compatible with any form of deterministic mechanicism? If this very claim were also predetermined by the machinery, we would be running around in a vicious circle. We cannot freely claim that free claims do not exist; and we certainly could not convince or persuade anyone else that this is true. I will just leave it at this.

Second, there are some nasty philosophical questions emerging: Can machines produce themselves? Can machines put themselves into action? The problem is that the real machines we compare ourselves with are always the product of human beings. So the question emerges as to who or what made these "machines" that we call human beings? Did they make themselves? But that wouldn't make sense, for nothing can cause itself. To say that a machine created itself is in fact philosophical nonsense, for such a machine would have to exist before it came into existence. A hand may draw a picture of itself, but it can never produce the very hand that does the drawing – as little as a projector can project itself.

Third, the machines made by human beings are, curiously enough, always made for a purpose. So to use the machine metaphor to claim there is no purpose in this universe is a bit odd, to say the least. The world of technology is per definition based on purposes that designers and engineers have in mind. In a world without purposes, there couldn't be any machines, at least not man-made machines.

Fourth, our bodies make for something so different from our minds that the question forces itself on us as to how a mind can work as if it were merely body material. The most ancient and simple answer consists of plainly denying that human beings are anything more than mechanical motions of material particles. This materialistic and mechanistic solution is hard to defend, though, partly because of one particular counter-argument advanced by the great German philosopher Leibniz. His idea was to picture the brain so much enlarged that one could walk in it as in a mill. Inside, we would only observe movements of several parts, but never anything like a thought. Hence thoughts and the like must be completely different from simple mechanical movements of parts and particles.

Some philosophers have come up with another reason to defeat mechanicism by calling upon the *incompleteness theorem* that we mentioned earlier. The logician and mathematician Kurt Gödel proved in this theorem that no complex mathematical theory can be both consistent and complete; if it is complete, it cannot be consistent; if it is consistent, it cannot be complete, for its consistency cannot be proven within the system. How does this relate to mechanism? If the human mind were equivalent to a machine, and if this machine is consistent, then Gödel's incompleteness theorem would apply to it as well. His proof suggests that there could be some higher-level entity, the *mind*, involving concepts which do not appear on lower levels of the *brain*, and that this higher level might explain what cannot be explained on lower levels. If so, the *mind* would escape explanation in terms of mere *brain* components. Gödel himself concluded that the power of the mind exceeds that of any finite machine. As a result, human beings with a spiritual *mind* must be more than automated machines with a physical *brain*. In chapter five, we will delve deeper into this issue.

A: You are *only* a bag of genes

Here we have another one: You have no creativity, no choices, no destination, for all you have is your genes – you are nothing but your genes. I must admit, though, that science is good at breaking things down into parts – and for geneticists those parts are genes. We have learned more and more about those genes. We even understand better how chromosomes, which carry the genes, are copied and then pulled to opposite ends of the cell, before the cell splits in two, but further details are still fuzzy. What we do know, though, is that a gene can carry one of several variants called alleles. Since genes always come in duplex, one of the two goes to the next generation – but as to which one, that is supposedly a matter of chance. When George Bernard Shaw was approached by a seductive young actress who cooed him in his ear, "Wouldn't it be wonderful if we got married and had a child with my beauty and your brains," Shaw replied: "My dear, that would be wonderful indeed, but what if our child had my beauty and your brains?" Yes, genetics can go either way; it works with chance and probability.

It shouldn't surprise us then that many biologists love what they call the *gene pool model* – basically a glorified bag of genes. The atheist and biologist Richard Dawkins, for instance, is one of them.

He loves to use this model to simulate a process of natural selection among the different variants of a gene (alleles) in a population. What he "sees" happening in the gene pool model is a change of allele frequencies, generation after generation, which basically changes the organism into a "survival machine" for its genes. He even speaks of a "selfish gene" that is in a constant "survival battle" with other genes.

Some people call this kind of approach disrespectfully "bean-bag genetics": a bag of genes in a bag of chromosomes in a bag of cells. And from there on, humans have become a bag of genes as well – nothing more, nothing less. They are completely at the mercy of those genes, shackled by what genetics dictates. We are supposed to dance on the strings of our genes.

R: We are *more* than bags of genes

Is what genetics tells us really all there is? Or is there another side to the story? I think we deserve to hear the rest of the story. Even science itself can show us that we are more than a bag of genes: You and I are surely more than the sum total of our genes. In chapter 6, we will see how limited the power of genes is.

Yet, some biologists love to glorify the all-inclusive power of genes. When Richard Dawkins, for instance, promotes his gene-pool model, he concludes that the actual unit of selection is the gene. In reality, though, genes are not units of selection. The late biologist Stephen J. Gould pithily rebuked, "Selection simply cannot see genes." Alleles, for example, that do not show up in the phenotype of a heterozygous organism can never be subject to natural selection. In reality, the real unit of selection is the *organism*, but not the *gene* and its alleles – contrary to what the gene-pool model suggests.

What is wrong with Dawkins' approach? He doesn't seem to realize is that we should never exchange the complexity of reality for the simplicity of one of its models. In addition, we also need to learn some important lessons from philosophy. Whenever geneticists speak of chance and randomness, we must be aware that the term chance can carry many different meanings, so each time a biologist says that something happened "by chance," we should ask: How do you mean? Biologists can define randomness in many ways, but they can never define it as meaningless or purposeless, as those words do not exist in science but derive from philosophy and religion. Yet, some geneticists love to adorn the scientific term *chance* with a capital C – changing it into some kind of goddess, the goddess of *Chance*, a sort of whimsical providence secretly worshipped and to be forcefully defended against rival deities. However, the concept of chance in genetics not even comes close to fate, destiny, doom, or meaninglessness. Chance is part of the model, but do not confuse the model with reality.

Religious people have always known this. What appears to science as a mere "random" event may in fact very well be a directed, indeed providential process from a religious point of view. As Saint Padre Pio once said to a man who claimed such-and-such event had happened by chance: "And who, do you suppose, arranged the chances?" On the same note, John Henry Cardinal Newman wrote in an 1868 letter that accidental events in science are "accidental to us, not to God." In religion, there is just no place for good or bad "luck." As a matter of fact, St. Thomas Aquinas once said, "Whoever believes that everything is a matter of chance, does not believe that God exists."

A: You are *only* a string of DNA

If this were true, you would have no self, no dignity, no calling, for all you are believed to be is a stream of DNA molecules. Since DNA comprises more than genes, this is the latest of the latest slogans. It sounds better to be a string of DNA than a bag of genes, for the one-time idea of DNA holding only genes has been refined by the discovery that protein-coding regions of genes can be interrupted by DNA segments that play more of a *regulatory* role by producing proteins that either activate or repress the activity of "regular" genes. Some of these regulatory genes are actually very short and do not produce proteins at all but short strands of mRNA capable of blocking the mRNA of a "regular" gene from creating its protein; they are called micro-RNA-genes. So the DNA picture is more intricate than the gene picture.

In addition, genes may be separated by long stretches of DNA that do not seem to be doing much. Some of this "non-coding" DNA is repetitive DNA, usually replicated from regular, coding DNA, and perhaps a rich source from which potentially useful new genes can emerge in evolution.

Because of these discoveries, many people now think that it is DNA that holds the script for a person's entire life, so they would like to know their "personal genomics." The science journal *Nature* listed "Personal Genomics Goes Mainstream" as a top news story of 2008. No wonder one of the DNA pioneers said he could compute the entire organism if he were given its DNA sequence and a large enough computer. And out you are – literally! DNA seems to have become the definitive controlling agency behind our lives.

The ultimate goal of most scientists seems to be an explanation of life in terms of DNA: therefore, the "secret of life" is supposed to reside in DNA. In their view, all that counts is DNA; so with the human genome project finished, we are supposed to know all there is to know about human beings.

R: We are *more* than strings of DNA

Is what DNA-gurus tell us really all there is? Or is there another side to the story? Again, all forms of reductionism reduce the complexity of the whole to the simplicity of its parts, and then claim there is nothing else than those parts, those DNA molecules. They actually curtail our outlook by not seeing the forest for the trees.

Scientists who defend the primacy of DNA essentially demote organisms to merely being DNA's way of creating more DNA – a form of "selfish DNA," so to speak. What they forget, however, is that DNA is useless in itself, unless it is part of a larger, very intricate system which includes enzymes and other cellular components located in separate cellular compartments. DNA cannot even replicate itself without an elaborate cell machinery that is made up of proteins. As a result, DNA looks more like an *archive* with instructions, but *what* to use from this archive *when*, *where*, and *how* is determined somewhere else.

In other words, we cannot possibly compute an organism, for the simple reason that an organism doesn't compute itself from its DNA. DNA is only a small link in a complex process of protein synthesis, and this system, in turn, is part of and is regulated by an even larger system – the elaborate system of an organism that switches genes on and off with hormones, and the like. As it turns out, the statement that the secret of life resides in DNA has its mirror image in the following, equally valid, yet less popular statement: Life is as much the secret of DNA as DNA is the secret of life. Think of viruses, which are essentially pure DNA or RNA; their DNA or RNA cannot do anything until it penetrates, like a Trojan horse, the environment of a "living" cell.

The reductionists' creed says: After dissecting them, things are much simpler than they appear. But we should ask them why explanations must always go one way, in the direction of "smaller," "lower," and "simpler" things. If the "smaller" can explain the "larger," why couldn't the "larger" explain the "smaller" as well? Would it really be "better" to explain the working of DNA in terms of its (smaller) molecular structure than in terms of its (larger) surrounding cellular structure?

Then we have an important philosophical question left: Did DNA discover itself? Here is my reason for asking this question: If all we are is DNA, and we are the ones who discovered DNA, then DNA must have discovered itself! That is like a camera taking a shot of itself (not through mirrors of course!). A copier makes copies, but not copies of itself; a projector can project pictures, but it cannot project itself. In other words, a world-view that portrays us as solely being a DNA chain is as fragile as the DNA structure that presumably generated this world-view; it cannot be worth more than its molecular origin.

To put it differently, if we were only a chain of DNA, we have in fact cut off the very branch that even science itself needs to sit on. We would have lost our reason for reasoning and for trusting our own rationality. Hence, we must be "more" than the molecules we are made of. We need something bigger than ourselves – certainly something "higher" than DNA. We cannot pull ourselves up by our own bootstraps. In chapter five, we will find out that our Christian religion has an answer to this problem.

A: You are *only* a blob of cells

There we go again: You have no personality, no morals, no significance, no destiny, for all you are is a bunch of cells. Another present-day slogan! True or false?

Science may give us the impression it is true. The power of science is that it makes scientific problems soluble by creating a test-tube-like shelter in a laboratory, removed from the complexity of nature, so that the various factors under investigation can be isolated and manipulated on an individual basis. Research is "the art of the soluble" according to Nobel Laureate Peter Medawar. Well, thanks to this artful technique, scientists have been able to *isolate* parts of living organisms in order to study them better. That is how they came across cells (and other entities such as genes and hormones).

A visit to an immunological laboratory, for instance, may show us immune cells (*B lymphocytes*) in test tubes (*in vitro*) attacking so-called antigens by producing antibodies all by themselves. No doubt, the test-tube approach makes things just easier "soluble." But this same observation may also be deceiving, giving us the false impression that the immunity system is really an isolated self-regulating system, until we learn from other research that the immune system interacts extensively with other bodily systems (*in vivo*) – which fact, in turn, makes things much more complicated.

Yet, many scientists often forget, or are just not willing, to place those parts or pieces back into the *whole* they came from. So we end up being nothing more than a blob of cells. If that were right, we could even be cloned in a Petri dish.

R: We are *more* than blobs of cells

Is what cell-biologists tell us really all there is? There must be more to the story than those blobs of cells! What we stated earlier concerning genes and DNA, we should also say about cells: Most cells do not operate on their own but are embedded in a much wider framework, the framework of an organism. Just as DNA is part of genes, and genes are parts of cells, so cells are typically parts of organisms.

Perhaps philosophy can help us understand this problem better. Bear with me for a moment! Our universe is "stuffed" with *substances* which are endowed with *properties*, and which are mutually connected by *relationships*. In other words, there appear to be three different kinds of entities in this universe. First, we have things (often called *substances*) such as molecules, cells, and stones. Next we have *properties*, making certain things inorganic and others organic, some heavy and some light, and so on. Finally, we have *relationships* between things, such as the relationship a mother has to her daughter, or football players to their team. When we say "Joe is tall and single," – unlike "tall" – "single" is not a property; it is about a (missing) relationship.

Why is this discussion so important for us? Well, the basic question is this: How can we be more than what we are made of? According to some, the *whole* (say, an organism) is nothing more than the sum total of its *parts* (say, its cells); only the parts are presumably "real," and the rest is considered fiction. But others would object to this and claim that a cell is certainly "more" than the collection of its molecules, or that an organism is "more" than the collection of its cells – or more in general, that the whole is "more" than the sum total of its parts. I think these latter people make a good point, but the question is how we should take this "more." If we consider this "more" to be an added, new "thing" or substance, we actually make the same mistake as our opponents do by only focusing on substances and properties, without paying any attention to the *relationships*, the interactions, between all components.

If that is a valid point, then the properties of the "whole" cannot be found in its composing parts alone, but they arise from interrelating or interacting activities *between* the parts, making for some kind of synergism depending on the way the whole is organized. That is why "lower-level" DNA can properly function and do its work, because it is harnessed inside "higher-level" cells, and those cells, for their part, can even function more intricately when they are harnessed inside an organism at a still higher level. That is why the "secret" of DNA is life – as much so as the "secret" of life is DNA, or perhaps even more so.

The same holds for cells: The world of cells turns out to be a highly interactive world that has developed new properties based on new relationships. St. Paul would put this view in a more down-to-earth way: "The eye cannot say to the hand, 'I have no need of you,' nor again the head to the feet, 'I have no need of you.'" (1 Cor. 12:21). Let no one ever fool you by claiming that we are just a blob of isolated cells.

A: You are *only* a pack of neurons

If this were true, you would have no mind, no free will, no personality. All you are believed to be is a network of neurons. It was the DNA co-discoverer Francis Crick who dared to tell us this – in his own words, "You're nothing but a pack of neurons."

The people who say something to this effect are actually proclaiming that the mental state of the *mind* is nothing but the neural state of the *brain*. In other words, a brain scan can presumably tell you everything about what is going on in your mind. If so, neurologists should be able to read your mind! Are they really? Do brains really make up their minds? It is a "nothing-buttery" claim again – this time, of reducing the mental to the neural.

This flawed idea has been reinforced by the observation that the brain works in the same way as a computer operates, because both use a binary code based on "ones" (1) and "zeros" (0); neurons either do (1) or do not (0) fire an electric impulse – in the same way as transistors either do (1) or do not (0) conduct an electric current. So it does appear as if the brain "thinks" like a computer "thinks." Therefore, you are not only a pack of neurons, but also a mere stream of binary code. Poor you!

R: We are *more* than packs of neurons

Is what Francis Crick tells us really all there is? Or is he, like many others, just telling us parts of the truth, thereby missing an essential part?

First of all, the mind doesn't go away when we try to explain it away. Picture yourself watching through a mirror how a scientist is studying your opened skull for "brain waves." The philosopher

Ludwig Wittgenstein once noted correctly that the scientist is observing just *one* thing, outer brain activities, but the brain-owner is actually observing *two* things – that is, the outer brain activities via the mirror as well as the inner mental processes that no one else has access to. In order for them to make the connection between "inner" *mental* states and "outer" *neural* states, scientists would depend on information that only the "brain-owner" can provide.

My second point is this: There is something wrong with this analogy of a stream of binary code in the brain. True, our thoughts may have a material substrate that works like a binary code, but it would not really matter whether this material substrate works with impulses (like in the brain) or with currents (like in a computer), because such material is only the physical *carrier*, merely a vehicle that carries something else – in the way trains can transport people or goods. One and the same thought can be coded in Morse, Braille, hieroglyphics, impulses, or whatever code language; it doesn't really matter, for these codes are just physical carriers, vehicles, or tools. But thoughts are not something physical.

So what is it then that sets the thought apart from its carrier? Well, thoughts are more than a binary code; they also have sense and meaning, and that is what the binary code really carries. Thoughts are about something else, something mental, which is something beyond themselves. And it is this very "about-ness" that a computer lacks; anything that shows up on a computer monitor remains just an "empty" collection of "ones and zeros," until some kind of human interpretation gives sense and meaning to the code and interprets it as being *about* something.

So the question is then: Who "reads" and "interprets" the neuron firings that take place in our pack of neurons? Could we perhaps say that the *mind* reads, writes, and uses the neurons in the *brain*? I would say so, for something has got to be in charge. If that is true, then we may, someday, be able to understand the human *brain*, but that doesn't mean we will ever fully understand the human *mind*. The mind can study the brain, but never could the brain study itself! The knowing *subject* must be more than the known *object* – for it requires a mind to understand the brain, as it requires a subject to study any object. We will discuss this more extensively in chapter five.

Then I have a third objection. If the mind were nothing but the brain, we have lost an entire world of thoughts and truths. That would be a tremendous loss! As I said before, thoughts are more than the code that carries them; they also have sense and meaning; we don't just think, we always think something. If the brain merely carries thoughts, but doesn't create them, then our thoughts somehow "use" the vehicle of the brain. Thoughts are about something else, something mental, which is something beyond the code that expresses them. However, if the mind were just a brain issue, thoughts could not be right or wrong and true or false, as neural events simply happen and that is that. Interestingly enough, denying the existence of mental activities is in itself a mental activity, and thus would lead to a detrimental contradiction.

But where does the mind come from then? I would say not from the brain, but from something or rather Someone transcending all of this. If humans were only a pack of neurons, and if humans are the ones who study neurons, then neurons would be studying themselves… We obviously need something "higher" than neurons – something beyond them, something that transcends them. One would need a mind before one can study the brain!

A: You are *only* a bundle of instincts

All you are is a bundle of suppressed instincts, so you have no self, no personality, no morals, no freedom. Sigmund Freud is probably the best know representative of this view. The 19th century could be called the century of Freud, either in support of his new "depth-psychology" or in opposition to the new psychoanalysis.

Freud is part of a long history. Descartes had been very explicit: Animals have no soul, cannot think, and are mere bundles of instincts, prepackaged by God – but humans are essentially different. Then Charles Darwin demoted the human race to a species that had evolved from other forms of animal life. In this line of thought, Freud viewed humans as animals with animal instincts, although he saw repression of (sexual and aggressive) instincts as necessary to the preservation of human community and order. But this repression supposedly came with costs: neurosis, depression, phobias, psychosomatic conversions, plus many other pathologies.

So Freud ended up with a new form of reductionism: Man is only a bundle of conflicting impulses, each one of which is striving for control, whereas the mind is just the passive onlooker. If Freud were right, we would be fully at the mercy of our instincts.

R: We are *more* than bundles of instincts

Dr. Allers, a Viennese by birth and head of the Laboratory of Medical Psychology in Vienna after World War II, who joined in 1938 the faculty of the Catholic University of America, said about Freud: His view of man is not a person, but "a bundle of instincts". He also said that the principles of this Freudian psychology are utterly materialistic, born from the spirit of naturalism and materialism. No wonder, Freud once remarked about Professor Allers that it was "a shame such a brilliant intellect had gone wrong."

There can hardly be any dispute, I think, that animals are bundles of instincts, impulses, affinities, and appetites, without the extra gift of reason. Humans also are a bundle of instincts, but supplemented by the gift of reason; then there are other features exclusively human, such as awe, veneration, humility, reverence, self-sacrifice, shame, modesty, and many others that are characteristic of what we call our moral nature. The Catechism of the Catholic Church would speak of "passions" – which are "emotions or movements of the sensitive appetite that incline us to act or not to act in regard to something felt or imagined to be good or evil" (1763).

Some animals may out-see us, out-smell us, out-hear us, out-run us, out-swim us, because their lives depend more upon these special powers than ours do; but we can out-wit them all because we have the resourcefulness of reason, and are at home in many different fields. As a matter of fact, humans enjoy freedom, rationality, and morality – all of which find their origin in God, as we will se further on.

On the other hand, if the slogan "You are only a bundle of instincts" were true, the ethical fallout would be tremendous. It makes the topic of sexuality, for instance, look like a purely psychological issue – a matter of instincts and feelings – whereas in fact, it also has wide moral and religious ramifications, including sinfulness. Do we call pedophilia an illness, or is it, in the words of the psychiatrist Thomas Szasz, more comparable to rape – a moral issue? Are we talking pathology here or morality?

It seems to me that psychology and psychiatry, under Freud's lead, have become an alternative for religion, a counterfeit religion so to speak, thoroughly based on the worship of the "self." As a consequence, many kinds of behavior – especially morally good or wrong behavior – have been turned into diseases, into some kind of pathology: Grief became depression, apprehension became anxiety, rape became sexual frustration, and so on. What is in a word? A world of differences!

Isn't it amazing what slogans of reductionism can do? In response, I would say religion may be the most effective anti-depressant there is, and the best weapon against sinful behavior! Chapter seven has much more on this complicated issue.

A: You are *only* a termite in a colony

If you are only a statistic, an insignificant member of the larger colony, then you have no rights, no individuality, no personality. You would just be a member of the herd. Here is the situation: Sometimes we do feel part of a herd. Each one of us has the feeling of being confronted with some power in society; this power may provoke in us feelings of rejection or acceptance, but there is no easy way of avoiding or ignoring this power. Society restrains me physically, and also interferes with my thinking and feeling; it stamps even my spiritual life, at least to some degree.

This has led some to take society – instead of the individual – as a *substance* on its own. If this were true, there would only be one thing in society, only one substance – which is the *whole* of the colony. The individuals would only be *parts* of this substance, and therefore do not qualify as complete entities. Just like the hand of a person is not complete in itself, but only a part of the whole, part of the person, in the same way an individual person is believed by some to be only a part of society – in the same way as worker bees only exist for the sake of the colony.

If it is so that society is the only truly real entity that enjoys full existence – whereas persons are only a part of this entity

– then it should be obvious that human beings have no rights of their own. After all, they live their lives as part of society, through the power of society, and for the benefit of society. In this view, the whole, the state, is more "real" than its parts, the individuals. As a consequence, the state is presumably in full control of its individuals; it determines how many children you can have, how much you can earn, how much care you can get, and even how long you can live. Sounds familiar?

The end-result is some kind of socio-ethical collectivism, actually totalitarianism, turning a human being into a mere means for the sole end of advancing the "colony" of human society. The ultimate consequence of social collectivism is the following mantra: "You do not exist at all." In this view, individual human beings do no longer really exist. They should always be used and relentlessly exploited as a means for accomplishing the purposes of the whole. They are like termites that only exist to make the colony survive. We all know of societies where this view was rigorously enforced and of the suffering it has caused. The only argument used to defend this claim is a bullet.

But even without bullets, this way of thinking has quietly pervaded modern society more than you might think: We have become mere numbers in a vast colony. The influential biologist Garrett Hardin, for instance, used this kind of thinking in his teachings on human ecology: "The real world is a world of quantified entities" – and so are human beings. The more people there are, the more insignificant they become. As a consequence, an individual life is "cheap, very cheap," as he calls it, because there is such an abundance of it – in his terms, "a surplus of demanding human flesh." An individual human life would only become *more* significant if there were *fewer* people. This lopsided view explains why he vigorously campaigned for population control.

R: We are *more* than termites in a colony

Is what Communism and related ideologies tell us really all there is? There must be another side to the story! Looking around in society, we do not perceive a society but only human beings – individual human beings, that is. So what to say about the "colony" we are supposed to work for? Is that perhaps just a collective term for all its members? Or is it the other way around – and is the colony indeed more real than the individuals, as the totalitarian view wants us to believe?

To answer this question, let's use the terminology we introduced earlier. If *substances* were the only real entities that exist, then we have to face a dilemma: Either the society is a real substance – with its members being a fiction without any rights – or the members are the real substances – with the society being a fiction without any rights.

I would say most people see in all clarity that individuals do have their own rights, yet they should also observe some duties toward society. In other words, neither individuals nor society are mere fictions. How can this be? The answer is that societies consist of individuals plus their *relationships*; which makes a society more than the sum total of its individuals. This sound philosophical view was widely promoted by the late philosopher Fr. Joseph Bochenski, O.P.

So we should come to the conclusion that the individuals are the sole full reality in society, but the society, in turn, is more than the sum total of its individuals, because it also includes the real relationships individuals have with each other and with their common goal. As human nature is social, some of our duties will be social. Therefore, our individuality remains upright; we are a community of persons. You and I are not a quantity or statistic, but a quality – the quality of being made in God's Image. Each one of us was created in God's image and likeness; and that is where our human dignity and human rights stem from – and no society can take those away.

But at the very moment we glorify the "colony" over the "termites," individuals lose all their rights and become enslaved to the "rights" of the totality – which is pure totalitarianism. The Church explicitly rejects "the totalitarian and atheistic ideologies associated in modern times with 'communism' or 'socialism'" (CCC 2425). The horrors placed on human beings by totalitarian regimes – in the labor camps run by Nazis, Soviets, Japanese, and Chinese – tell us how ugly this ideology can get. They turned their "citizens" into cattle and "cheap meat."

A: You are *only* a 3-dimensional being

You have no depth, no foundation, no destination, no Maker, for all you are is merely a tiny element of this three-dimensional world. People who think this way have become completely focused on what they can see, feel, hear, or touch in a physical sense. So God has disappeared from their radar – out of sight, out of mind. Such people have lost the fourth dimension – the dimension of the invisible, the dimension of the supernatural, the dimension of the spiritual and divine. They live in a vacuum that was once filled by faith in God.

More and more people in our society are no longer aware of this growing vacuum, as they have no memory of the way life used to be; they live obliviously in complete religious ignorance. They are like electrical appliances during a power outage. Here we have atheism in its simplest form: I just never think of God. Without evangelization, religious illiteracy would be rampant.

As we discussed in the previous chapter, this version of atheism has become very prevalent in our modern society. Pope Benedict XVI calls it "secularism," which leads to a lifestyle marred with complete unawareness of God. He also calls it "paganism," turning us into complete heathens. It doesn't deny God, doesn't fight God, it just ignores God. Its only commandment is "You shall never invoke the name of God, unless you do so in vain." We used to unify people with the motto "one nation *under* God," but now they try to unify us under the banner of "one nation *without* God."

R: We are *more* than 3-dimensional beings

Here we have reductionism in optima forma. As with all forms of reductionism, their claims are not plainly false, but they are *half*-truths. The problem with half-truths is that a partial truth in itself seems to make so much sense that it actually keeps us from seeking the full truth.

I would describe the situation as follows: The bottom has fallen out, our legs have been cut from under us, our fourth dimension was taken away, our sixth sense got lost. We ended up with a "God-shaped hole" that nothing and nobody can fill but God. I myself feel ripped off. What about you? How long can we stay afloat with the bottom taken out? Well, here is my answer – not really mine, but God's answer, Jesus' answer, the Church's answer, and perhaps some day your answer.

First, as humans, we have been endowed with *rationality*, which goes far beyond what reductionism has come up with. As said before, the knowing subject has got to be more than the known object. Thank rationality for it! Second, as humans, we have been endowed with *morality*, which again goes far beyond what reductionism can discover. Third, both rationality and morality need something – *Someone* – far beyond themselves to lend them a stable footing. The Catechism quotes the early Church Father Tertullian who said "Alone among all animate beings, man can boast of having been counted worthy to receive a law from God: as an animal endowed with reason, capable of understanding and discernment, he is to govern his conduct by using his freedom and reason, in obedience to the One who has entrusted everything to him" (1951).

If rationality were only based on DNA, we would have no longer any *reason* to trust our own reasoning; we would not be able to distinguish true from false. Einstein was well aware of the fact that, without God, we cannot even explain why nature is comprehensible at all, why nature is so orderly and logically consistent. We will get back to this in chapter five.

And the same holds for morality. If morality were only rooted in our genes, we would have no *right* to tell right from wrong. Even the atheist and philosopher Jean Paul Sartre was aware of the fact that, without an eternal Heaven that would make values objective and universal, there can be no absolute or objective standard of right and wrong. We will delve deeper into this in chapter seven.

I would say it is quite something what religion is claiming here! Let's find out in the rest of this book how Catholicism can maintain such claims and how the Church answers to those who deny the validity of these claims.

3

Science in Dialogue with Religion

A Match Made in Heaven

For centuries, science and religion used to live in harmony. But times have changed. Nowadays there is a breed of scientists who are very vocal atheists; they promote their new "religion" with extremely popular books and they preach their "gospel" in schools and universities. No wonder the faithful feel personally attacked. Although Christians did launch some counterattacks (often against science itself, though), they mostly retracted to their new catacombs, the church pews.

I believe it is about time to revive the old dialogue between science and religion, for those "worshipping atheists" deserve to be challenged. I like to compare them with football fanatics who think that the only thing that counts in life is a football game. There is certainly nothing wrong with football, but let us not make it our new "god." Let's also apply this to science: Do not throw science away but put it in its proper place.

This chapter tries to simulate a dialogue between a *skeptical* scientist (S) and a *religious* scientist (R). I hope and pray it is going to open any blinded eyes for what is at stake. No one can break us who didn't make us – and certainly not a skeptical scientist.

A *skeptical* scientist (S) interrogates
a *religious* scientist (R)

S: Religion? What is religion? I thought religion was on its way out a long time ago. We scientists took care of that!

R: No, religion is still very much alive. But I am glad you have some memory left of the way it used to be, for science was actually born in the cradle of religion – like it or not. Think of St. Albert the Great, Fr. Roger Bacon, Fr. William of Ockham, and Bishop Robert Grosseteste, all of whom started scientific experiments as early as the 13th century. And they were not even the first ones. At the end of the 1st millennium, Pope Sylvester II had already used advanced instruments of astronomical observation, in his passion for understanding the order of the universe. But we can even go further back: As early as the 8th century, the English Benedictine monk St. Bede the Venerable had studied the sea's tidal currents.

Why had no other cultures before them come up with such novel ideas? The answer is rather simple: The Bible and the Church teach us that the universe was created by a rational intellect capable of being rationally interrogated, even through experiments. These early scientists wanted to illuminate the mysteries of the Creator, the "Cosmic Orderer." Only in such a cradle could science be born.

S: Didn't other, non-Christian cultures and societies start science as well?

R: Not really. Interestingly enough, there is growing evidence that the "scientific revolution" in the 15th and 16th century had its roots more in the Christian Middle Ages than in the world of ancient Greeks such as Aristotle and of Islamic scholars such as Avicenna. The latter may have been masters in geometry and mathematics, where pure reason reigns, but this made them think they could generate scientific results deductively from passive observation, which would make those conclusions seem logically necessary. I admit that the Greek and Muslim traditions of logic and mathematics did provide the tools that science would badly need in order to make its ascent, but do not confuse these tools with science itself. There was a different environment needed for applying these tools in a scientific context – and that environment was the Judeo-Christian concept of Creation and a Creator God. There is no way around it, science was born in a Judeo-Christian cradle and is still living off Judeo-Christian capital.

Because the Judeo-Christian God is a reliable God – not confined inside the Aristotelian box, not capricious like the Olympians in ancient Greece, and not entirely beyond human comprehension like in Islam – the world depends on the laws that God has laid down in creation. That is where the order of the universe ultimately comes from. And the only way to find out what this order looks like is to "interrogate" the universe by investigation, exploration, and experiment. Through experiments we can "read" God's mind, so to speak. Even the nuclear physicist J. Robert Oppenheimer, who was not a Christian, was ready to acknowledge this very fact when he said, "Christianity was needed to give birth to modern science."

One might in fact claim that the scientific project and its scientific method are an invention of the Catholic Church. It was precisely during the high Middle Ages that the great European universities were founded. One of the first scientists, Bishop Robert Grosseteste, introduced the scientific method, including the concept of falsification, as early as the 13th century. The Franciscan friar Roger Bacon established concepts such as hypothesis, experimentation, and verification, so science would be free from foreign authorities and habitual bias. In other words, what some consider a period of darkness was actually the birth of the light of reason.

S: Well, that is how it may have started, but science is grown-up now and has become fully independent.

R: I do not think so. Science started as a faith-based enterprise, and it has stayed that way. Copernicus' achievements were based on his religious *belief* that nothing was easier for God than to have the earth move, if He so wished. And Kepler's Christian *belief* told him God would not tolerate the inaccuracy of obsolete circular models in astronomy. It was in God that these scientists found reason to investigate nature and trust their own scientific reasoning. Even contemporary scientists still hold similar beliefs, although they may be unaware. Faith gave scientists their job, and so it still does!

In one sense, though, you're right: Science would gradually articulate more clearly what its actual territory is. In 1650, scientific societies began to blossom. The fellows of the *Royal Society of London*, for instance, received from King Charles II the privilege of enjoying intelligence and knowledge, but with the following important and crucial stipulation "provided in matters of things philosophical, mathematical, and mechanical." Notice that explicit limitation.

Everything else was given away for others to handle, as long as their own members, the future scientists, were permitted to "know" what can be known by *counting* and *measuring*. That is how the "division of the estate" was executed. By accepting this, science bought its own territory, but certainly at the expense of inclusiveness. The rest would for ever remain part of a different territory, beyond the reach of science, and therefore outside its scope. Most scientists realized very clearly that religion would always be off-limits to them, and that science just has an inborn "blind spot" for God – which makes some scientists nowadays think there *is* no God. However, you may *neglect* what is outside your scope as a scientist, but that doesn't entitle you to *deny* its existence. God cannot be found by flashlight.

There is so much that science is "blind" for – a vast invisible world. Science may be everywhere, but science is certainly not all there is. There is more to life than science, for science is not by any means a know-all or cure-all. Science purchased success at the cost of limiting its ambition. The rest of the "estate" was reserved for others to handle. That is where faith, religion, ethics, and philosophy come in. The unfounded claim that "the real" world" is a world of quantified entities ignores the fact that not all that counts in life can be counted. Again, you may neglect what lies outside the scientific range, but you cannot just deny its existence. That would be like denying the existence of infrared and ultraviolet, because our eyes cannot capture those wavelengths.

S: Even if I would admit there is another part to the "estate," it seems so fickle to me. That is why I would agree with the physical chemist Peter Atkins that science liberates, whereas religion obfuscates.

R: It may seem so because the domain beyond the reach of science is indeed not countable, quantifiable, and measurable

– which doesn't mean it isn't *real*. As I said before, not everything that counts can be counted. Science cannot account for all that needs to be accounted for. I do agree with you that if science doesn't go to its limits, it is a failure, but I must also add this: As soon as science *oversteps* its limits, it becomes arrogant – a know-it-all. We should never forget that there are so many aspects of life that are off-limits for science. Things that are located outside the scientific realm of visible things may be more or less invisible, but that shouldn't make them disappear from our "radar screen." Science has purchased success at the cost of limiting its ambition. Even science itself depends on elements that are more or less invisible and do not belong to its own territory but come ultimately from other parts of the "estate." Let me clarify this.

It is a fundamental "rule" in science that everything it tries to explain or predict is based on laws – laws of physics, biology, chemistry, and so on. But the fundamental question is where such a "rule" comes from. The "law" that everything is based on laws definitely doesn't come from science itself, for science cannot explain its own rules, as little as chess can explain its own rules. Science can explain things by using laws, but it certainly cannot explain those very laws. So where do those laws come from then?

Be aware, we are leaving scientific territory here! How come our universe is orderly and lawful? How come only certain biological designs could pass the filter of natural selection? How come those designs work successfully? Why is there some-thing rather than no-thing? Science has no answer to such questions; they are undoubtedly beyond its reach. Science raises questions it cannot answer itself. They are part of an invisible realm.

S: Where would the answer come from then, in your opinion?

R: The answer does not come from physics, but from *meta*-physics, and ultimately from religion. We either accept that there is *no* explanation at all for the order and design we find in nature (which is basically irrational) – or we look instead for a *rational* explanation of this cosmic order and design. I would say it is much more rational to go for the latter.

Again, science itself cannot *explain* order and design but must *assume* them, for without these assumptions, science would be impossible. Everything science does is based on the fact that there is order in this universe; otherwise nature would be a long chain of inexplicable and unpredictable events; that is why we demand further explanation when scientific laws seem to be violated; but without an underlying order, there wouldn't be such a thing as a violation of laws and there would be no falsifiable evidence.

Only philosophy can explain these assumptions by stating: There has got to be an underlying order in this universe, some kind of *cosmic order*. And religion would add to this that it is a Divine Creator who created this cosmic order according to an intelligible plan accessible to the human intellect through the natural light of reason. To paraphrase Saint Augustine: We need faith in order to understand – even so in science, I would add.

S: Don't tell me that philosophy and religion are essentially the same.

R: No, that is not my point. Philosophy is capable of showing us that this world would be irrational and incomprehensible if there were no orderly and lawful Creator – a God of order so to speak. It is "nature's God," all-powerful, all-knowing, and all-present. That is basically the point *deism* asserts, but that is also where philosophy reaches its boundaries. The Catechism acknowledges that "Human intelligence is surely already capable of finding a response to the question of origins. The existence of God the Creator can be known with certainty through his works, by the light of human reason, even if this knowledge is often obscured and disfigured by error" (286).

Religion, on the other hand, is about our *personal* relationship with this Creator God – the God of the Covenant, a God of Love, not only all-present, all-powerful, and all-knowing, but also all-loving. That is where *theism* comes in. In the words of the Catechism, "Beyond the natural knowledge that every man can have of the Creator (Cf. Acts 17:24-29; Rom 1:19-20), God progressively revealed to Israel the mystery of creation. He who chose the patriarchs, who brought Israel out of Egypt, and who by choosing Israel created and formed it, this same God reveals himself as the One to whom belong all the peoples of the earth, and the whole earth itself; he is the One who alone 'made heaven and earth'" (287).

This is not to say that philosophy and theology are miles apart from each other. They may have their own approach, methodology, and vocabulary, but they also need to intersect properly. Some philosophers are too much of a philosopher to be understood by theologians and some theologians are too much of a theologian to be understood by philosophers, but others, such as Pope Benedict, have the right blend and appeal to both sides of the discussion. When in Athens, St. Paul saw an altar inscribed "To an Unknown God," so he invited the Athenians to take the step from deism to theism: "What therefore you worship as unknown, this I proclaim to you" (Acts 17:23). I invite you to take that step too.

S: I don't need God to do science. I have my own scientific reasons for trusting science.

R: I am curious to hear your reasons, for I have never heard of any valid ones. If you base your trust in science on scientific evidence, you are running around in a vicious circle. No experiment can do such a trick! Science cannot pull itself up by its own bootstraps. An electric generator cannot run on its own power.

In order to counter your objection, I couldn't do better than quoting Albert Einstein when he said, "The most incomprehensible thing about the universe is that it is comprehensible." Indeed, it is an incomprehensible thing to scientists, a mystery, but not so to religious believers, for they know why we can *comprehend* this universe.

There is only one reasonable explanation for this: All scientists – perhaps willy-nilly or unknowingly – do uphold the biblical conviction that God created the world according to an intelligible plan that is accessible to the human intellect through the natural light of reason. Reason is not a product of ir-rationality but it comes forth from the great Intelligence that is behind everything. As Pope Benedict XVI said to the Bishops of Washington, DC during their *ad limina* visit on Jan. 19, 2012, we have "the ultimate assurance that the cosmos is possessed of an inner logic accessible to human reasoning."

Let me put this more specifically for scientists: In science, one must just assume and trust that nature is law-abiding and comprehensible in principle. To put this in different terms, this world is best understood as an "intelligent project." That is the faith behind reason. Therefore, denying that God is our Creator is actually an acid eating away the foundation of science and rationality. In other words, science is a faith-based enterprise. Whether they like to admit it or not, all scientists are still living off monotheistic, Judeo-Christian capital. It is capital that we cannot value enough! It is priceless!

S: I am afraid that you are beginning to make *reason* a matter of *faith*.

R: Not really, but I do think they are strongly intertwined. Reason requires faith (otherwise reason has no basis) and faith seeks understanding (otherwise faith becomes incoherent). The Catholic Church has a long history of asserting that faith and reason can never contradict each other. It was actually St. Thomas Aquinas, a *Doctor of the Church*, who stressed that faith and reason can never arrive at a conclusion in opposition to each other, because it is the God of our faith who created the reasoning mind. Although faith is above reason, there can never be any real discrepancy between faith and reason (CCC 159). On the one hand, reason requires faith, otherwise reason would have no basis. On the other hand, faith seeks understanding, so that we understand better what God has revealed to us (CCC 158) – so that faith doesn't become incoherent like a blind impulse of the mind (CCC 156). In other words, "Since the same God who reveals mysteries and infuses faith has bestowed the light of reason on the human mind, God cannot deny himself, nor can truth ever contradict truth" (CCC 159).

The First Vatican Council clearly condemned the doctrine that faith is irrational; it insisted that faith is always in harmony with reason (but that does not mean it would be subject to scientific demonstration). Then in 1879, Pope Leo XIII issued the encyclical *Aeterni Patris*, in which he reaffirmed a central principle of the Catholic intellectual tradition: the harmony of faith and reason. Nevertheless, some people still think that when we begin to use reason, we have no choice but to abandon faith; conversely, they think that if we have faith, we cannot use reason. The Church teaches differently: Discovering the truth through reason can never destroy faith. Pope John Paul II even wrote an encyclical on this very issue (*Fides et Ratio*); and Pope Benedict relentlessly followed in his footsteps. When we search for truth, we must have the confidence that its discovery will not destroy our faith, lest we reject the gift of reason.

As a consequence, Catholics are supposed to be "reasonable" in their faith, and "faithful" in their reasoning, so their minds should be "directed" by the light of *faith* as well as by the light of *reason*. Reason and faith need each other in order to discover horizons they could not reach on their own.

Although science is a specific form of using reason, based on a specific methodology, we could say something similar about the relationship between faith and science: Good research in all branches of knowledge can never conflict with the faith, because the things of the world and the things of faith derive from the same God (CCC 159). That is why Catholicism doesn't see any conflict between religion and science, while many Protestant denominations still do! Discovering the truth through reason, even when done through strict scientific procedures, can never destroy faith. It is faith that makes us understand and it is reason that makes us believe. But we do need to put science in its place, as we also should put religion in its place.

S: Don't tell me there is a happy relationship between science and religion!

R: I think there should be, but you are right, there hasn't always been. The ideal situation would be that there is never a conflict between the two.

It shouldn't surprise us that, given its motto of *Faith and Reason*, the Catholic Church doesn't see any conflict, and therefore makes a distinction between the *Book of Scripture* and the *Book of Nature*. By the words of St. Augustine "It is the divine page that you must listen to; it is the book of the universe that you must observe." Whereas the *Book of Scripture* tells us how to go to heaven, the *Book of Nature* tells us how the heavens go. Since both books have the same Author, they cannot possibly contradict each other. According to Catholic faith, they are a match made in Heaven.

As early as 1893, Pope Leo XIII said in his encyclical *Providentissimus Deus,* "no real disagreement can exist between the theologian and the scientist provided each keeps within his own limits." No wonder that, even before the year 1000, Pope Sylvester II had become a famous astronomer. He wanted to understand the order of the universe by illuminating the mysteries of the Cosmic Orderer. And so do we.

S: I would say then the first test case was the Galileo conflict. And didn't religion suffer defeat during that trial?

R: I am not so sure it did. The case is a bit more complicated than it looks at first glance.

Copernicus was the first to publish the idea of a heliocentric model in 1543, suggesting that the earth orbited the sun. But because, like Ptolemy (c. A.D. 90–168), he insisted on *circular* orbits, his heliocentric model was no more accurate than Ptolemy's geocentric one. Johannes Kepler improved the model by using the Copernican system but adding *elliptical* orbits. Then Galileo entered the scene. In 1632, he published, with papal permission, a book in which he supported Copernicus rather than Kepler, so Galileo's heliocentric model was also not any better than Ptolemy's geocentric one.

As a matter of fact, the scientific case was not as clear as some think. If we use Aristotelian theories of impulse and relative motion, the theory advanced by Copernicus, as well as by Galileo, appears to be falsified by the fact that objects fall vertically on earth rather than diagonally – the famous so-called tower argument, forcing Galileo later to "reinterpret the facts." Additional facts seemed to confirm that the earth did not move, for if it did, the clouds would be left behind (as Galileo himself had remarked in a lecture of 1601). Apparently, Galileo had introduced theories that are inconsistent with well-established facts. The observation that objects fall vertically on earth required a new interpretation to make it compatible with Copernican theory. So Galileo was in fact going *against* reason at the time.

Galileo even had to reluctantly admit that his mentor Copernicus had committed, as he described it, "a rape of the senses." And when Galileo demonstrated his "tube" to 25 professors in Bologna, most were unable to see what they were "supposed" to see with the new tool. Later on, he conceded in a letter to Kepler that many people were unable to see what they were "supposed" to see through his telescope. So understandably, many scientists thought that all the things the new telescope showed them were merely artifacts or optical illusions. A tube that shows what cannot exist presumably would not make for a very reliable tube, for tools must prove their reliability first (something Isaac Newton would do later on!). Imagine, some fixed stars were even seen double through Galileo's tube!

So there were many reasons to doubt what Galileo was claiming at the time. But I admit that also personal and theological issues came into play, which further complicated the case. In his speech of Oct. 31, 1992, Pope John Paul spoke of a "tragic mutual incomprehension." As we learn more new facts, we also learn more about the methods to discover those facts.

S: But why do we still have all those tensions then between science and religion?

R: I would say that is because of extremism. Many scientists still think that once we begin to use reason, we have no choice but to abandon faith. And many Christians still believe that if we have faith, we cannot use reason. I would say both viewpoints stem from extreme ideologies – I would call them *"isms."* All "isms" tend to confuse the vast complexity of reality with the limited models used to simplify that complexity; "isms" make for half-truths – totalitarian, one-sided, and narrow-minded.

Fundamentalism is one of them; it takes the Bible in a literal – that is, semi-scientific – way. It reads the *Book of Scripture* as if it were the *Book of Nature*. So it glorifies faith and then tries to silence reason and science. No wonder it considers all scientists "despicable" atheists. That is where religion goes overboard, I would say. We have a distorted form of faith here – faith without reason.

Scientism is another form of ideology; it accepts science as the only valid way of finding truth. It acts like the drunken man who thinks that his lost car keys must be near the lamp post, because that is the only place where he can see in the light. Scientism proclaims that truth can only come from the *Book of Nature*, but never from the *Book of Scripture*. It pretends that all our questions have a scientific answer phrased in terms of particles, quantities, and equations. Thus it glorifies science and tries to silence faith and religion, declaring all believers "weird" fundamentalists. That is the point where science goes overboard. It makes for a distorted form of reason – reason without faith. To best characterize this attitude I like to borrow an image from the late psychologist Abraham Maslow: If you only have a hammer, every problem begins to look like a nail. So do not idolize your "scientific hammer," for not everything is a "nail."

S: I am sure that scientism should emerge as the winner in your contest.

R: But it shouldn't! Scientism is also a baseless, unscientific claim that can only be made from *outside* the scientific realm. Science itself can never prove it is the only way of finding truth; there is no experiment that could do such a trick. So what is the claim of scientism based on then? Quicksand! Let's knock science off its pedestal and put it where it belongs – back in its cage.

Why is it quicksand? Never confuse a scientific "map" or "model" of the world with the world itself; maps and models are only a limited surrogate for "the real thing," so do not replace the real world then with one of its surrogate maps or models. If you do, you would be ripped off with a stripped version of reality. The fact that highways are missing on railroad maps, for instance, doesn't entitle us to deny their existence. Therefore, my advice to fundamentalists would be: Don't strangulate scientists and don't fight science, for that is a hopeless battle; use your energy instead to fight *scientism*, because that is a battle you can easily win.

In short, scientific knowledge is not a superior form of knowledge; it may be easier testable than other kinds, but it is also very restricted and therefore requires additional forms of knowledge. Mathematical knowledge, for instance, is the most secure form of knowledge but it is basically about nothing.

Consider this analogy: A metal detector is a perfect tool to locate metals, but there is more to this world than metals. That's where scientism goes wrong; instead of letting reality determine which techniques are appropriate for which parts of reality, scientism lets its favorite technique dictate what is "real" in life.

S: I think you are quite biased and too easy toward the other side of the debate, the fundamentalists.

R: No, fundamentalism is definitely wrong too! Fundamentalists are just out to silence science. At the moment we would allow fundamentalists to stifle science, scientists would be denied to study the *Book of Nature*. Fundamentalists violate the motto of the Church – *Faith* AND *Reason* – by saying that we cannot use reason if we have faith. Let me quote St. Augustine one more time: "It is dangerous to have an infidel hear a Christian [...] talking nonsense." And fundamentalists do talk nonsense...

Catholics, on the other hand, are not forced to make a choice – either for scientism or for fundamentalism – since they consider that to be a false dilemma. Pope Benedict XVI put it very clearly, "nature [is] a book whose author is God in the same way that Scripture has God as its author" (Oct. 31, 2008). To say differently creates a conflict that the Holy Father calls "*an absurdity*." What we "know" in science and what we "believe" in religion can and should live together under the same roof, in the same human being, in harmony with each other. The First Vatican Council had already condemned the doctrine that faith is irrational; it insisted that faith is always in harmony with reason (but need not be subject to scientific demonstration).

S: It seems to me that science and religion must have a hard time to live together in Catholics who still go to church.

R: Sadly enough, Catholics in the pews have been bombarded from two opposite sides. On the one side, there is the fact that non-Catholic fundamentalist Christians, and evangelicals in particular, now have an enormous impact on our culture – and so has their rejection of science, making Catholics feel they must be suspicious of science if they want to be "faithful" in their religion.

On the other side, there are those very vocal attacks of atheists who use science as their favorite tool in battling Christian faith; several of them are influential writers – atheists such as Richard Dawkins, whose books have sold millions of copies all over the world. Many evangelical Christians easily bought into that clash, attacking science as the greatest threat to their beliefs – instead of taking on these "worshipping atheists."

No wonder Catholics feel right in the middle between fundamentalists and atheists! They are surrounded by extremism on both sides, making it hard for them to remain clear-headed and determined.

S: Well, they *should* feel being in the middle, for science tells them about one primordial event, the Big Bang, whereas the Book of Genesis talks about seven creation days. These do not go together!

R: Be careful when you read the first chapter of Genesis; it doesn't really give us a chronology of seven days, for the simple reason that creation cannot follow a timeline, as time itself is a product of creation. Our *universe* has a beginning and a timeline, but *creation* itself doesn't have a beginning or a timeline. It is very hard to interpret creation as a step-by-step process unfolding in a temporal order, for "creation at the beginning of time" is impossible, since there is no time until time has been created. Creating time "at a certain time" is tough to do! In other words, creation is not an event in time, because time is something that, in and of itself, would also require creation. For us creatures, creation had a beginning, but God Himself is time-less. Creation isn't something that happened long ago in time, and neither is the Creator someone who did something in the distant past, but the Creator does something at all times – by keeping a contingent world in existence.

Consequently, it is hard to take the creation account as a *chronological* description of the initial stages of this world, for without creation, there wouldn't be any world at all. Therefore, creation may create chronology, but it cannot become part of chronology, nor can chronology be the framework of creation. In other words, creation is not exclusively focused on the *beginning* of this world, but more so on the *origin* of this world. Creation is both giving a beginning to all that exists and sustaining in being all that exists (CCC 290).

Let me explain this a bit more extensively. When St. John says, "In the beginning was the Word," he is not speaking of the beginning of all things, as one of the first things to be created, but "beyond" the beginning of all things, "before" there was even time. Do not read "*in* the beginning" as "*at* the beginning." The first chapter in the Book of Genesis is not about what happened *at* the beginning, but it is about what everything is based on to begin with – that is, *in* the beginning. Consequently, Genesis is not a *scientific* theory of the world's *beginning*, but rather a *monotheistic* creed about the world's *origin* and foundation – which is a creed directed against the widespread polytheism and idolatry of ancient and modern times. Genesis 1 offers us a theo-logy of creation, not a sciento-logy of creation. Its core message is this: God is the creator of everything, and there are no other gods beside Him.

S: I wonder whether this creed against polytheism still has any meaning for us living in the 21st century.

R: For many people, the world is still a divine and godly entity, populated with little gods – such as deities in the sky (astrology), occult forces, fertility gods, the mammon, etc. In contrast, Genesis tells us that GOD is the creator of everything – and He alone, so there are no other gods beside Him. God is in charge, and nothing else.

Put differently, God's creation is good, it is even very good, but it is certainly not divine. The Bible actually takes all divinity out of nature – it de-deifies the universe. The sun doesn't rise because it "wants" to rise; instead, it rises because if follows the laws laid down in God's creation since He spoke His creative Word. The rainbow is not some kind of whimsical deity, but it follows the laws laid out in God's cosmic design; that is why we can create rainbow effects ourselves. Zeus and Jupiter no longer explain lightening, but God's laws do. God is the ultimate source of all there is in this universe. God's eternal and creative reason is the only power over the world and in the world. As Pope Benedict XVI puts it in his book *Jesus of Nazareth* (Part I, 174), the world is now seen as something rational. Faith in the one God is the only thing that truly liberates the world and makes it "rational."

I say it yet again, it is only thanks to the Bible that science could even begin to emerge. Whereas religion is in search of *God* Himself, science is in search of God's *laws* – that is, of the cosmic design He placed behind and beneath our universe. The Catechism puts it this way: "The order and harmony of the created world results from the diversity of beings and from the relationships which exist among them. Man discovers them progressively as the *laws of nature*" (CCC 341; italics are mine).

S: I would say the Big Bang was the real revolution. You make it sound like the Book of Genesis is rather revolutionary, don't you?

R: Yes, that is my strong conviction. Just imagine what the sweeping consequences are if we take the Book of Genesis seriously. All processes in nature are supposed to follow physical and biological laws. It is these laws – in fact *God's* laws – that control everything in the universe. If there is such a thing as a Big Bang, those laws of nature must have already existed before the Big Bang came along, making for a framework in which even the Big Bang had to take place. These laws are part of the intelligent cosmic design of creation and have their origin in an intelligent, lawgiving Creator.

But there's also another side to this: Never should we bring God back in again as an intervening agent to adjust or redirect His own given laws – which would degrade Him into what they call a god-of-the-gaps " – of scientific gaps, that is (but this doesn't mean that God cannot intervene with genuine miracles). God doesn't need to keep the planets moving; they just follow their God-given laws. Even Newton didn't fully realize this; he thought God had to periodically correct irregularities in the solar system, but now we know better; God's laws take care of that. Yet, make no mistake, creation keeps everything in existence until God takes

His "breath" away. To sum up, the universe is a *created* entity, not a *divine* entity.

S: But how can religion and science ever live together in the same person?

R: On the one hand, believers shouldn't be afraid of science. Pope Pius XII expressed the same stance in 1951, "[...] true science discovers God in an ever-increasing degree – as though God were waiting behind every door opened by science." On the other hand, scientists shouldn't be afraid of religion either, for religion sees the universe as a law-abiding, explainable structure created by a lawful God. It was faith that gave scientists their job!

So we need BOTH of them. As Albert Einstein, a scientific authority once said, "Science without religion is lame, religion without science is blind." Or in the words of Pope John Paul II, a religious authority: "Science can purify religion from error and superstition. Religion can purify science from idolatry and false absolutes." Do not ever pressure anyone to choose between these two. Do not turn science into a pseudo-religion, or religion into a semi-science. Science was invented to give glory to God by examining His laws of nature, not to erase Him from existence.

S: Sounds cozy, but I do not think I want, or even need, religion as a neighbor.

R: Without that neighbor, science would basically fall apart or at least lose its foundation, as I said before. Without God, scientists would basically lose their *reason* for trusting their own scientific reasoning. Without the notion of the universe as a *created* entity, science would be a shaky and problematic enterprise. It is faith that makes us understand, as I said before. Just think of this:

- How could nature be intelligible if it were not created by an intelligent Creator?

- How could there be order in this world if there were no orderly Creator?

- How could there be scientific laws if there were no rational

Lawgiver?

- How could there be design in nature, if there were no intelligent Designer?

- How could there be human minds, if the universe were mindless?

My point is that I want to hear the *whole* story – not just the part that science tells me. There is so much more to life than what meets the (scientific) eye by means of thermometers and spectrometers; there are other ways to look at things; there is so much more to the story...

I like to compare the relationship between science and religion with the idea of "separation of church and state." The state should be protected from the church as much as the church should be protected from the state. In other words, render to Caesar what is Caesar's, but never render to Caesar what is God's. In his book the *City of God*, St. Augustine had already declared the Christian message to be spiritual rather than political. Christianity, he argued, should be concerned with the mystical, heavenly city, the New Jerusalem — rather than with earthly politics. As Pope Benedict XVI wrote in his book *Jesus of Nazareth* (Part II, 170) about the separation of religion and politics, "In his teaching and in his whole ministry, Jesus had inaugurated a non-political Messianic kingdom and had begun to detach these two hitherto inseparable realities from one another." And elsewhere (Part I, 40) he says that, when the two fuse, "faith becomes the servant of power and must bend to its criteria." Only a clear separation can strengthen *both* sides.

Something similar holds for the relationship between religion and science. They are autonomous and independent from each other, but still need to be in harmony inside each one of us. Together they make us whole and wholesome, whereas in isolation, they are incomplete and under-performing. But I also want to add one more remark: Caesars come and go, whereas religion stays forever.

In other words, science should stay away from religious territory in attempting religious interventions as much as religion should stay clear of science in attempting scientific interventions. Nevertheless, science should protect religion from errors, and religion should keep science within moral bounds. Render to science what is measurable and visible, but do not render to science what is God's. So honor the "fences," but do not forget that, no matter on which side of the fence you happen to be, you do have a "neighbor."

S: I still maintain religion and science are like neighbors in strong competition with each other. The gain of one is the loss of the other.

R: I agree science must go to its limits, but it should never overstep its limits and become arrogant. The same holds for religion. That is why there is no real competition between the two. The philosopher Peter Kreeft compares this situation with that Western in which one cowboy says to the other: "This town ain't big enough for both of us. One of us has to leave." He is right in questioning why one of them would have to leave. They deal with two different worlds – the visible world versus the invisible world, the supernatural world versus the natural world. They have different "books," but unlike the biblical books, science books need constant revision, whereas the certainty of faith doesn't depend upon scientific-historical verification (for then it would always remain open to revision as well).

In other words, do not consider the relationship between science and religion as a "battle field" that resembles a *football* field – where advancements on one side make the other side retract. They are neighbors, but the expansion of one is never at the cost of the other party. Instead, I would say the dialogue between science and religion takes place on a field that is more like a *tennis* field, where each party should stay on its own side to do its "performances."

S: Well, my point is then that there's nothing left outside the range that science covers. Science keeps expanding at the cost of religion.

R: You are still talking in terms of a football field. You equate God with a "god of the gaps" who serves as a provisional explanation for what science has not yet explained. However, such a god is indeed a fleeting illusion, for when the frontiers of science are being pushed back, such a god would be pushed back with them as well. That is how Zeus and Jupiter left the scene, but they are not God.

In religion and philosophy, on the other hand, the "real" God should never function as a "missing link" in our scientific explanations. Otherwise you would be putting God on the same level as your scientific explanations, but God is far above and beyond any of those – God is the very origin of all that science discovers. God should never be the "victim" of scientific expansion, nor should He be at the "mercy" of scientists. God is *transcendent* to His creation – not an element or part of it, but its overarching source and foundation (CCC 300). God is not a player on stage, but He is the *Author* of the play. Without God, there would be no universe at all.

S: You are talking in riddles for me. What do you mean by "transcendent"?

R: Let me try to explain this in more philosophical terms. St. Thomas Aquinas calls God a *"Primary* Cause" and all the causes science deals with he refers to as *"secondary* causes." The physical causality of science reigns "inside" the universe, linking causes together in a chain of (secondary) causes, whereas God reigns from "outside" the universe as a *Primary* Cause, thus providing a "point of suspension" for the chain itself, so to speak. So God is not a super-cause among other causes, but He lets the secondary causes do their work. It is only thanks to the Primary Cause that creatures can become secondary causes. God is not a deity like Jupiter or Zeus – not a being stronger than other beings and superior to all other beings, yet acting like all other beings. Instead, He is the very source of all being. This Primary Cause is *un*-caused, not self-caused, but the Source of all being; not some super-being among other beings but an *Absolute* Being; not a cause prior to and larger than other causes, but a *Primary* Cause.

To put it differently, God is not a super-power among other powers or a super-power that beats all other powers. God's power does not exceed other powers but it *transcends* those other powers. His power is of a different kind of magnitude in such a way that other powers could not even exist outside His power. In that particular sense, God is all-powerful, all-knowing, and all-present. He is infinitely greater than all His works (CCC 300).

Let me use the following example. Science knows of oxygen; it is a *secondary* cause that some creatures depend on. If there were no oxygen, there would be no birds, for instance. Religion, on the other hand, knows of God. He is a *Primary* Cause that all creatures depend on. If there were no God, there wouldn't be any creatures at all. Everything in this world is *contingent* and dependent on God; that is why it is so appropriate to call us "creatures." God is not a super-being among other beings, but the *absolute* Source of *all* being. As Pope Benedict XVI put it in his book *Jesus of Nazareth* (Part II, 91), "the 'name of God' meant his 'immanence': his presence in the midst of men, in which he is entirely 'there,' while at the same time infinitely surpassing everything human, everything to do with this world." How true it is that only a transcendent Being can fully envelop and embrace each and every one of us.

S: Now I also need to understand better what you mean by the term *contingent.*

R: We are contingent because we could easily not have existed, as the reason for our existence can not be found within ourselves. All physical causes and events in our universe are contingent in the sense that they depend for their existence on an overarching, transcending "ground" – a "First Cause," if you will. This First Cause is uncaused itself, yet it is the "cause" or "ground" behind all other, secondary causes. It is "first" in origin – that means "*in* the beginning" – but not first in time – that would be "*at* the beginning." God is the "ground" and "source" of all that exists – think of something like the framework surrounding a spider's web. Likewise, God as the ground of my being is the One who supplies the "framework" that supports the "web of my life" It is in Him that we are grounded – otherwise we couldn't even exist. God provides the "framework" in which "we live and move and have our being," says St. Paul (Acts 17:28). Therefore, God cannot be found *in* science, but He can certainly be found *behind* and *beyond* science – in the "vacuum" or "residue" science necessarily leaves behind, in the questions science has no answer for.

Let me explain this important distinction with an example that C.S. Lewis uses. Just as architects are not part of their buildings, yet are somehow "part" of every part of them, so is God *transcendent* – that is, not a physical part of what He created – and yet He is *immanent* – that is, actively involved with each and every part of it. God transcends creation and yet is present to it (CCC 300). As a consequence, though, God can never act like an element or part of His own creation. That is why we should never degrade Him to a "missing link" in our scientific explanations, a cause among causes. We are just God's creatures – not "next" to God but "under" God, not "outside" God but "in" God. "Outside" God, there's nothing.

Therefore, God does not compete with any creature, not even my parents. My parents are the natural cause of my being here (a *secondary* cause, that is), but God remains the transcendent *Primary* cause of my being in existence and alive. That is why we should always say that children come *through* us but not *from* us. Even our own children are not "our own," but they come ultimately from *God*, the source and ground of all that exists. God is "part" of everything, but without being a physical "part" of it. The Catechism puts it very concisely, "God is the first cause who operates in and through secondary causes" (308).

S: When you talk about creation, aren't you actually referring to the Big Bang? Wasn't it the Big Bang that started everything?

R: No, creation isn't some trigger event like the Big Bang; in fact creation isn't an event at all, so we found out. On the contrary, creation must come "first" (first in order, not in time; *in* the beginning, not *at* the beginning) before any events, even a Big Bang, can follow. In other words, creation is not so much about the *beginning* of this world, but about the *origin* of this world (including its beginning and all its subsequent stages). The world may have a beginning and a timeline, but creation itself doesn't have a beginning or a timeline; creation actually makes the beginning of the world and its timeline possible. Creation creates chronology, but it cannot become part of chronology. In other words, creation is not a "one-time deal," but it deals with the question as to where this world comes from; it doesn't come from the Big Bang, but may have started with the Big Bang.

So the Big Bang may be the beginning of the *universe*, but it certainly is not the beginning of *creation*. Creation isn't something that happened long ago in time, and neither is the Creator someone who did something in the distant past, but He does something at all times – He keeps a *contingent* world in existence. Our contingent reality depends on an *Absolute* Reality. If God would take His "breath" away, everything would immediately vanish. In the words of the Catechism, "With creation, God does not abandon his creatures to themselves. He not only gives them being and existence, but also, and at every moment, upholds and sustains them in being" (301).

In short, without creation, there couldn't be a Big Bang at all. Creation sets the "stage" for this and keeps this world in existence. The "rest of the story" would be something for science to tell.

S: Why would we need more than the Big Bang? I think the physicist Stephen Hawking was right when he spoke of a *spontaneous* creation.

R: Some scientists have indeed fallen into the trap of arguing that the Big Bang has replaced what we call creation. Stephen Hawking does indeed speak in terms of a spontaneous creation: "Because there is a law such as gravity, the universe can and will create itself from nothing. Spontaneous creation is the reason there is something rather than nothing." No wonder, this made the physicist Carl Sagan exclaim, in the preface of one of Hawking's books, that such a cosmological model "left nothing for a creator to do." Others, such as the cosmologist Lee Smolin, made sure there is no space for a Creator left by proclaiming that "by definition the universe is all there is, and there can be nothing outside it."

I agree that the word "universe" stands for the whole of all that is physical and visible, but I need to also point out that the idea of a spontaneous creation is sheer philosophical magic; for something to create itself, it would have to exist before it came into existence

– which is logically impossible. Imagine, the universe creating itself from nothing! That is pure philosophical nonsense! How could the universe "create" itself from nothing – let alone cause itself? That is philosophically impossible, for a cause just cannot cause itself; it would have to exist before it came into existence. As the saying goes, nothing comes from nothing in this world. It would surely be nice if gold could create itself from nothing, but that is not the way it is.

When Hawking tells us that gravity would be able to create the universe, I would counter that the law of gravity would have to exist before there was gravity. Albert Einstein hit the nail right on the head when he said: "the man of science is a poor philosopher." And there are many more of those. The physical chemist Peter Atkins, for instance, has the audacity to state that "there is hope for a scientific elucidation of creation from nothing" after he had said earlier that science has a limitless power and must even be able to account for the "emergence of everything from absolutely nothing."

S: Some physicists believe that CERN's famous *Large Hadron Collider* may help us unravel the "mystery" of the beginning of this universe. Wouldn't that also be the end of the "mystery" of the creation of this universe?

R: Again, there are two very different kinds of mystery here; one is a scientific *puzzle*, the other a real *mystery*. The Big Bang "out of nothing" is a puzzle, very different from the creation "out of nothing." When the Church speaks of creation out of nothing (*ex nihilo*, CCC 296), it is not talking science. "Nothingness" is not a highly unusual kind of stuff that is more difficult to observe or measure than other things are; it is not a thing, but the absence of anything. Science is about producing something from something else, whereas creation is about creating something from nothing (according to an old, solid distinction that St. Thomas Aquinas already made centuries ago). Science is about changes in this universe, but creation is certainly not a change; it is not a change from "nothing" to "something." Creation has everything to do with the philosophical and theological question as to why things exist at all, before they can even undergo change. Creation – but not the Big Bang – is the reason why there is something rather than nothing (including something such as the law of gravity).

Aquinas made very clear that science and religion differ from each other but can never be in conflict with each other. His reasoning goes as follows: God is the author of all truth; the aim of scientific research is the truth; therefore, there can be no fundamental incompatibility between the two. Provided we understand Christian doctrine properly and do our science well, we will find the truth. So if we perceive a conflict it is because of a failure to distinguish between cause in the sense of a natural change of some kind and cause in the sense of an ultimate bringing into being of something from no antecedent state whatsoever. To be the complete cause of something's existence is not the same as producing a change in something. The Creator does not create something out of nothing in the sense of taking some nothing and making something out of it. This is a conceptual mistake, for it treats nothing as a something.

Apparently, if we do not distinguish scientific questions from philosophical and theological questions, we would be in for a real mix-up. If we would give scientists the limitless power that some of them think they have, we would give most of our lives away. Not only would they claim that there is no corner in the universe beyond their reach, but also no dimension of reality and no feature of human existence. We would be robbed of many things that count in life but cannot be counted. We would, for instance, end up with a universe without any *purpose*. And that is a high price!

S: You keep coming up with new notions and elements unknown to science! Where does your new idea of a "purpose" suddenly come from?

R: The core problem is that you have a rather meager concept of reality. Hamlet said it so plainly, "there are more things in heaven and earth [...] than are dreamt of in your philosophy." In fact, reality has many different "levels", seen from different "angles" or "perspectives." It is just plain truth that there are many ways of looking at things. Each approach reveals a distinct aspect of reality. There are many more "dimensions," "windows," and "aspects" to this world than science can account for.

If you still wonder why science has left so many aspects untouched – well, we found out science decided to limit itself to what can be counted and measured. The astonishing successes of science have not been gained by answering every kind of question, but precisely by refusing to do so. Its success is bought at the cost of limiting its ambition, thus leaving a huge area untouched. So there is no reason for megalomania in science. Always keep asking for "the rest of the story" – the rest that science fails to see. And that is where "purpose" keeps coming back in – from outside the domain of science.

The Catechism speaks of "a question of another order, which goes beyond the proper domain of the natural sciences. It is not only a question of knowing when and how the universe arose physically, or when man appeared, but rather of discovering the meaning of such an origin: is the universe governed by chance, blind fate, anonymous necessity, or by a transcendent, intelligent and good Being called 'God'?" (284).

S: I must say you are very consistent in trying to suggest that there are other than scientific ways of looking at the world. But how "real" are these various aspects?

R: Forgive me for using the following cruel example: What was the "driving force" behind Hitler's gas chambers? There are many ways of looking at this tragedy.

- I think we all agree it was the cyanide-based insecticide *Zyklon B* that did the devastating work in the gas chambers – at the level of science, that is.

- But that wasn't all. Also playing a role here were strong emotions of anger and hate, plus feelings of superiority, all operating at another level, steering the use of *Zyklon B*. This is the level of emotions and passions.

- But the story doesn't end here either. These emotions were propelled and reinforced by something on yet another level – a racist ideology as voiced in the book *Mein Kampf*. This is the level of reasons and intentions, albeit a bigoted form of reasoning.

- But we should definitely also point at Hitler's immoral behavior, his lack of having any sound moral values to correct and curb his view. This is the level of morality.

- But ultimately, the real fuel behind all of this is to be found at even a deeper level: Some satanic force engaged in a battle against God's creation gave Hitler more than mere human power.

If you deny the reality of any of these levels, you miss at least part of the whole story. You would be like those tourists who see their tourist destinations only through the lens of their cameras, while missing out on all the other parts of their trip.

S: I still remain skeptical about the reality of all these levels...

R: Radical, hard-core skeptics actually doubt whether *any* outlook on life can be trusted; they deny the validity of almost all aspects of knowledge, because we are not supposed to know any truth with certainty, not even in science. *Skepticism* makes for a very restrained view on the world – actually so restrained that absolute skeptics cannot even know if they have a mind to doubt with. I always wonder how some can be so *certain* that nothing is certain.

Ultimately, skepticism leads us to the edge of an abyss, claiming that there is no law, no authority, no rationality, no morality, and no purpose to life. Skepticism rejects any authority but still wants to be the new authority. People who have lost the sense of God tend to lose the sense of man and man's dignity as well. I consider this a detrimental loss. What would we do without religion, when disaster strikes us, when things do not go the way we had planned, when we become victims of injustice – in short, when bad things happen to good people? Swallow hard? It is clear that life doesn't owe us a living.

4

Adam's and Eve's Bellybutton

The Way Creation Unfolds

At the moment we take science seriously, we run into many new questions. For instance: Did Adam and Eve have bellybuttons? Why would they, if they didn't have parents? And if they did have parents, they should. Curiously enough, all Catholic artists portray them as having a bellybutton. Was this perhaps the Creator's seal of approval saying "you are done"? Or did they in fact have parents?

This chapter is about evolution. I know this a very contentious issue in religion, but I do not want to leave it out, for there is hardly any school or college left where they do not teach evolutionary theory. How do Catholics deal with the question "Where do we come from?"

- Are our roots in the animal world, or are we rooted in God? Or are both perhaps true?

- What should we believe as Catholics living in the 21st century? Should it be both evolution and creation, or just one of these?

- What should we preach in our churches?

- What do we teach in our Catholic schools?

- And as Catholic parents, what do we say to our children who are being bombarded with evolution in their classrooms?

Obviously, this is an issue of life or death. If evolution has the last word, then death is ultimately the end of the story. But if there is creation, then eternal life is the light at the end of the tunnel. Let this chapter be your solid guide, bolstered with many citations from Church authority.

Q: I don't think we can have it both ways. If there is evolution, there is no creation; and if there is creation, there is no evolution. Right?

A: I think you are creating a false dilemma. Pope Benedict XVI calls this contrast even an "absurdity" (7-26-07). Let me explain why it is a misleading standoff. St. Thomas Aquinas may help us make some clear distinctions here. He distinguishes "creating" (*creare*) from "producing" (*facere*). The Creator *creates* the world, which means that He makes something from *nothing*. The potter, on the other hand, *produces* a pot, which means he makes something from something *else*.

As we saw in the previous chapter, our world may have been *produced* by the Big Bang, but it was *created* by God. In other words, creation is something completely unique; only God can create – that is, bringing something into existence that didn't exist in any way before. Perhaps we could say something similar about evolution: Our world may have been *produced* by evolution, and yet it was *created* by God. Evolution would not be a process of creating something from nothing; instead, it would be a process of producing something from something else. It could very well be that human beings were created from nothing, and yet they were produced from something else in the animal world. This may look like a daring statement, but it is philosophically sound in the tradition of St. Thomas Aquinas.

Q: Has the Church ever clarified this distinction? Would the Church accept such a statement?

A: It certainly would. As we saw in the previous chapter, there is this powerful tradition in the Catholic Church of distinguishing between the *Book of Scripture* and the *Book of Nature*. By the words of St. Augustine: "It is the divine page that you must listen to; it is the book of the universe that you must observe." (*Enarrationes in Psalmos*, 45, 7). This distinction was a belief shared in the past by many authors: from the Apologetic Fathers to St. Basil; from St. Gregory of Nyssa to St. Augustine, from St. Albert the Great to St. Thomas Aquinas.

Pope John Paul's Encyclical *Faith and Reason* revived this dialogue between the two "Books." Then on 10-31-2008, Pope Benedict XVI, reinforced the same message when he said, "Galileo saw nature as a book whose author is God in the same way that Scripture has God as its author. It is a book whose history, whose evolution, whose 'writing' and meaning, we 'read' according to the different approaches of the sciences."

Well, creation is definitely part of the *Book of Scripture*, whereas evolution would be part of the *Book of Nature*. Since God is the Author of both books, they can never contradict each other. Science studies only the *Book of Nature*, including the process of evolution. The Catechism clearly acknowledges this: "The question about the origins of the world and of *man* has been the object of many scientific studies which have splendidly enriched our knowledge of the age and dimensions of the cosmos, *the development of life-forms and the appearance of man*" (283; italics are mine).

Q: How come the conflict of creation versus evolution is still raging in the Church, whereas you say there's no conflict?

A: Not so long ago, many Catholics in the pews understood that evolution was somehow consistent with Church teaching. What has changed is not Church teaching, or science, but the fact that non-Catholic fundamentalist Christians, and evangelicals in particular, now have an enormous impact on our culture, especially in the USA – and so has their rejection of evolution, making Catholics feel they must be suspicious of evolution if they want to be "faithful" in their religion. As we saw before, these fundamentalists are out to silence science. But we should ask them: What makes you think that science is wrong if religion is right?

Besides, something else has changed as well: the very vocal attacks of atheists who use *evolution* as their favorite tool in battling

Christian faith. Several of them are influential writers – biologists such as Richard Dawkins, whose books have sold millions of copies. Many evangelical Christians easily bought into that clash, attacking evolution as the greatest threat to their beliefs – instead of taking on these atheists, who are out to silence religion. But we should ask them: What makes you think that religion is wrong if science is right? Catholic scientists do not have to renounce their science or their faith.

If you have the feeling science is pulling you away from your faith, do not blame science – but maybe some particular scientists who want you to feel that way. Religion and science, or creation and evolution, can live in peace, since God is the Author of both the *Book of Scripture* and the *Book of Nature*. That is the Catholic view, dating at least as far back as St. Augustine.

Q: If you are right, Catholics again end up in the middle of two extreme viewpoints, trying to find a middle ground.

A: You say that right, they are smack in the middle of two extremes. Extremes are always one-sided; they are "isms." As I said before, all "isms" are *ideological* doctrines that focus on one side of the story, and want you to believe there is no other side. In our present discussion, this leads to *creationism* on the one side and *evolutionism* on the other side.

Creationism basically rejects the *Book of Nature*, since it claims to find all answers to all our questions about the origin of life in the *Book of Scripture*, more in particular in the first chapters of the Book of Genesis. People who take this view call themselves creationists, but are also often called fundamentalists who take the Bible literally as if it were also the *Book of Nature*.

Evolutionism is the opposite worldview. It rejects the *Book of Scripture*, as it claims to find all answers to all our questions about the origin of life in the *Book of Nature*, more in particular in neo-Darwinism and evolutionary biology. Proponents of this ideology glorify the theory of evolution and use it as the exclusive foundation of their worldview. Therefore, they want to silence religion, because they reject creation and worship evolution instead.

Q: How can one ever glorify evolution, for I think the theory of evolution has very poor credentials?

A: I would say the credentials of the theory of evolution are actually pretty strong. There may be some controversy as to the mechanism of evolution (for instance, natural selection), but the fact that there is indeed evolution is very hard to deny. And why would we anyway? Even as early as 1950, Pope Pius XII said in his encyclical *Humani Generis* "The magisterium of the Church does not forbid that [...] research and discussions [...] take place with regard to the doctrine of evolution." Then in 1986, Pope John Paul II expressed a similar view, but more strongly: "[...] from the viewpoint of the doctrine of the faith, there are no difficulties in explaining the origin of man in regard to the body, by means of the theory of evolution."

And in 1996, Pope John Paul II was even more definite saying "Today, [...] some new findings lead us toward the recognition of evolution as more than a hypothesis. [...] The convergence in the results of these independent studies [...] is in itself a significant argument in favor of this theory." I think we should conclude from this that we cannot just throw the current theory of evolution away in the dumpster.

Q: Do you really think that biology has a case to make in favor of the theory of evolution?

A: Yes, arguments come from many biological disciplines. First of all, there is *taxonomical* evidence. Human beings are animals and have characteristics all animals have. Just like all other animals, we breed, feed, bleed, and excrete; we are flesh of their flesh; we are made of the same "cloth." This makes some animals look like close relatives and others like more distant family – which is the first indication of common descent and ancestry, but with some modification.

Second, there is *morphological* evidence. All mammals share more or less the same morphological structure. Just the fact that all mammals have consistently seven cervical vertebrae illustrates this point – no matter whether it is in the sturdy neck of a rhino or the long neck of a giraffe. Some of those common basic structures may have become "overdeveloped," some "underdeveloped." Structures that have lost their functionality are called rudimentary; such "left-over" parts only make "sense," if we assume that all mammals derive their same build from common ancestors.

Third, there is strong *paleontological* evidence for evolution as well. The general observation is that the deeper the layers from which fossils originate, the more they differ from their current counterparts. Additional evidence comes from the fact that the current location of continents is allegedly the result of a drastic transformation. Originally, all continents formed one large continent (*Pangaea*), but parts of it drifted away from each other to reach their current position (which is the so-called continental drift based on the plate tectonics theory). Australia, for example, had been isolated already before mammals appeared on stage; consequently, marsupials could flourish in the Australian fauna by lack of mammalian competition.

Phenomena like these only make "sense" if we assume that isolated continents and regions had their own evolutionary processes, independent from other areas. Madagascar, for instance, has a very peculiar fauna due to its longtime isolation. It would be very hard to explain these "odd" facts without the assumption of some kind of evolutionary process. In short, evolution is a strong unifying concept in biology.

Q: I still consider these facts arguably ambiguous. I know that creationists dispute many of them. Isn't there any stronger evidence for evolution?

A: I would say the strongest evidence comes from genetics. Chimpanzees, for instance, have 24 pairs of chromosomes, whereas humans have only 23 pairs (actually 22+XX for females or 22+XY for males). This change from 24 to 23 pairs of chromosomes can be explained if we assume that two ancestral chromosomes have fused together to form the human chromosome #2. This is even more likely the case since gorillas and orangutans also have 24 pairs, just like chimpanzees.

What makes it even more likely that chromosome #2 came forth from a head-to-head fusion of two shorter chromosomes is the fact that the tips of all primate chromosomes have a special sequence of DNA code which is rare elsewhere. Well, this very sequence is also found right in the middle of our fused chromosome #2. The fusion has left its DNA imprint behind, so to speak, making it hard to explain this phenomenon without postulating common ancestry and descent. Amazing, isn't it? It is like Adam's and Eve's bellybuttons; they tell us something about their past.

And then we have even more compelling evidence from further DNA research. Comparing DNA from different species tells us more in detail about their genetic affinity, which is often very striking. And then we have those so-called pseudo-genes; they resemble a regular DNA packet of a functional gene, but have been affected by one or more glitches that change their script into "nonsense." They were once functional copies of genes but have since lost their protein-coding ability. In a way, pseudo-genes are like rudimentary organs. When comparing humans and chimps, we do come across some pseudo-genes. A striking example is the gene for a jaw muscle protein (MYH16), which has become a pseudo-gene in humans, but is still very functional to develop strong jaw muscles in other primates. Another example would be the DNA code for an enzyme that produces vitamin C in most animals. Many primates, including humans, have a defect in this DNA code, so they must acquire vitamin C through food, but they did hold on to this code in the "silent" section of their DNA. Again, such phenomena are hard to explain without some kind of evolution. As there are still people who deny that humans landed on the moon, there will always be people who deny that there is evolution.

Q: How could such evolutionary changes ever come along?

A: That is where the theory of evolution becomes more controversial. At this point, most biologists would say that the changes originate mainly from genetic changes caused by mutations in DNA. This leads to genetic diversity. Based on this genetic diversity, natural selection promotes the good designs more so than the bad designs, which makes them increase their frequency in future generations.

It was Charles Darwin who introduced the causal mechanism of natural selection based on the fact that organisms differ with regards to their chances of survival and reproduction. The more an organism is adapted to its environment – making for a better design fit to solve a problem posed by the environment – the more likely this organism is to contribute to the genetic constitution of the next generations. Somehow, natural selection promotes the better designs by "weighing" the benefits against the costs like an engineer, economist, or architect would. A good design for nest animals – several helpless young at birth – is not a good design for herd animals; the latter usually have only one young that could develop well in the womb so it can get up fast after birth and follow the herd.

What a great insight Darwin had: As comets and planets follow the laws of nature, so does evolution by following the law of natural selection (and some other laws).

Q: Natural selection may work fine within the boundaries of a species, but has it ever been shown to produce a *new* species?

A: Let me define first what a species is in biology: a population of organisms that can breed with one another, but not with members of other populations. So the theory of evolution has to "prove" how natural selection can create a new species that is reproductively isolated from the old species – which process is called *speciation*. How often do I hear lay people say that no one has ever seen a new species emerge in the laboratory – or even in nature, for that matter. But they are wrong!

First of all, hybrids (e.g., mules that are hybrids between a horse and a donkey) tell us that speciation may very well be a process that is still on its way but has not been completely finalized yet. Second, we know of new species that carry fused chromosomes (like our chromosome #2), or genes transferred to different chromosome sections, or newly inserted repetitive DNA segments. Well, such changes may at some point prevent pairing of chromosomes, and even mating between organisms – which, in turn, would isolate their carriers reproductively. Such cases have been documented and are rather common.

Q: But did we ever really *observe* a new species emerge in nature?

A: Biologists would say that speciation is usually a long-winding, large-scale, step-by-step process – too slow for us to see changes accumulate, too gradual to locate any clear thresholds, and too massive to be simulated in the lab. (This is something similar to the way different languages came forth from a common language source.) Nevertheless, speciation has been shown in the laboratory with fruit flies – organisms that have a short life cycle.

In addition, we do find clear cases of speciation in nature. In California, for instance, the *Ensatina* salamander forms a horseshoe shape of populations in the mountains surrounding the Californian Central Valley. Although interbreeding can happen between each of the 19 populations around the horseshoe, the salamanders on the western end of the horseshoe cannot interbreed with the salamanders on the eastern end. This poses the question as to whether we should consider the whole ring a single species, or each population a separate species instead. This much is clear: If enough of the connecting populations within the ring perish to sever the breeding connection, the remaining members would have become two distinct species.

Perhaps a comparison with a less controversial issue might help. Hardly anyone doubts that languages such as Sanskrit, Greek, and Latin – no matter how different they look and sound – have a common source. After much study, it was found that all three are descended from some mother language, called Proto-Indo-European. Changes that occurred during this evolutionary process were subject to laws as strict as those of the natural sciences. Ultimately we ended up with a huge diversity of languages, which leads us to the question as to when a language becomes a language on its own. Dutch and South-African Dutch, for instance, are pretty far on their way to separation, but Dutch and Flemish are still so close that some consider them dialects rather than separate languages. However, at some point in time, and after extended isolation, regular speakers of those two dialects may not be able to understand each other anymore. Well, something similar happens in biological evolution: populations may become separate species.

Q: Sometimes I hear the objection that evolution requires not only variations within existing genes (alleles), but also the formation of *new* genes. Is there any evidence that such a thing is possible?

A: There certainly is. The best known example is the bacterial flagellum, which is an "outboard motor" that propels bacterial cells in various directions. Comparison of protein sequences from various bacteria has revealed that several components of the flagellum are related to an entirely different apparatus used by some bacteria to inject toxins into other bacteria. The explanation for this similarity can be found in those long stretches of DNA that are located between functional genes; they do not seem to be doing much – that is why they are often called "junk DNA," but "silent DNA" would be a much safer term. Some of this DNA is repetitive DNA, often replicated from regular, coding DNA. Gene duplication is a very common process in genetics. Well, this "silent" DNA could be a rich source from which potentially useful *new* genes can emerge in evolution. Since components of the flagellum resemble closely the components of an apparatus that injects toxins into other bacteria, it is very likely that elements of this latter structure were duplicated in the "silent" parts of DNA and then recruited for a new use, the flagellum.

Perhaps an even better example is the intricate cascading route of human blood-clotting, involving lots of proteins. Most of these proteins turn out to be rather similar at the level of amino acid sequence – another indication of gene duplications. Since new copies were not essential for the original function, they could gradually evolve to take on a new function, driven by the force of mutation and natural selection. That this is really the case can be exemplified by the fact that we find only partial clotting cascades in fish: Some of these proteins have a long history in the animal world, but the cascading series of proteins got gradually longer and longer: When it needed to stop possible leaks much more quickly, our current blood clotting mechanism evolved from a low-pressure to a high-pressure cardio-vascular system – which became possible due to additional, modified gene replications.

Science is making more and more progress in explaining such

facts, but let us not forget that this is an ongoing process, for science always remains open to revision. But no matter what the outcome is, we have nothing to fear from genetics and evolutionary theory as long as they stay within their boundaries, because there can never be any conflict between science and religion in the view of the Catholic Church.

Q: Despite all the evidence you offer, I maintain that the opposite view, creationism, also makes a strong case. Just think of all the data in the Book of Genesis.

A: I have my doubts. My first objection is that the *Book of Scripture* is not the *Book of Nature,* and should therefore not be read as a scientific treatise. It has a different message to tell. Second, the Book of Genesis has not one but *two* creation accounts – and they are quite different. Genesis 1 paints an immense world, with an abundance of water, carrying a tiny human being who appears at the eleventh hour (the 6th day) while everything is ready for this human being. But then in Gen. 2:4b, it is almost as if the Bible starts all over again by painting a mirror image: a tiny world, short of water, in which a human being is stalking about like a giant, and nothing really starts until this being is around. In Genesis 2, everything is on hold until humankind arrives; all the earth is thirsty until there is a human being to cultivate it; the animals do not have a name until this human being gives them one. That's quite a contrast! To harmonize them "scientifically," we would have to make quite some mental acrobatics. "Theologically," however, they portray the same message: Everything comes from God, but human beings come from God in an even more special way.

The Catechism (289) acknowledges that "From a literary standpoint these texts may have had diverse sources. The inspired authors have placed them at the beginning of Scriptures to express in their solemn language the truths of creation." I always wonder, though, why creationists usually choose the 1st account in their fight against evolution instead of the 2nd account. I have never heard a convincing argument. If you want to read Genesis "literally," you cannot read it "selectively" at the same time.

Q: Still, evolution speaks in time spans of millions of years, whereas Genesis mentions a time span of only seven days at the most.

A: You are right, if you do go by the first creation account alone. But do we really interpret that account correctly when we take it as a *chronological* report? There are several problems with such an interpretation. Let me just mention one.

In a chronological version of creation, God needs time, actually six days, in order for Him to create everything, including time itself – which is a bit odd seen from a logical viewpoint, since time cannot be created at a "time" there is no time yet. Thomas Aquinas actually denies that creation is some chronological episode, located somewhere back in time, when he says, "God brought into being both the creature and time together" and "Before the world, there was not time." As I said before, God didn't create the world "*at* the beginning" but "*in* the beginning." In other words, creation is not exclusively focused on the beginning of this world, but on the origin of this world; creation is both giving a beginning to all that exists and sustaining in being all that exists (CCC 290).

As we discussed before, creation cannot follow a timeline, for time itself is a product of creation, so it is hard to figure out how creating time can be done at a certain time. Creation creates chronology, but it cannot become part of chronology, nor can chronology be the framework of creation. God certainly doesn't need time, not even a week, to create everything, let alone to create time! So I do not think Genesis 1 offers us a *chronology* of creation within the time span of six days.

Q: If Genesis 1 does not offer a *chronological* report, how else can we read that chapter?

A: As Pope Pius XII told us as early as 1943, "[…] the ancient peoples of the East, in order to express their ideas, did not always employ those forms or kinds of speech which we use today; but rather those used by the men of their times and countries." In ancient literature, it was common to place historical material in a *sequential* order according to a particular structure or framework, rather than in strict *chronological* order. The Catechism explains it this way: "Scripture presents the work of the Creator *symbolically* as a succession of six days of divine 'work,' concluded by the 'rest' of the seventh day" (337; italics are mine).

This opens the door for a *structural* interpretation: The seven days of creation are not intended to be taken literally as a chronology of how God made the world. Rather, Genesis 1 tells us *what* it is that God did, not *when* and *how* God did it. Therefore, the act of creation has been fitted into the structure of a single Hebrew week (the 7-day week was a novelty that didn't exist yet in prior ancient cultures). Each "day" is concluded by God saying that what He created was good. The main theme here is theological: Nothing is good without God.

Q: I still do not see how we could read Genesis 1 in what you call a *structural* interpretation.

A: For many centuries, it has been recognized that the six days of creation are divided into two sets of three:

—In the first set, God divides one thing from another: on Day One, He separates the light from the darkness (thus giving rise to day and night); on Day Two, He divides the waters above from the waters below (thus giving rise to the sky and the sea); on Day Three, He divides the waters below from each other (thus giving rise to the dry land). Classically, this section is known as the work of *division*.

—In the second set, God goes back over the realms that He produced by division in the first three days and then populates or "adorns" them. On Day Four, He populates the day and the night with the sun, moon, and stars. On Day Five, He populates the sky and sea with birds and fish. And on Day Six, He populates the land (between the divided waters) with animals and human beings. Classically, this is known as the work of *adornment*.

By the way, do not dismiss this interpretation as a modern version of biblical liberalism. We find this idea already in the writings of St. Thomas Aquinas.

Q: What makes you think a structural split into two sections is correct?

A: Genesis itself tells us so when you read it carefully, for it says that "the earth was without form and void" (Gen. 1:2). Well, the work of *division* cures the "without form" problem, whereas the work of *adornment* fixes the "void" (empty) problem. Likewise, at the end of the account we are told "the heavens and the earth were completed [i.e., by *division*], and all the host of them [i.e., by *adornment*]" (Gen. 2:1).

Therefore, creation is not about the *beginning* of this world, but about its *origin*. Creation means that everything that exists depends on God for its existence. In other words, the very first words of Genesis – "In the beginning" – do not refer to a "trigger" event at the beginning of time (something like a Big Bang), because creation must come "first" before any events (including a Big Bang) can follow. "In the beginning" should not be taken in a temporal, chronological, or sequential sense, but rather in a transcending sense – that is, more in the sense of "originally" (before any beginning, which is *in* the beginning) than "initially" (which would be *at* the beginning).

Q: It is obvious that you have a *biblical* problem with creationism. But some say there are also *philosophical* issues.

A: I would certainly agree with those people. Creationists do not distinguish, let alone accept, that the doctrine of creation is about the meta-physical grounds of life, and that the theory of evolution, on the other hand, is about the natural, physical causes of life. St. Thomas Aquinas would explain this difference with is famous distinction between a Primary Cause and secondary causes: Regular, physical causality reigns "inside" the universe, linking causes together in a chain of *secondary* causes, whereas creational causality reigns "outside" the universe as a *Primary* Cause, thus providing a "point of suspension" for the chain itself, so to speak. As a consequence, creation is about the Primary Cause behind this world, whereas evolution is about the secondary causes working in this world. They do not and can not even "bite" each other.

If Aquinas had known about evolution, he would probably have said that evolution offers us a *scientific* account of how a later state of the material world might have emerged from an earlier state – whereas creation offers us a *meta-physical* account of where the material world itself comes from. Creation is about the Primary Cause, whereas evolution would be about secondary causes. In contrast, creationism makes God, who is the Primary Cause, act as if He were also a secondary cause on each "creation day."

People who confuse the Primary Cause with secondary causes always remind me of that man in the middle of a flood, who begged God to rescue him. When God sent him someone in a rowboat, then someone in a motor boat, and finally someone in a helicopter, the man refused each one of them and kept waiting for God – apparently unaware of all the miracles God was performing for him in vain through secondary causes.

Q: Does this mean that creationists do not accept the distinction St. Aquinas introduced?

A: Correct! Creationists actually talk about God, the *Primary* cause of this world, as if He were also a *secondary* cause who performs a series of miraculous, supernatural interventions. In this way, God would act more like a demiurge who works a series of events, step-by-step, in the course of six or seven days. Creationism degrades God to some kind of "hands-on" god that we know from pagan mythologies. Instead, God is the First Cause, the ground and origin of all that exists – not a cause superior to all other causes, not a super-being among other beings, but an *Absolute* Being. So God is not the One to physically interfere in the universe and in the process of evolution, as if He were a "cause" prior to and stronger than any other causes, but instead He lets the secondary causes do their "job." Evolution follows biological laws as much so as planetary motions follow physical laws.

God does not make things Himself but He makes sure they are made. Belief in evolution does not preclude belief in creation but actually needs it. Pope Benedict put it this way (10-31-08): "creation is neither a movement nor a mutation. Instead, it is the foundational and continuing relationship that links the creature to the Creator, for He is the cause of every being and all becoming." In the words of St. Paul, "In Him we live and move and have our being" (Acts 17:28). Without God, there would be nothing, not even evolution. God is the Alpha and the Omega.

So let us be clear from now on: the Big Bang may be about the beginning of the universe, and evolution may be about the unfolding of the universe, but creation is about the origin of the universe.

Q: Do you have also *scientific* objections against creationism?

A: Creationists probably do not accept scientific arguments, because they usually reject science, but let me try. First of all, all the evidence from taxonomy, morphology, paleontology, and genetics that I mentioned earlier pleads *against* creationism. Besides, if we would follow creationists and take Genesis 1 as a biological exposé on the origin of species, we would run into trouble as soon as we want to explain hybrids in nature. In a world of fixed species, presumably created once and forever, there is no place for hybrids such as mules.

Besides, the "taxonomy" Genesis uses is not a *biological* taxonomy. Plants need sun, yet they were created prior to the sun. Birds and fish were created on the 5th day in order to "adorn" the firmament and the waters that were separated on the 2nd day, whereas the land animals were created on the 6th day after the land and its vegetation had been separated from the water on the 3rd day. Seen from a biological point of view, this kind of "taxonomy" wouldn't make much sense; obviously, the *Book of Scripture* has a *theological* message here instead. Genesis 1 is not so much a historical and scientific report as it is a creed, or perhaps even a prayer.

Nevertheless, creationists love to give a *biological* interpretation to the verses that say God created all creatures "according to their own kinds" (Gen. 1:12; 1:21). So they assume that God "must" have created all species once and forever. However, we cannot read Genesis as if it were a textbook on biology. It is more about *kinds* than about *species*; its classification is more practical than biological; that is why it distinguishes swimming creatures and winged birds in 1:21, and again cattle, creeping things, and wild animals in 1:24. Besides, seen from a biological kind of view, you wonder what makes cattle qualify as a separate "kind."

Later on in the Bible, we find even a theological classification. It mentions, for instance, two kinds of water creatures – with or without fins and scales – and two kinds of land animals – with or without cloven hooves (Deut. 14) – that is, kosher kinds vs. non-kosher kinds. Such distinctions are more theological than biological. If Genesis were really about biology, you should ask yourself why God created more than 350,000 species of beetles. The late biologist J.B.S. Haldane once said, "God must love beetles, because He created so many different kinds of them." Biology knows better.

Q: But isn't creationism correct that everything in nature is so beautifully designed?

A: There is certainly beauty in nature, but biology also tells us that not all biological designs are perfect, because natural selection promotes *optimal* designs – which are usually not *perfect* designs, because there are compromises to be made when balancing the benefits against the costs. Natural selection always goes for the best available design under the given circumstances. As a result, designs good for life in the Sahara may not be good for life in Alaska, and designs good for living in the trees may not be good for living on the ground, and so on. All that matters for an optimal design is reproductive success. In biology, success breeds success!

No wonder many designs did eventually become *outdated*, because the needs and circumstances kept changing. The list is endless: useless wings in flightless birds such as penguins; the tiny pelvis of whales; the problem of a dysfunctional appendix; the problem of our wisdom teeth, because we have the same set of teeth as other primates, yet a much flatter face. All such *rudimentary* designs are not perfect, but they are "footprints" or "traces" of common descent. Once they did have a function, but no more. To put it briefly, nature is beautiful, often optimal, but rarely perfect. As the Catechism puts it, God's creation is "in a state of journeying toward an ultimate perfection" (302). God wills perfection but allows imperfection.

Q: I still have my doubts. Doesn't the idea of evolution actually downgrade God's creation?

A: Not really. God's creation works under the laws of nature–actually *God's* laws. Thanks to creation, our universe has a cosmic order and design that regulates how things "work" and which biological designs "fit." It is the *cosmic* design that determines which *biological* designs are possible, and then it "selects" those designs that fit best; it is the cosmic design that contains the laws and constraints regulating which biological designs are successful in reproduction and survival – as much so as they regulate which bridges are successful designs. Because organisms differ in biological designs, partially based on genetic diversity, natural selection can promote those designs that are better in terms of the cosmic design.

I do not think this would downgrade God's creation, though. Isn't there immense beauty and splendor in the laws that govern our world and in the design our Creator has placed upon the universe? Just look at the beauty of what the laws of evolution have produced: a bewildering diversity of organisms living together in a rich variety of well-balanced ecosystems. It is only because the *cosmic* design is so beautiful that natural selection can produce some beautiful, yet limited *biological* designs.

The Catechism summarizes this well: "The order and harmony of the created world results from the diversity of beings and from the relationships which exist among them. *Man discovers them progressively as the laws of nature.* They call forth the admiration of scholars. The beauty of creation reflects the infinite beauty of the Creator" (341; italics are mine).

Q: I think the main objection of creationists against the theory of evolution is that it is "God-less."

A: You are probably right – that seems to be their deepest motive for fighting evolution. I would say Pope John Paul II worded it perfectly when he stated, "Scientific culture today requires Christians to have a mature faith." We should realize that science can never detect God, because it doesn't have the tools to do so – just as the eye cannot detect sound waves and ears cannot register odors. In that strict sense, science is indeed "God-less." But creationists go one step farther by calling Darwin an atheist, or at best an agnostic. Whether that is true or not, that in itself wouldn't disqualify his scientific theories. The fact, for instance, that the physicist Marie Curie was an agnostic doesn't disqualify her for having discovered radioactivity.

But there is probably more to it: Creationists also reject Darwinism because they think it made Darwin turn from a religious believer into an atheist. But I must say, even if he did become an atheist, such may have happened *after* he developed his theory, but not necessarily *because* of his theory; in his own words, it was the devastating loss of his ten-year-old daughter Annie that made him an agnostic. Whatever the real story is, I do not consider this an argument against evolutionary theory.

Q: So you keep maintaining that creationism is wrong?

A: I consider it a one-sided ideology that tries to silence science and thus gives religion a bad name. Fortunately, I am in good company in the Catholic Church. As early as 1868 (only 9 years after Darwin's famous publication), Cardinal John Henry Newman, recently beatified by the Church, said in one of his letters, "Mr. Darwin's theory need not then to be atheistical [sic], be it true or not; it may simply be suggesting a larger idea of Divine Prescience and Skill." I would say those words came from a very clear, wise, and trustworthy Catholic mind, refined by faith and reason.

In July 2007, Pope Benedict XVI discussed the debate raging in some countries of creation versus evolution, saying "This contrast is an absurdity." Yes, he actually called it an *absurdity* that "whoever believes in the creator could not believe in evolution, and whoever asserts belief in evolution would have to disbelieve in God." I couldn't agree more; let no one force you to make a choice between the two.

There is no competition between the *Book of Scripture* and the

Book of Nature. They rather complement each other and make us whole in unison. Those who pray for healing shouldn't throw away their medication, and those on medication shouldn't stop praying. Medication and meditation go very well hand in hand; they both come from God. Something similar holds for the twosome creation and evolution. Creationism is not the Catholic view, nor is evolutionism. The Catholic view is "faith *and* reason," "faith *and* science," "creation *and* evolution."

Q: So far, you have been very silent about the opposite ideology, evolutionism. I hope you have much to say *against* that ideology as well.

A: I am glad you mention this, for evolutionism certainly shouldn't be off the hook. I do agree with Pope John Paul II, though, that "some new findings lead us toward the recognition of evolution as more than a hypothesis" (10-22-96). But evolution-*ism* goes much farther than that. It is as one-sided and extreme as the opposite view of creationism is. It is also an "ism," and all "isms" look at the world from one specific perspective, claiming this makes you see everything. They are monopolistic by nature, and do not tolerate competitors. Evolution-ism is one of them: It declares to have found a "Grand Theory of Everything" in terms of natural selection – a theory that explains literally everything in life.

I would say in reply that biology certainly is no know-all or cure-all. I know of a Jesuit biologist who used to tease his parishioners and challenge his students with a quip: "You don't need to tell me anything about life – I am a biologist." It was a joke! But to some scientists it is not! Students in our schools – from elementary school to university – deserve to be taught genuine science, so they and their parents should not settle for some kind of ideology. Hence, in teaching the science of evolution and natural selection, we must also make clear what its limitations are – such is part of teaching genuine science as well. *Teach* it, but do not *preach* it.

So the question is then what the limitations of science are and where evolutionism goes overboard. The famous late geneticist Theodosius Dobzhansky, a dedicated member of the Orthodox Church, was wise to stress that it is in biology that nothing makes sense except in the light of evolution. But he was very aware of the fact that there is more to life than biology. Darwin may be to biology what Newton or Einstein is to physics, but we do not need to worship at Darwin's altar like evolutionists tend to do. Render to religion what is divine, but never render to science what is God's.

Nevertheless, the ideology of evolutionism sees everything exclusively in the light of evolution, and therefore it regards any other worldview as a rival, as a competitor claiming its own exclusivity. It knows no bounds or fences, so it is hostile to religion, including its doctrine of creation; it actually likes to down-grade religion to the status of being itself the mere product of natural selection – and nothing more. It is a very demanding doctrine that ultimately devours itself.

Q: So tell me then where evolutionism goes overboard. How would it ultimately devour itself?

A: Let me answer your question in several steps. My first step is to repeat my argument that evolutionists suffer from megalomania and tunnel-vision. They claim to have all the answers to all possible questions – including the answer that evolutionism is all there is and all that counts. They have a very myopic view on the world, declaring everything else in life outside their narrow scope as a mere illusion. They claim that, as scientists, they know everything about the universe, based on some esoteric knowledge that everyone else lacks, but they fail to remember they are just specialists like any other specialists – specialists in doing scientific research regarding the material and physical aspects of this world, leaving everything else to other "specialists."

My second reason for rejecting evolutionism is the fact that it is self-destructive and devours itself. Let me explain. Since the theory of natural selection is a product of the human mind – Darwin's, to be precise – we should ask ourselves where the human mind comes from. Evolutionism will tell you that the human mind is just a product of natural selection, like everything else in life. In their view, natural selection is supposed to explain everything in life, including the human mind. But if that were really so, we would find ourselves trapped in a vicious circle: The mind explains things with natural selection, but natural selection in turn would explain the mind? That is trouble!

Darwin himself was somehow vaguely aware of this thorny implication (good for him, I would say!). He says in his *Autobiography*: If the theory of natural selection comes from the human mind, one might wonder whether "the mind of man, which has, as I fully believe, been developed from a mind as low as that possessed by the lowest animal, [can] be trusted when it draws such grand conclusions." And again in a letter to W. Graham in 1881, "Would anyone trust in the convictions of a monkey's mind, if there are any convictions in such a mind?"

Q: You are right: How can we trust a mind generated by natural selection? That looks like a boomerang to me!

A: It certainly is! If natural selection were the origin of all there is in life, including the human mind, it would act like a boomerang that comes back to its maker (in a vicious circle), knocking out the truth claims of whoever launched it. How could we ever trust the outcome of mere natural selection when it comes to matters of truth? On the contrary, natural selection must *assume* the human mind, but it can neither generate it nor explain it. On its own, natural selection would be just a powerless and useless concept. If the theory of natural selection were the mere product of natural selection, it would be worth nothing; we wouldn't even be able to know whether it is true or false.

Science is based on rationality, and rationality is a feature of the human mind. Let me put it very clearly: If one cannot trust the rationality of human beings, one is logically prevented from having confidence in one's own rational activities – with science being one of them. Obviously, evolutionism has undermined itself – by cutting off its very *reason* for reasoning!

The only reason we have to trust our reasoning, even in science, is the fact that God is our Creator and that we were created in His image as a take-off of the Divine Mind, because our human understanding "shares in the light of the divine intellect" (CCC 299). As a matter of fact, denying that God is our Creator is an acid that eats away the foundation of rationality, and therefore of science itself. We cannot pull ourselves up by our own bootstraps. To those who claim that the mind created God, I would say they have it upside down: It is God who created the mind.

Q: Don't evolutionists claim, though, that natural selection has replaced God's work?

A: If they do, they have a very weak case. Natural selection "promotes" the fittest biological design. This means it doesn't really create anything new but just sorts out what is already there. In doing so, natural selection may be able to explain that a fine working design has a better chance of being reproduced, but ultimately it cannot explain why such a design is working so well.

That is where *teleology* comes in, for design is a teleological concept. Teleology is about goal-directed phenomena. There is teleology in the biological world because the animate world is design-like – just as there is teleology in the technical world of designers, because the world of technology is design-like as well.

Be aware, though, we have left physical territory here and have entered *meta*-physical terrain. There is "something" in successful biological designs that carries them through the filter of natural selection. In other words, natural selection on its own cannot do the "job" unless it works within a framework of cosmic design. Without this "cosmic design," there could be no natural selection. Natural selection can only select those specific *biological* designs that follow the rules of the *cosmic* design. Natural selection follows the "path of least resistance" in the landscape of the cosmic design. So evolutionists cannot really deny this design nor its Creator.

Q: And yet evolutionists do deny the cosmic design of an Intelligent Designer.

A: Somehow, evolutionists feel very uncomfortable with teleology. The physiologist Ernst Von Brücke used a rather risqué but telling analogy when he said that biologists treat teleology like a lady without whom they cannot live, yet they are ashamed to show themselves with her in public. And it is this very teleology that leaves us some thorny meta-physical questions – whether evolutionists admit this or not. Darwin may have believed that he took "purpose" out of science by explaining it in terms of a physical mechanism, but at the same time he left it in as a meta-physical presupposition. Anyone who rejects metaphysics can only do so on metaphysical grounds.

Leon Kass, M.D., chairman of the President's *Council on Bioethics* from 2001 to 2005, couldn't have said it better: Organisms "are not teleological because they have survived; on the contrary, they have survived (in part) because they are teleological." In other words, the causality of natural selection doesn't explain teleology, but *assumes* it. Put differently, without the "arrival of the fit," there wouldn't be any "survival of the fittest." Without order and design in nature, there couldn't be any natural science.

But be careful. This is not to say that the Intelligent Designer of the cosmic design must periodically intervene in His creation in order to bridge, for instance, the gaps in the fossil record – as if God's original creation contains gaps or omissions that require God to later fill or repair. Such a spurious conclusion would violate again the distinction between creation and evolution. Unlike the causes at work *within* nature, God's act of Creation is a completely non-temporal and non-progressive reality. God does not periodically adjust or "fix up" natural things, because that would downgrade Him to a "hand-on" god. Instead, He is the ultimate divine reality without which no other reality could exist. God is indeed the Author of nature, but as its transcendent ultimate cause, not as another natural cause alongside other natural causes.

Q: But what about the highly controversial issue of "chance" in evolution and evolutionary theory?

A: You're right, that is a hot topic in biology, as evolutionary theory often speaks of *randomness*; mutations, for instance, are supposed to be random, environmental changes are considered to be random, and Mendel's genetic laws act at random. However, this view is not in conflict with the idea of creation. St. Thomas Aquinas even argued in his *Summa Theologiae* that the presence of chance and contingency in nature shows that nature requires a divine Creator in order to exist (I:2:3).

But there is more to it. We can easily replace the phrase "at random" with the expression "by chance" However, the term chance can carry many different meanings, so each time a biologist says that something happened "by chance," we should ask: How do you mean? Randomness and chance in biology can stand for various interpretations: A random outcome can be unpredictable, and/or unrelated to other causes or effects, and/or arbitrary without any preferences, and/or opportunistic without any foresight, and/or undirected without a certain preset outcome. But no matter how we define *chance* in science, we can never define it as meaningless or purposeless, as those words do not exist in science but derive from philosophy and religion.

Yet, evolutionists love to adorn the scientific term *chance* as it is used in evolutionary theory with a capital C – the goddess of *Chance*, a sort of whimsical providence secretly worshipped and to be forcefully defended against rival deities. However, the concept of chance in evolutionary theory not even comes close to fate, destiny, doom, or meaninglessness. Science has nothing to say about chance with a capital C. Fate is far beyond its reach; fate is in essence a worldview notion that doesn't belong in scientific vocabulary.

Q: Can you give me an example of this illegitimate use of the word *chance*?

A: Evolutionists love to take the word *chance* out of its scientific context and interpret it as "senseless" and "meaningless" – which changes the whole of life into a mere play of whimsical and fortuitous events. By so doing, they turn "Chance" into a capricious, blind agent, actually a deity, or a "blind watchmaker" at best. So we end up with the deity of chaos versus the God of order. After that, they claim that evolution is a senseless and meaningless process – which is a dogmatic worldview again, nicely disguised in the garment of science. Science has thus been turned into a pseudo-religion: omni-potent and omni-present.

If all of this were true, there is only one conclusion left, namely that – in the words of the paleontologist George Gaylord Simpson – "man is the result of a purposeless and natural process that did not have him in mind." No wonder Oliver Wendell Holmes Jr.

could write "I see no reason for attributing to man a significance different in kind from that which belongs to a baboon or a grain of sand."

My response to Simpson's proclamation made from his "quasi-scientific" pulpit at Columbia is actually very simple: Simpson says there is no God, and Simpson is His prophet! As I said before, do not take the word *chance* out of its scientific context by interpreting it as "senseless" and "meaningless" – which would change the whole of life into a mere play of whimsical and fortuitous events. Those who argue that evolution is a senseless and meaningless process are just promoting a dogmatic worldview, nicely disguised in the garment of science. So we end up with the deity of chaos versus the God of order.

Besides, seen from a *meta*-physical viewpoint, there is nothing "random" in evolution. The Catechism puts it this way: The world "is not the product of any necessity whatever, nor of blind fate or chance" (295). True, human beings are *contingent* – that is, they could easily *not* have existed, since the reason for their existence cannot be found within themselves – but that doesn't mean they are *random* or mere products of blind fate. They may have come through a process of evolution, but ultimately they must come from creation, or else they couldn't be here at all. Although evolution didn't have humanity "in mind" – for it has no mind – our Creator did. Otherwise, we wouldn't and couldn't even be here. Thanks to our Creator, each one of us is not just an evolutionary nobody but rather a significant somebody. We are not a quantity but a quality – which is the quality of being made in God's image. As Benedict XVI put it in his 1st homily as Pontiff, "We are not some casual and meaningless product of evolution. Each of us is the result of a thought of God." Although we came into this world alone and will leave this world alone, we are not really alone, for we came here from our Maker and will eventually return to our Maker.

Q: They always say that "purpose" was taken out of astronomy by Copernicus, out of physics by Newton, and out of biology by Darwin. But you are bringing it back in!

A: Purpose was indeed taken out of science by scientists such a Copernicus, Newton, and Darwin, but that doesn't mean it has completely disappeared from view. It didn't really disappear but went into hiding. I always find it startling that evolution has produced some human beings devoting their entire career to the very *purpose* of proving that evolution has no purpose whatsoever. Or – to paraphrase one of C.S. Lewis' discoveries – if there were no light in the universe and therefore no creatures with eyes, we should never know it was dark. Similarly, if there is no purpose in the universe, how were we ever to know there is no such thing as purpose?

Besides, denying that there are purposes in life defeats its own claim. If it is your purpose to remove all purposes from life, you are also wiping out your own purpose for doing so. Those whose purpose it is to eradicate *all* purposes from life have lost even the very purpose for doing so. That is why it always strikes me how some people made it their main purpose in life to claim that there are no purposes in life.

Please be aware that issues of sense, meaning, and purpose do not belong in scientific vocabulary. The question as to whether evolution has a meaning, destination, or purpose takes us into the domains of philosophy and religion. Science has just no answers to these kinds of questions – no matter what evolutionists proclaim, or like to proclaim. Scientists do not have the competence to declare us as casual and meaningless products of evolution, but they should leave that verdict up to others.

Q: Nevertheless, evolutionists maintain evolution was steered by disorder. The physicist and cosmologist Stephen Hawking even goes as far as postulating that the entire process the universe is going through runs on its own power. He speaks of something like "spontaneous creation.".

A: You are right, the doctrine of evolutionism – based on evolutionary biology, but stretched far beyond its limits – takes evolution as an autonomous process running its own course, based on random mutations and natural selection and evolving from simple entities to complex entities. Many take this process as the gradual development of biological order out of physical chaos. No wonder, atheists like Daniel Bennett think that religion has it wrong

– "upside down" in his own words – by claiming that science places order at the *end* of an evolutionary process, whereas God's creation is supposed to start with order from the very *beginning*.

It is true that evolution seems to have a time arrow moving from "what is less complex" to "what is more complex," but the simple is in no way less orderly than the complex; a simple snowflake actually shows a very intricate order. In other words, there is no reason to think that the process of building more order begins with and is being steered by "disorder." Although science tries to explain that order comes from *below*, religion keeps maintaining that order comes from *Above*. The order we see in nature does not and cannot come from chaos, but must come from a more fundamental, preexisting order at a deeper level – which is the cosmic order of Creation governing everything that happens in the universe, including the process of evolution.

Think of the following experiment. Shaking jars of variously shaped candies won't create much more order, but shaking a jar with *round* candies would, as round candies have an underlying order – that is, at a "deeper" level" – which allows for a "hexagonal closest packing" structure. It is the cosmic design that is at the basis of this kind of order. I call this the reversed approach. Such an approach would reveal to us that evolution has an underlying order of biological designs and genetic constraints – making the stream of evolution run in the bed of a cosmic design. Like water, natural selection follows the path of least resistance.

There "must" be some form of preexisting order, as no order could ever come forth from a purely chaotic universe. In a world of chaos, there wouldn't even be room for science, because science is a very orderly enterprise that studies order by definition. Those who believe order emerges from chaos see chaos as "pre-order." But as C.S. Lewis once said, "Before you switched on the light in the cellar, there was (if you want to call it so) 'pre-light'; but the English for that is 'darkness.'" Chaos is what it is – chaos!

Chaos and chance can never create the order found in the living and nonliving world—as little as blindness can create sight. As the old saying goes, "what chance creates, chance destroys," because there is no purpose or direction to chance (just test it at a slot machine). It is the other way around: Chance is only intelligible in terms of the order which it lacks; a previous order must exist before any chance event can even occur. If there were no order, there could be no chance, because chance needs the order of preexisting causes coming together to produce unexpected results (which is called coincidence).

Q: How come evolutionism still remains a very strong ideology in modern society?

A: I wonder myself, for its basis is fundamentally shaky and flawed. A world-view that portrays us as solely being a DNA chain produced by evolution is as fragile as the DNA structure that presumably generated this world-view; it cannot be worth more than its molecular origin. Evolutionism is resting on the quicksand of molecular structures, but the foundation of science cannot be built on a foundation of molecules. In a world of molecules, there is no talk of being true and false, but only of being hard, stable, strong, and what have you. The late biologist J.B.S. Haldane couldn't have said it better, "If my mental processes are determined wholly by the motions of atoms in my brain, I have no reason to suppose that my beliefs are true ... and hence I have no reason for supposing my brain to be composed of atoms." Evolutionism is caught up in this vicious circle.

Don't forget that a worldview claims to be all-inclusive – in this case, the only thing acceptable would be science, nothing else; but if nothing outside science is permitted, we have cut off the very branch science sits on. So the dream of an all-knowing, all-powerful worldview based on sheer science is bound to be an illusion as well. It has lost its *reason* for reasoning and for trusting its own rationality. The advocates of evolutionism are not ignorant, of course, but they know so much that isn't so. Yet, they are quite powerful and produce such popular books that many do get snowed by this new counterfeit "religion."

Q: Some say they are promoting even more... What I am referring to is *eugenics*.

A: Eugenics may not be a direct result of evolutionism, but it is certainly one of its offshoots. Eugenics is the study and practice of selective breeding applied to humans, with the aim of improving the human gene pool by a specific form of natural selection, *artificial* selection. This idea is a consequence of degrading humans to animals. The slogan is: If you can breed animals, why not humans! Some have even said that it is only with mankind that the "worst animals" (in a biological sense) are allowed to "breed."

At the beginning of the previous century, eugenics flourished – not only at universities and on the editorial boards of scientific journals, but also in politics. The Virginia Justice Oliver Wendell Holmes declared in *Buck v. Bell* (1927) that "three generations of imbeciles are enough," and launched a massive campaign of forced sterilizations. Eugenicists started giving IQ tests to Jewish immigrants on Ellis Island and reported that forty percent of them were "feeble-minded." The 1924 Immigration Act drew heavily on ideas from eugenicists such as Madison Grant and Harry Laughlin.

Eugenics has since become a brutal movement which inflicted massive human rights violations on millions of people. The "interventions" advocated and practiced by eugenicists involved a wide range of "degenerates" or "unfits" – the poor, the blind, the mentally ill, entire "racial" groups such as Jews, Blacks, Roma ("Gypsies"), and the "dysgenic" victims of Margaret Sanger's *Planned Parenthood*. All of these "misfits" are deemed "unfit" to live according to their despotic dogma called "survival of the fittest." This, in turn, led to practices such as segregation, sterilization, genocide, euthanasia, pre-emptive abortions, designer babies, and in the extreme case of Nazi Germany, mass extermination. Eugenicists are living happily on a boat, more than willing to shove others back into the water. G.B. Shaw predicted that "part of eugenic politics would finally land us in an extensive use of the lethal chamber."

Q: Isn't eugenics something from the past, though?

A: Let me say this first: Perfectly in line with evolutionism, eugenics is dedicated to the dogma that humans are solely animals, which means we could breed humans like we breed animals. But it is also dedicated to the evolutionist creed that all men evolved un-equal. If natural selection is all there is, human beings can only *evolve* un-equal, so they can only be *treated* accordingly as un-equal; and since there is presumably no such "thing" as creation, they are certainly not *created* equal. Making the weak be at the service of the strong is a consequence of this worldview. It is the cause of today's atrocities, but can easily become tomorrow's routine. That is eugenics in a nutshell – and it is still very much alive.

It came, for instance, alive again as the major ideology behind our so-called Reproductive Genetic Technologies (RGT), often connected with in-vitro-fertilization procedures (IVF). Here we have a new breed of eugenicists who urge parents to have the "best" children by using what they call a pre-implantation genetic diagnosis (PGD). In this procedure, a single cell is extracted from an IVF embryo and then tested to see which embryos make the genetic cut. The embryos that "fail" the test are discarded or donated to research. The ones that "pass" have a chance to be transferred into a womb.

All these technologies are modern versions of eugenics and were introduced as a way to eventually eradicate diseases within the embryo, not only by genetic engineering, but also by destructing human life. Their defenders cleverly swap one value, the sanctity of life, with another value, the prevention of suffering. Since words are inherently flexible, they can easily be adapted to any ideology. No wonder, some ideologists have put a nice label on this kind of abortion: "eugenic abortion." Others have chosen to say that abortion is a "cure" for the "disease" of pregnancy. Then again, others call abortion and abortive contraceptives a "health care" issue, but none of this has anything to do with the health of the mother, let alone the health of the aborted unborn baby. Keep in mind that moral values can never be put against each other and weighed like we weigh coins. There are no gradations in good and evil; there is no "lesser evil" or "greater good." How could "a greater good" ever permit "minor evils," for how could good ever originate from evil? We will get back to this in chapter seven.

No matter how you look at it, these "eugenicists" have charged themselves with the grave duty to decide who is to live and who is to die. I would say they are lucky they have already been born;

so they made it to the "boat" and are happy to shove other people back into the water by following their own, man-made "moral" laws – which are actually immoral laws. They think that, since genes are in control of our lives, they, in turn, should be in control of those genes. Isn't that a vicious circle?

Q: What does the Catholic Church have to say about eugenics?

A: Today's main critic is Pope Benedict who warned us of a new eugenics mentality on 2/21/2009. He condemned this "obsessive search for the 'perfect child'," and added in response that "Man will always be greater than all that which makes up his body."

Indeed, eugenics places the final end of human beings in biological worth, but the Catholic teaching places it in eternal life. Put differently, the Church makes human culture subordinate to morality, whereas eugenics makes morality a mere product of human culture. When it comes to slavery, abortion, genocide, or what have you, evolutionism can only talk in terms of "winners" and "losers"; there is no longer talk of "good" and "bad," because those terms are not only outside its scope but are even declared illusory. That is why it eventually dehumanizes and leads to what C.S. Lewis called "the abolition of man." As Pope John Paul II once observed, "When the sense of God is lost, there is also a tendency to lose the sense of man, of his dignity and life."

Q: After all the nice things you have said about the biological evolution of humankind, I think many Catholics would still not be too happy about their "new" pedigree.

A: Indeed, we do not have a very impressive pedigree given the fact that we trace our ancestors back to the "dust" of the earth and the animal world. As we hear on each Ash Wednesday, "You are dust, and to dust you will return." Our bellybuttons are a lasting reminder of this fact. But we are also more than dust – a living soul – and that is thanks to God's breath. So we have another "lifeline," reaching directly into heaven, because we have Adam and Eve in our family tree; and since they were created in God's image and likeness, so were we.

We could also say that we came here *through* evolution, and yet we came here *from* God – in the same way as our children come through us but not from us. Let me word it in this way: We are earthy, made from earth, and yet we are heavenly, made in God's image. Evolution gave us "roots," but creation gives us "wings." We can spread our spiritual wings and fly, no matter how earthbound our feet seem to be. Our bodies may look "ape-like" and will return to "dust," but Catholic faith promises us that our souls are "angelic." The Catechism says about this soul "that it is immortal: it does not perish when it separates from the body at death, and it will be reunited with the body at the final Resurrection" (366). There are better things ahead of us than any we leave behind. Let's try then to live up to God's expectations.

In the upcoming chapters, we will study what it is in us that doesn't derive from the animal world, but only comes with being made in the image of God.

5

A Beautiful Mind and Soul

Made in God's Image

The human mind and soul have been under attack for quite a while. I do not quite understand why, but it is my educated guess that it has something to do with the fact that many of us nowadays do not like the idea that we have been made in the likeness of God. But there is probably much more to it.

You may wonder, though, how the human mind could ever be seriously attacked and damaged. Indeed, it is amazing how some people love to downgrade the human mind while touting their own minds. Yet they keep trying – with their minds and in their minds – to damage the human image as a replica of God's image. They maintain, for instance, that human beings are nothing but glorified animals, and so must be their minds. Or they attempt to prove that the human mind is nothing but a neuronal network that runs like a computer, worth nothing more than a machine, or an animal at best.

This chapter wants to scrutinize those claims and seek to restore the human mind and soul as something made in Heaven. Those who think that the mind creates God will learn that it is God who creates the mind. It is a chapter written for mind-full people. I hope and pray it is going to enrich your mind as well.

Homo sapiens (S) in discussion with *Homo religiosus* (R)

S: My name is *Homo sapiens*. I was given this name because I am an evolutionist who belongs to a biological species rooted in the animal world. I came from the animal world and was modeled after the animal world. My body tells you my entire story.

R: Well, my name is *Homo religiosus*. I prefer this name because I was created in God's image and likeness. I have a bond with Him, I come from Him, I was modeled after His divine image, and I will return to Him. The fact that I have a mind tells you where I come from. Perhaps my body came from the animal world, but I am more than my body. The word "Man" goes back to the Sanskrit, "Manu" meaning "thinking" or "wise" – for that is indeed the essence of my being. No wonder we are sometimes called thinking animals. As the philosopher Immanuel Kant put it, "Man is distinguished above all animals by his self-consciousness, by which he is a 'rational animal'."

When I say I come *from* God, I am not denying that I came here *through* my parents, and that they came here through their parents, and that perhaps their far ancestors came here through evolution. No matter what, we all came here from God. It is not so much our bodies that were made in God's image, but first of all our minds and souls. I am not denying what you say, but I am adding a deeper dimension to your claims.

S: How are we ever going to communicate with each other? We are light years apart. I have already a problem with the way you use the word "mind" – let alone the word "soul." You are suggesting your mind is different from your body, but all I can see and experience is my body.

R: That is a very common viewpoint nowadays. We have been brought up with cameras, TV-sets, iPods, and what have you. And these seem to determine what is "real" in life. However, a camera can only capture what is *physical* – hard-rock entities, including bodies, and bodily things such as X-rays, EKG's, EEG's, brain scans, and so on. We live in a world of "visible" things. So we have been brain-washed: What cameras cannot capture can not and does not exist. Period!

My response would be: Wait a minute! Not only has science been masterful in discovering things we never thought existed, but there is also so much in life that instruments can never capture – things such as emotions, thoughts, hopes, dreams, beliefs… Are they perhaps not real, because they do not show up on EEGs and brain scans? They may not be physical, and yet they are definitely based on facts and have shaped human history to the core; they have even enabled our technology and most of what is surrounding us. Think of this: A camera may not be able to capture the difference between a blinking eye and a winking eye, but we all know they are different. Behind this visible world of material things that can be counted, measured, and recorded, there is a vast invisible world of immaterial things that elude our recordings and measurements. Curiously enough, when you deny the existence of anything immaterial, you also deny the existence of your very own immaterial denial. So be careful as to what you say!

S: But how real can these non-physical things be if they cannot be made visible?

R: Those who hesitate to call them real I would advice to keep in mind how much Hitler's intentions, thoughts, beliefs, and his bigoted reasoning did shape human history. Were those less real than his gas chambers? Or picture what would happen if a majority of people make an immaterial decision to withdraw all their money from the bank. Are those decisions not real? Just watch their outcome! I know it is hard, actually impossible, to capture thoughts by camera, but do not tell me they are therefore not real.

And then there are moral values. Without those, there wouldn't be good and evil; yet, we all know that evil is an ontological reality, something real, something to watch out for. How different would our world be if everyone would do to others what they want to be done to themselves! Wouldn't the world be a much better place if everyone would see God's image in everyone else!

And what to make of issues like meaning and destination – a destination in this life, even beyond death? I could even make the case that people who have lost a purpose in life may run into psychological trouble. If we had no religion, what would we do when disaster strikes us, when things do not go the way we had planned, or when we become victims of injustice – in short, when we are no longer in control?

In short, there are so many things in life that are not material and physical, and yet they are undeniably real – things such as thoughts, values, decisions, and purposes. They do not belong to the visible, material world but to the invisible, spiritual world.

S: You seem to be saying that reality is not a monolithic thing, right?

R: Correct! Reality is like a jewel with many facets; you can look at it from various angles, with different eyes, through different windows. As a consequence, physicists perceive primarily physical phenomena, whereas biologists see mainly biological facts – but all of them are often "blind" for other aspects of reality. Be aware, though, what they call the "scientific world" is just *one* aspect of the "real world." The fact that other aspects are beyond the scope of science doesn't make them less "real" or less "factual" or less "objective" or less "valid." What you choose to neglect you cannot just reject.

There are many more perspectives than what science tries to cover with its barometers, thermometers, and spectrometers. Just like the "physical eye" sees colors in nature, so the "moral eye" sees moral values in life. All these "eyes" are in search of reality, but each one "sees" a different aspect of it. There's so much more to life than what meets the (scientific) eye; there are many more ways of looking at things; there's so much more to the story. There are many kinds of blindness: Not only can you be physically blind, but also morally blind and even spiritually blind.

Picture yourself walking around a statue; what you see in the back is different from the front, not because you *wish* the back to be different but because the back *is* actually different from the front. In a similar way, there are many perspectives and outlooks on the world surrounding us, making for different points of view, different conceptual frameworks, different aspects of reality, different facts—all of which can be equally "real," "factual," "objective," and "valid" (albeit not equally "tangible"). Yet, each one offers only a one-sided interpretation of reality.

S: I would say the "aspects" you are speaking of are just made up by us in our brains.

R: That is a position hard to defend, for if you were right, you may have to give up much more than you probably would be willing to. Many people believe that, by giving a mighty kick to a stone, they have proved the reality of a "hard fact," but they do not realize that what comes to our senses is transformed by our brains into a mental model of the external world. So reality is not only a matter of kicking and touching – there is much more to it. If you choose to be such a matter-of-fact person, you may not have much left. Let me explain to you why not.

There are no facts without *interpretation*. Every fact is interpreted within a specific framework or – to put it differently – is seen from a specific perspective. In other words, we don't just bump into facts; instead, we generate "facts" ourselves and then test them. In observation, one is both a passive "spectator" and an active "creator" at the same time. We look at *events* as spectators, and then change them into *facts* as creators. Animals, for instance, just do not know about any *facts*. Animals live in a world of events, but humans also inhabit a world of facts – which are mental interpretations of those events. The world of animals is only populated with what their senses can capture. But capturing facts requires a human mind.

So I am coming back to my previous point: Cameras may capture physical things, but there is much more in reality than they can capture. At the moment we look at pictures taken by a camera, we still need to *interpret* what we see on the picture, as pictures in themselves are just worthless pieces of paper. That is where the human mind comes in – so as to make sense of the dots seen on a newspaper picture. Behind the visible world is an invisible world.

S: I am sure you are suggesting that "mind" is one of those

things a camera cannot capture.

R: You got it! There is often more going on behind the scene than we can physically register. Here is my simple example again: *Blinking* is something we can capture with a camera, but *winking* is of a rather different nature; it is not just a single blink with one eye (unless you suffer from a winking "tic"), but there is a very particular *intention* behind winking. What does a "wink" add to a "blink" then? The answer is straightforward: My wink tells you to read my *mind* as kidding. Yet, a camera cannot register the difference between a wink and a blink.

Would you still maintain that winking is less "real" than blinking? True, winking at someone is undoubtedly a physical process, as much as blinking is, but it is also very different from blinking an eye, as it surpasses a series of physical causes. In contrast to blinking, there is something else behind a wink – call it an "I" or a "mind" or a "soul." From now on, I will use these three terms interchangeably, for I want to stay away from the difficult and technical discussion as to how they differ; yet what they do have in common is that they are *spiritual*, definitely beyond what a camera can capture. They are part of what is "unseen."

In the rest of this discussion, I will therefore use the word "mind" as a collective term to refer to my self, my mind, my soul, my spiritual side – and the word "I" acts like a shortcut for all of these. The Catechism defines the soul as "the spiritual principle in man" (363). Perhaps it helps if you take the mind as the *intellectual* part of the soul; yet both belong to our *spiritual* side. The mind is the power of the soul by which we know truth; the mind is the soul's "eye," its "light," so to speak.

S: **Sorry, but what you call "mind" would still need a bit more "body" for me.**

R: Let's start with "I" – the "I" of the human body, mind and soul, the "I of the beholder." There is something very enigmatic about this "I." You may, for instance, think or say to yourself "I cannot help what I do, because the activity of my brain cells is said to be determined by physical and biological laws." If this were true, we would end up with a form of circular reasoning – something like "There is no God; so all proofs for the existence of God must be flawed because there is no God." In this case, we are saying "All I do is determined by laws; so I cannot change what I do because everything is determined by laws." There is only one way out of this vicious circle: It is your very "I" who is thinking all of this.

Somehow, we are talking here at two very different levels. In my thoughts, I am always a step "ahead" of myself, or "above" myself – which has been called the "systematic elusiveness of *I*," leaving science behind in the dust. So when I ask myself the question "Who am I," I certainly do not do so from a desire to find out my own name, gender, age, etc. Instead, I am searching for something "behind" these personal details – something unique that doesn't and cannot belong to anyone else. When I reflect on myself, it is always "I" doing this. Imagine a missile being its own target, or your index-finger pointing at itself! That is impossible, and yet, *I* – my "self" – can do so.

S: What you call "I" reminds me of what I call "Ego."

R: Please do not confuse your "I" with your "Ego." Whereas "Ego" arrogantly dominates, "I" humbly reflects and corrects. "I" stands for the "transparency of the self," whereas "Ego" represents the "grandeur of the self" – something that humanism promotes. "Ego" is self-made, self-centered, part of a so-called me-society, whereas "I" belongs to the "City of God." "Ego" has forgotten who "I" is… God and Ego cannot live together in the same person. As John the Baptist says about Jesus, "He must increase, but I must decrease" (Jn 3:30).

"I" is a "take-off" of Someone else, whose Name is I-AM, in whose image and likeness "I" was created. So it is our calling to determine and develop our self more and more in line with God's image. It shouldn't surprise us then that, in contrast, human history has mostly been a history of huge and super "Egos," a history of leaders with the biggest fangs, of cowboys with the fastest guns, of oil sheiks with the largest harems. Saint Ambrose loved to say that "the great" of this world put off being humble until death humbles them." That is what happens when we confuse "I" with "Ego." My brain may make me a genius, but my mind could turn me into a sage with a soul and a spirit.

S: Your "I" is indeed very enigmatic! I do not know how to picture such a "thing."

R: You are probably being sarcastic, but I do agree it is enigmatic. We cannot put our fingers on what this "I" stands for. It is like my shadow – always a pace ahead of me, leaving open what my next step will be. The shadow of oneself will never wait to be jumped on; it evades capture, and yet is never very far ahead. It is here that we come in touch with this astounding capability of the human mind – the capacity of reflecting on itself. I may notice, for instance, that I am clumsy; I may even notice that I am laughing at myself for being clumsy; and then I may decide to tell others that I noticed how I was laughing at my own clumsiness. This is in fact an iterative or recursive process of *self-reflection*, making "I" act like my own shadow; I can never get away from it in the same way as I can get away from someone else's shadow. I can think about myself, correct my own actions, comment on my own actions, and even revise the comments on my own actions. In short, I have this unique desire to learn about myself through *self-reflection*.

We have a fascinating situation here: I-as-a-subject (*I-now*) can reflect on I-as-an-object (*I-past*). I remember my past because *I-now* is more than and ahead of *I-past*. As a subject, I may investigate I-as-an-object and then realize, for instance, that I-as-an-object made a mistake. In contrast, I-as-a-subject is never open to investigation because its future possibilities are beyond its current actualities – and therefore, I-now is always a pace ahead of I-past.

That is why I can never blame my glands or hormones for what I did wrong, because I-now is always a pace ahead of I-past (including my glands). Whenever I reflect on myself as an object, there is "some I" doing all of this as a subject; it is as if another "I" is "looking over my shoulder." That is why the mind itself is not an object like other objects in this world, for it is their very origin that makes the world intelligible. Without the mind, there wouldn't be any objects of knowledge comprehensible to us. No wonder the human mind is just an elusive entity in this universe – surely immaterial and spiritual.

S: I do not like the words "immaterial" and "spiritual." They sound too lofty to me. They refer to an invisible world, and that sounds spooky to me.

R: Well, these words might make more sense when you realize that the human mind has also the capacity of *transcending* itself. When I say or think "I am only human," I am not comparing myself with something "below" me (such as a cat, a dog, or an ape), but I am comparing myself with something – or rather Someone – "above" me and transcending me.

When I call myself "only human," I am actually comparing myself with Someone who does not have the limitations I experience myself. In some mysterious way, I am reaching out into the realm of the Absolute, far beyond myself. In so doing, the "finite" catches a glimpse of the Infinite. Somehow, I share "in the light of the divine mind," as Vatican II puts it.

No wonder God's name in the Bible is "I AM." Our "finity" can only be identified in comparison with God's infinity. I would say we certainly need the words "immaterial" and "spiritual" to capture this mysterious reality of *self-transcendence*. Therefore, it shouldn't surprise us that our hungry bodies also have a hungry soul.

Because of our capacity of self-transcendence, self-reflection can also be used for *self-examination*. Whereas self-reflection allows me to know more about myself, self-examination also enables me to compare what I know about myself with moral standards beyond myself: Is what I did in conformity with what God wants me to do? This is where the will comes in. We tend to think that intellect is the key thing – that if we know what is right, we will pursue it. But this fails to account for weakness of will – that is, when we know what is right but fail to do it. Self-examination is an examination of conscience – an honest assessment of one's life. It examines my "finity" in the light of God's Infinity. We will get back to this in chapter seven.

S: I am curious to hear where this power of self-transcendence would come from then.

R: Obviously, I cannot transcend myself on my own, but because I myself was made in the image of God, I perceive more than myself whenever I perceive myself completely – and in this process, I may become more like God. That is where *Homo sapiens* turns into *Homo religiosus,* who is a being in a bond with God.

All of a sudden, there is a new dimension in our lives – God! God is not one of the persons among other persons, just as He is not a cause among other causes. In the words of St. Augustine, God is "higher than my highest and more inward than my innermost self" (Conf. 3, 6, 11). Therefore, submitting ourselves to God, the Maker of Heaven and Earth, is not like submitting ourselves to a dictator, who is just another person in our midst. On the contrary, the more we become like God, the more we become like ourselves, for we were made in His image. That is the enigma of Christianity: We do not try to become followers of a dictator, but followers of God, through His Son Jesus Christ. And by following Him, we become more like *ourselves.*

However, all of this is only possible if the human mind is a "take-off" of the Creator's Mind. "Being in the image of God the human individual [...] is capable of self-knowledge" (CCC 357). Here we stumble upon another elusive part of the human mind and soul. No wonder atheists are out to destroy this human image, because it is a divine image, a reflection of God's image.

Nevertheless, it is our very humanity that is at stake here. It shouldn't surprise us then that science had to drop out of this race, for even if science wants to study the human mind, it needs to start from the minds of those very scientists. Let me put this in more general terms: The *knowing subject* must be more than the *known object,* for all knowledge of objects is based on a subject that apprehends those objects, but the subject itself can never be fully captured by making it an object. It is for that reason that biology can never fully comprehend the human mind, because biology itself depends on the working of the human mind. I consider that mind-boggling.

S: You are still mystifying the human mind. You are ignoring the fact that scientists have come up with some great discoveries in studying the human mind.

R: Yes and no. Biology can study the human *brain*, and perhaps explain it, but I doubt whether it could ever fully explain the human *mind*. I realize many scientists think they are studying the human mind, but it would be safer to say they study the human brain. Neurologists and neuroscientists can read brain scans but they cannot read your mind. We need some terminological clarity here. The brain is the *material* tool used by the *immaterial* mind. If the mind were the same as the brain, thoughts could never be right or wrong, as neural events simply happen and that's that. Whereas thoughts can be true or false, brain waves can *not*.

Therefore, we should never confuse the mind with the brain. Intelligence, for instance, is a brain issue, but rationality belongs to the domain of the mind. The same holds for morality; it is not a brain product, but it is a mind issue. We are not rational and moral by nature, so we need to be *taught* to be rational and moral. Even after we are grown up physically, we still need to grow mentally and morally, aided by good examples, by prayer, and by God's grace.

At the moment we mix these things up, rationality and morality suddenly and erroneously become part of our physiology and would soon end up in our genes. Our anatomy and physiology and neurology may be based on DNA, natural selection, and the like, but there is another side to the story: Our rationality and morality derive from *Above* – beyond the reach of science, and yet they are at its very basis. Rationality and morality are gifts of creation, not products of evolution; they come with our minds and souls that possess the rational power of our intellect and the moral power of our conscience – a pure gift from God, written in our hearts (CCC 362-368). They set us apart from the animal world; when you take them away, we are mere animals again. When I lose God, I also lose my mind. It is only in light of God that a human being can be fully understood.

When scientists try to understand the working of the human brain by studying the brains of animals, they may get some better insights into what is going on in the human *brain* as well, because our brains do derive from our animal ancestry, as we discussed in the previous chapter. However, the human *mind* adds a completely different dimension to the brain, which creates room for mental concepts. No wonder, animals do not study brains like we do because they lack a mind, not to mention a soul.

S: With your distinction between brain and mind, you are taking us back to the old Cartesian dualism of body and mind. I do not want to go there!

R: I must admit it may seem this way, for I do consider the mind as very different from the brain – immaterial, invisible, unseen, and not-physical. Whereas the body has characteristics such as length, width, height, and weight, the mind doesn't have any of those; thoughts are true or false, right or wrong, but they are never tall or short, heavy or light. Just as we have five senses for the material aspects of this world, we also have two senses for the immaterial aspects: the rational sense of true and false as well as the moral sense of right and wrong.

That is the reason why the brain is very different from the mind. C.S. Lewis said something along these lines: If my mental processes are determined wholly by the motions of atoms in my brain, I have no reason to suppose that my beliefs are true ... and hence I have no reason for supposing my brain to be composed of atoms. I would add this to it: Even if we consider the brain as a scientific, neuronal model of the mind, there still has got to be more to the mind than just the brain. Without the mind, we would never be able to distinguish truth from untruth, or right from wrong. Granted, human beings are living beings, but unlike other living beings, they are *rational* beings, and *moral* beings besides.

You probably call this dualism, but I do not think it is! I am certainly not promoting a dualism of soul and body, of mind and body, for the human person is a composite unity of soul and body (CCC 362). What I am trying to stress instead is that the "knowing subject" is "more" than any "known object." All knowledge of objects is based on a subject that apprehends those objects, but the subject itself can never be fully captured by making it an object. Therefore, I consider body and mind two aspects of the same human being; you can *tell* them apart but you cannot *set* them apart. The body belongs to the world of objects, whereas mind and soul are part of the world of subjects. Therefore, I consider body and mind two *aspects* of the same human being – two aspects that you can *distinguish* but not *separate*.

S: But it is so common to put the body against the soul. One of my favorite writers, C.S. Lewis, says "You do not *have* a soul. You *are* a soul. You *have* a body." Aren't you doing this as well?

R: I would be very careful to put it the way Lewis did. We are so hung up on possessions that we view even personhood in terms of ownership, saying that we *possess* our bodies. St. Thomas Aquinas, for instance, would warn us for this kind of terminology. He taught us that the human body is an essential part of the human person. If a human being consists of both soul and body, I cannot say that a person "has" a body. If I were the "owner" of my body, I could do with it as I please. That is not the Catholic view: "The human person, created in the image of God, is a being at once corporeal and spiritual" (CCC 362) and "spirit and matter, in man, are not two natures united, but rather their union forms a single nature" (CCC 365). If you do want to say you "have" a body, then you must add that you also "have" a soul with a mind.

Yet, in spite of the fact that my "self" cannot be defined principally in terms of one or the other, people tend to take sides – exclusively for either the body or the soul. Those are extreme positions which are not in line with Catholic teaching. On the one hand, some people excel in glorifying the soul by denigrating the body. They stress that the body gradually weakens, often sickens, and eventually dies. But what ultimately remains is the soul, in their view. However, I am not just a soul temporarily nesting in a shell of irrelevant flesh. If I am essentially both, then neither is about to disappear. The body is a "temple" for the soul. As Jesus said, "Destroy this temple, and in three days I will raise it up" (John 2:19). Therefore, the soul "does not perish when it separates from the body at death, and it will be reunited with the body at the final Resurrection" (CCC 366).

On the other hand, there are also people who reject or at least neglect the soul as part of a human being. At best, they talk about the body as something temporarily animated by some vital principle that religious people supposedly call a soul. Yet, all we can see and touch is that one particular body, so they counter. It is the body that we feel, the body that aches, the body that responds to medication – and not something as esoteric as the soul. Stick with the visible, not the invisible, is their recommendation.

This latter view has increasingly permeated our society and our beliefs. It is very prevalent in science. As a consequence, it remains a timeless temptation for scientists to reduce the mental to the neural – which I call a *nothing-buttery* claim of reducing mental states of the mind to mere neural states of the brain – or put in the words of the DNA co-discoverer Francis Crick, "You're nothing but a pack of neurons." However, the mind doesn't go away when we try to explain it away. If it did, we would lose a vital part of our humanity; not only would we lose our minds but also our souls.

The mind keeps coming back! My "inner" mental states are only accessible to me, the "brain-owner" endowed with a mind, whereas "outer" neural states are also accessible to the neurologist. Whereas the world of my body is public and accessible to others, the world of my mind is private and invisible. Even brain scans have no access to my private world like I myself do; all they can pick up is "brain waves," but never my thoughts, as those fail to show up on pictures and scans.

S: There you go again: You are placing thoughts in opposition to brain waves. I maintain they are essentially the same.

R: Sorry, I do question whether they are identical. Unlike brain waves, thoughts are always about something, about some "mental object" – no matter whether this "something" is fiction or non-fiction, real or make-believe. We do not just think, we always think something. It is this very fact that sets thoughts apart from what is physically going on in the brain, and that is why it is basically impossible to identify mental events with neural events. Let me try to explain this difference more extensively.

Some have argued that the brain works in the same way as a computer operates, because both use a binary code based on "ones" (1) and "zeros" (0); neurons either do (1) or do not (0) fire an electric impulse – in the same way as transistors either do (1) or do not (0) conduct an electric current. So it looks as if the brain "thinks" like a computer "thinks." If that were true, you would be right, and mental thoughts would indeed be just a stream of binary code.

In contrast, I would like to point out there is something wrong with this analogy. Our thoughts may have a material substrate that works like a binary code, but it would not really matter whether this material substrate works with impulses (like in the brain) or with currents (like in a computer), because this material is only the physical *carrier*, a vehicle that carries something else – in the way trains can transport people or goods. One and the same thought can be coded in Morse, Braille, hieroglyphics, impulses, or whatever code language; it doesn't really matter, for these codes are just physical carriers or vehicles.

But once we acknowledge that the same thought can be transported by different vehicles, we must conclude that a thought is different from its carrier. So it seems to me that the carrier doesn't *create* thoughts but merely *transports* them. Brains just don't make up their minds. The thoughts somehow "use" the brain as a vehicle – just like a radio carries news reports, but does not create them. The mind uses the brain as a programmer would use a computer. And yet, brain and mind, body and soul, are intimately united in a human person.

S: So what is it then that makes mental thoughts different from their physical carrier?

R: Well, thoughts are more than a binary code; they also have sense and meaning, and that is what the binary code really carries. As I said before, we do not just think, we always think something. Thoughts are *about* something else, something mental, something beyond themselves. And it is this very "about-ness" that a computer lacks; anything that shows up on a computer monitor remains just an "empty" collection of "ones and zeros," until some kind of human interpretation gives sense and meaning to the code and interprets it as being *about* something. It is like with a picture; a picture may carry information; but the picture itself is just a piece of paper that only makes "sense" when human beings interpret the picture and declare what it is about. The same with books: They provide lots of information for "book worms," but to real worms they only have paper to offer. Even a bank note would just be a worthless piece of paper, if humans didn't have a mental conception of money. All facts are mental interpretations of events. It always requires a *subject* with a mind to create mental *objects*. Physical objects do not make sense to us without mental objects.

Without a human subject, objects do not have any meaning, do not make any sense, and do not even exist – for these objects are objects of knowledge, based on mental concepts in the human mind. I am not saying here that those objects of knowledge are merely illusions, but they make the real world knowable and intelligible for us. Without a human mind as a subject, there wouldn't be any mental objects at all. Computers, radios, etc., do not have meaning or sense in themselves until a human subject uses them as carriers of information that was given sense and meaning by a human subject. What is more, without a human subject, a computer doesn't even have a binary code, but just two different states (on or off) that a human subject *uses* as a binary code (true or false) so it can carry and convey information that makes sense to other human subjects.

Let me repeat it again, the knowing subject must be more than the known object, in the same way as a projector must be more than the images it projects. Let me put it very crudely: When I bash my radio, the news report may stop, but this doesn't mean the news was created by the radio; it was only the news vehicle that broke down. Without human subjects, no computer, no radio, and no robot would be able to carry information. These machines do not create thoughts, but just carry thoughts that were created by the mind of a human subject. They only do what we, human beings with a mind and soul, make them do. A computer may play chess better than Kasparov or any other champion, but it plays the game for the same "reason" a calculator adds or a pump pumps

– the reason being that it is a machine designed for that purpose – and not because it wants to or is happy to do so. Why not? Well, a machine doesn't have an "I" behind it (other than the "I" of its maker). When a machine does amazing things, we shouldn't marvel at the machine but at its makers. Computers do not and can not have a mind, and our minds are not computers. Somehow, we are back at that famous systematic elusiveness of "I" again. How could the brain ever study itself? It is only the mind, "I," that can study the brain.

S: How would you explain then that certain brain areas do show more neural activity when we have specific thoughts?

R: True, in response to certain thoughts, some brain areas may become more active, but that doesn't necessarily mean that those areas *produce* the thought; all we can say is that they probably *carry* the thought and that is why they appear "active." Here is my same point again: Thoughts are more than brain waves. We can read and interpret an EEG, but looking at it doesn't show us any thoughts.

That is the reason why we may be able to physically induce specific pains, specific emotions, or certain memories by stimulation of certain brain areas, because they are physical and biological phenomena (even animals have them). But we cannot physically induce a specific thought, since thoughts are of a different nature, so we cannot stimulate specific brain areas to produce thinking, let alone specific thoughts. Memories of thoughts are a different issue, though. They can be physically stored in the brain, once produced by the mind, similar to the way thoughts can be "stored" on paper. Thoughts can be physically stored in memory, but they cannot be produced in a physical manner.

Thinking is pondering realities beyond that which we experience through our senses. Animals, in contrast, may have instincts, drives, and emotions, but they do not have thoughts. They do not have any thoughts about the past or the future. Only humans are conscious of time; they can study the past, recognize the present, and anticipate the future in their thinking; they can even transcend time, thinking about living forever. Only humans wonder "what caused or will cause what and why?" Only human beings have inquisitive minds asking questions such as "Where do we come from?" Only humans are constantly in search of some kind of worldview or explanation of life – which certainly goes far beyond their need for food. Only humans have a hungry soul. Only humans know of things unseen. And last but not least, only humans know of God.

As a matter of fact, humans are born philosophers. Philosophy may seem a pretty sophisticated enterprise to many, but is there anyone who doesn't philosophize? Each one of us is destined to start philosophizing at some point in life. Because we are "thinking animals," not only can we use our minds for philosophical ponderings, but we even have an obligation to do so; to do anything less is to reject the gift of reason. The first sentence of Aristotle's *Metaphysics* reads "All men by nature desire to know." Psalm 32 has God say: "I will instruct you and teach you in the way you should go; I will guide you with my eye. Do not be like the horse or like the mule, which have no understanding" (8-9). In other words, without our thoughts, we wouldn't be human. So do not dull your mind with mindless entertainment!

S: You keep talking about "mental objects," but what are they? They sound kind of hazy to me.

R: As I said earlier, mental concepts transform physical "things" and "events" into mental "objects" of knowledge, thus enabling humans to see with their "mental eyes" what no physical eyes could ever see before. That is where the deep divide lies between humans and animals. Animals do not have this capacity; a dog may have a *physical* image of its boss, but it has no *mental* concept of what a boss is like. Dogs will never "chat" about their boss, but humans almost certainly will. Animals live in a world of *events*, but humans also inhabit a world of *facts* – which are mental interpretations of those events. It is only through mental objects that physical objects can make sense to us and become intelligible. No wonder the animals closest in looks to us are still swinging from trees, while we ourselves are driving cars, flying planes, readings papers, and writing books. Thanks to our minds, we can spread our spiritual wings and fly, no matter how earthbound our feet seem to be.

What animals lack is the "I of the beholder." In other words, they lack a real "self." They do not have a self or a mind or a soul – which I call briefly the "I of the beholder." Although monkeys appear to be able to use mirror images to locate things and even other animals in space, they have been given months, not to mention years, in which to recognize *themselves* in mirrors, but they continue to either neglect their mirror image or treat it as a potential aggressor.

S: But chimpanzees and orangutans (unlike gorillas) do show some capacity of recognizing themselves in a mirror, as do elephants and dolphins. So they seem to have some self-awareness.

R: I know that the mirror test keeps ranking high on the agenda of some scientists, especially evolutionists, but passing the mirror-test doesn't entitle us to equate self-recognition to self-reflection, let alone to self-awareness and self-expression. Let me explain.

First of all, one could argue that passing the mirror test is merely evidence of superior neural capabilities, arguably based more on face-recognition than a sense of "self." Dogs, on the other hand, perform poorly on the mirror test, but they do seem to be able to recognize their own scent. We are dealing here, at least partially, with a form of learned behavior. When first exposed to a mirror, most apes react to their reflection as they would to another member of the same species; but eventually they may learn to recognize their mirror image as a reflection of their own body.

Second, animals are very well able to classify, distinguish, and recognize faces and scents; so why would they not be able to classify a face or scent as coming with one particular body, their own. The fact that birds, for instance, can clean their own feathers doesn't mean they have the capacity of self-awareness and self-reflection. Even if animals are able to recognize "themselves" in a mirror, they may have some body-recognition, but not necessarily self-recognition or self-awareness.

Third, the mirror test shows us that some animals can recognize their own body; but that shouldn't shock us, since animals drinking from water surfaces should be used to seeing a reflection of their own bodies. But do they also have a sense of "self," a sense of past and future, knowing that they exist in a particular time and place? I doubt, for the simple reason that mirrors mirror a body, but not a *self*. Animals won't make a trip to the water to just have a look at themselves in the "mirror."

Finally, the mirror test may tell us much more about ourselves than about the animal world. When we see apes recognizing "themselves" in a mirror, we hope (or fear) to see ourselves in them. It doesn't say much about an animal's "self." It is exactly because animals do not have a "self" that animals couldn't even follow the golden rule that says "what you do not want to be done to your self, do not do that to others."

S: I know of animals, though, who can express themselves in art.

R: Again, some have worked hard to let apes create paintings; yet the colorful mess apes produce under pressure is far from any representational kind of art that we know of. The human mind, on the other hand, does have this astounding capacity of *self-expression* in various forms of art – in literature, in paintings, in sculpture, in music. We find these expressions as far back as the early history of humankind. Of all animals in prehistory, only humans left stones behind with inscriptions; only humans dress themselves up, paint or tattoo their faces, decorate their surroundings, etc.

And then we have this astonishing art in prehistoric caves. Understandably, some considered such paintings fake for a while, because they could not accept such a high level of self-expression that early in human history. My wisecrack would be, "Even a cave man can do it!" Some of the first Cro-Magnon sites, dating from well over 30,000 years ago, have even yielded evidence for music: multi-holed bone flutes capable of producing a remarkable complexity of sound.

And what do you think of some very early evidence of elaborate burials? The amount of effort put into the aesthetic productions found in prehistoric graves suggests, I would say, a high level of *self-expression*. Burial of the dead with grave goods indicates a belief in an after-life, for the goods are there because they are considered useful to the deceased in their future lives.

How different this is in the animal world. In Guinea, W. Africa, for instance, chimp mothers have been seen in nature carrying and grooming their off-spring's lifeless bodies for up to 68 days. By the time the corpses were finally abandoned, the bodies had mummified and developed an intense smell of decay. Believe it or not, but some scientists give this observation their own twist: 68 days of mourning the dead! Only human beings could come up with such an explanation; I would rather describe this as 68 days of ignorance! Besides, I would like to question those scientists where the burial and the grave are. Apparently, only the "finite" human mind is able to catch a glimpse of the Infinite.

S: It is amazing how much power you give to the human mind. But that doesn't mean much if we do not have the power of *self-determination*!

R: We certainly do have that power. Unlike animals, human beings have this strong desire of becoming someone of their own making. True, animals may have drives, impulses, instincts, or motives, but these are very different from intentions or reasons, and they are always directly or indirectly related to sex or food (that is why behavioral experiments with animals usually enforce behavior with food rewards).

Humans, on the other hand, have many added kinds of goals in life; not only do they live their lives based on role models, but also do they steer their lives guided by reasons, plans, beliefs, values, hopes, and dreams – which shape them the way they are going to be. How different this is from animals. In the course of its life, an animal doesn't change much; it just looks and acts older and more worn-out. Humans, on the other hand, may have gone through dramatic changes in outlook on life, attitude, career, wisdom, faith, and beliefs – and hopefully for the better.

Apparently, there is quite an abyss between humans and animals! Only humans have the capacity to make free decisions in life. Human freedom means that one is able to choose and act according to the "dictates" of one's own will – which is the freedom of *self-determination*. "God created man a rational being, conferring on him the dignity of a person who can initiate and control his own actions" (CCC 1730).

You are right, though, if you are questioning how human freedom can "operate" in the rigid "law and order" world that we live in and that science tells us about. The answer is rather straightforward. By knowing how things are determined by the laws of nature, human beings are able to construct highly effective and successful designs on earth – in architecture, technology, and what have you. They can channel those "rigid" laws. Although chains of cause and effect appear to be very fixed and rigid, they can obviously be used and channeled within the settings of larger systems and designs. Even in a world ruled by the law of cause and effect, there is still our own ability to be the *cause* of events. In chapter six, we will discuss this issue more in detail.

Freedom of self-determination doesn't mean, of course, that we can do whatever we choose! When calling this universe orderly, I mean that it is law-abiding – but not necessarily pre-ordained. So the freedom of self-determination doesn't let us do whatever we want to do, but it leaves us a series of options, curbed by a set of lawful constraints such as those known from physics, biology, psychology, sociology, economics, or history. Human freedom cannot go *against* the laws of nature, but it certainly can go *beyond* those laws. The more you are aware of your constraints, the more you are actually free. In order to be free, "Know Yourself," says an old inscription in Delphi. The best we can do to reach this goal of self-knowledge is praying to God, "Lord, teach me about myself," so as to know the truth and choose the good.

S: Your "spooky" mind still reminds me of something like an "inner observer" located in the brain behind the cortex, or a "mental agent" steering the body like a piano player would play the piano." No wonder this idea has been dubbed as a "man in the machine."

R: No, that is certainly not my intention, for we would end up with "an observer in an observer" or "a piano player inside a piano player." Not only would this lead to dualism, but also to the infinite regress of "an observer in an observer in an observer..."!

Yet, the mystery remains. We cannot catch any "piano player" inside ourselves, but we do hear his or her "music." As a matter of fact, we all know and experience that mental events do exist and can make bodily events happen. In other words, when the mind "wills" something, a series of events starts: I make a decision | then my mouth talks | then my eyes water | then I make a new decision | then my hands wipe my tears...

What to make of this series of events? It is definitely not a chain of mere physical causes, since mental events are not physical events. It is more like a series of physical causes interrupted by "mental switches." Thinking of "two times three" doesn't physically cause the thought of "six"; perhaps you wish it did, for you could probably have skipped many years of school education. An "act of will in the mind," is not a *physical* cause, but it inserts a reason or intention into the closed causality of our body parts. In the midst of physical causes, the human mind still has the ability to become its own cause of events.

So what is the difference then between physical causes and mental causes? Because the mind does not occur on the physical map of the body, it may seem as if it is nowhere in the chain of bodily activities, yet it is the "soul" of it all and pervades the entire body. In contrast to blinking, there is a "soul" or an "I" behind winking – a mental cause behind the physical causes of a reflex circuit. But there is more. If thoughts were the physical outcome of bodily actions and causes, we couldn't tell truth from error – for they would all be equivalent brain-states.

That is why mental switches must be real! Take the shocking 9/11 attacks in New York City; the cause behind those events was not a physical cause – some kind of destructive defect in the plane engine – but a mental cause – a destructive intention in the minds of some people. In this context, I would like to quote what the Nobel-laureate and physicist Arthur Compton (known for the Compton effect) used to say: "If the laws of physics ever should come to contradict my conviction that I can move my little finger at will, then all the laws of physics should be revised and reformulated."

S: But how could mental switches ever interfere with physical actions? When you distinguish them, you are causing yourself a lot of trouble!

R: Well, the human mind does certainly not belong to the category of bodily functions. Bodily activities are undeniably related to each other by physical connections; a lot of running physically causes you to eat; cutting onions makes you cry. Mental activities, on the other hand, are not physically related. The brain does not harbor any detectable agent who plays the "piano" of the body – no matter how attractive it is for scientists to locate the mind somewhere in the body as a physical entity, hoping that by dissecting the human brain, they can dissect the human mind. Nevertheless, the mind keeps eluding the knife of the dissecting scientist, for brain-surgeons aren't mind-surgeons. Here we have that systematic elusiveness of "I" again.

All I can say at this point is that the physical and the mental – the material and the spiritual – appear to us as two different aspects or two different levels of some underlying reality, but I must admit this doesn't really explain much. As I said earlier, I like to tell them apart, but not set them apart. Thus, the mystery remains... Obviously, body and mind do not have a mental relationship; on the other hand, it is not a physical relationship either. Thoughts may make you cry, but definitely not in the physical way that cutting an onion makes you cry; and crying may make you think, but there's no physical causation here.

In other words, never should we degrade the mind's activity to a physical link in a network of physical causes between neurons, muscles, etc. If thoughts were mere products of the brain, we would never be able to declare our thoughts as true or false and our moral judgments as right or wrong – they would all be of the same caliber: matter. In other words, the mind is not one of the players on the neuronal scene, but it is the author as well as the producer behind this neuronal play.

S: Well, then there must be some kind of interaction between body and mind.

R: Apparently, there is an interaction between the two; the mind can create mental causes that interfere with physical causes, but it does so in a rather "mysterious" way. Somehow, the mental and physical aspects do affect each other, but we just do not understand the "mechanism" of their interaction; their interaction is part of the cosmic design of creation. This is not as strange as it may sound. Think of the relationship between mass and gravity; we really do not know how these two interact. Or take the case of electrically charged particles that interact with each other through the mediation of electromagnetic fields; the charged particles affect the fields and the fields affect the particles – but we do not know anything about the "mechanism" behind this interaction. Something similar happens when it comes to body and mind; we know *that* they interact but do not know *how*.

In other words, we can *tell* the mental and the physical apart but we cannot *set* them apart, for "spirit and matter, in man, are not two natures united, but rather their union forms a single nature" (CCC 365). And yet they are both real; there is a mental aspect of reality and there is a physical aspect of reality. The fact that we distinguish them doesn't entail that we can separate them, any more than the idea of a three-dimensional space means that we can separate those three dimensions. The same holds for the mental and the physical: We can distinguish them but not separate them. Those who torture others, for instance, try to get to the mind through the body, whereas those who bully others do the opposite – they try to get to the body through the mind.

Therefore, without the human mind and soul, we couldn't be ourselves. Only the mind has reasons and thoughts – they are not the product of the brain. Only the mind has moral values – they are not the product of the brain either. If they were, they would be worth nothing, or at least nothing more than the molecules the brain is made of. We would have no *reason* to trust our reasoning and no *right* to claim any moral rights. We would have no foot to stand on in order to decide between true and false reasoning or between right and wrong moral judgments. If our laws of nature and our moral laws were generated by the brain, they could never claim universal validity either. Let me quote J.B.S. Haldane again: "If my mental processes are determined wholly by the motions of atoms in my brain, I have no reason to suppose that my beliefs are true ... and hence I have no reason for supposing my brain to be composed of atoms."

The reason to trust our reasoning as well as the right to claim our moral rights can only be found in God. Reason is not a product of irrationality but of the great Intelligence that is behind everything. That is the enigma we have to live with for the rest of our lives, as we share in the light of the Divine Mind. Let's just thank God that we have been endowed with self-reflection, self-awareness, self-determination, self-transcendence, and self-expression. To quote the philosopher Immanuel Kant again, "Man is distinguished above all animals by his self-consciousness, by which he is a 'rational animal'" – as well as a "moral animal," I would add.

S: But you seem to ignore that so often the mind seems to be gone when the brain is gone. I am thinking of people in coma, with brain disorders, etc.

R: You are confusing the mind with the brain again. The mind may operate through the brain but is not identical with it. Even when people have "lost their mind," as they say, through dementia, Alzheimer's disease, autism, or insanity, they haven't really lost their mind or their soul, but there are certain defects in the physical network of neurons, neurotransmitters, etc., that prevent the mind from working through bodily activities the way it used to, or usually does. The mind has become an incarcerated mind; the soul is locked in the solitary confinement of the body. Therapy may often help such people to stay in touch with their soul, their "self." What comes to mind are also individuals who have a speech impediment, or people who are in a seeming coma; they just cannot say what they want to say. So do not overlook what is "behind" the human carrier: It is always a beautiful mind and soul! Together, body and mind form an intricate unity.

When the Bible tells us we were made in God's image and likeness, it is both referring to our bodies and to our minds and souls. As Vatican II says about Man, "he surpasses the material universe, for he shares in the light of the divine mind" (*Gaudium et Spes*, 15). And Psalm 8 tells us about human beings, "Thou hast given him dominion over the works of thy hands; thou hast put all things under his feet" (Ps. 8:6-7). Shakespeare's Hamlet summarizes this well, "What a piece of work is a man! How noble in reason! how infinite in faculties! in form and moving, how express and admirable! in action how like an angel! in apprehension, how like a god! the beauty of the world! the paragon of animals!"

S: I have one more question to ask you. You speak so highly about the mind with all these lofty words of self-reflection, self-awareness, self-determination, self-transcendence, and self-expression. But they all sound so self-centered to me…

R: Please do not take me wrong. When I speak of "self," it is the "self of I," not the "self of Ego." Human beings, unlike animals, do have a "self" made in the likeness of God. But during the Fall in Paradise, they decided to go for the dark side of "self," which is the Ego of "I, me, and myself," acting in opposition to God. Ego considers God a rival, even an enemy. That is the way of a fallen world.

Without a doubt, "Ego" is purely self-centered and narcissistic, and chooses to live in splendid isolation. In contrast, "I" is God-centered, made after His image, and fully connected with the rest of humanity – that is, with "we." This kind of "I" cannot live without God. In his book *Jesus of Nazareth* (Part I, 145), Pope Benedict XVI stresses that we must acknowledge first and foremost the primacy of God: "Where God is absent, nothing can be good." Some people erroneously believe that human beings lose their freedom when they live "under God." Quite the opposite! Because "I" was made in His image, "I" become more myself when I grow in God's likeness. Only those who are reconciled with God can also be reconciled and in harmony with them-selves. But when creatures separate from their Creator, they lose their identity. We were given the freedom to choose not whatever we *like* to do but what we *ought* to do.

So what comes to mind when we speak of this kind of "self," are additional concepts – words like self-control, self-denial, and self-giving. Self-giving means, in the words of Pope Benedict (54), "stepping outside the limitations of fallen humanity – in which we are all separated from one another [...] stepping outside the limits of one's closed individuality." This certainly requires self-control and self-denial. The Catechism calls self-control, also called self-mastery, "a training in human freedom"; and then it goes on as follows, "The alternative is clear: either man governs his passions and finds peace, or he lets himself be dominated by them and becomes unhappy" (2339). Be sure, all of this is a lifelong task and strenuous training for the "self of I." In the following chapters, we will see what this task entails.

6

How Determined Are We...

To Be Less Pre-determined
And More Self-determined

We live in a world dominated by science. Many of us are under its spell and therefore think that there are genes for practically everything in life: for being intelligent, for being an alcoholic, for being a homosexual, for being religious, you name it. I consider this an extreme form of determinism: The genes of parents inevitably and fully determine all the characteristics of their children, so the story goes! We are supposed to dance on the strings of our genes. Some geneticists have actually created phantom diseases and phantom genes to make their case.

What is wrong with this form of determinism? Certain parts of our destiny may indeed be determined by our genes and by our surroundings, but real determinism makes us full victims of our past, with no future in sight. Questions abound. Can we still make our own rational choices and moral decisions? How determined are we to become more self-determined and less pre-determined? Is there still room left for God's salvation and providence? That is a lot to tackle in such a short chapter.

Q: More and more I get the impression that our self-determination is very limited, because there are genes that determine practically everything. We seem to be trapped by our own genes.

A: I would feel trapped too if I didn't know better. We get

constantly bombarded with an ideology of complete genetic determinism. We are supposedly the mere product of our genes. Genetic determinism says that the *genotype* completely determines the *phenotype* – that is, the genes completely determine how an organism turns out. We could also call this view "puppet determinism," because we are supposed to dance entirely on the strings of our genes. The simplest form of genetic determinism holds that the genes of parents inevitably determine the characteristics of their children. If so, our next generation has already been fully predestined; there wouldn't be much freedom left, if any.

The problem is that genetics nowadays seems to have a strong case. We are learning more and more about those genes that are supposed to make up our bodies. Genetics seems to proclaim that it is hard to fight what comes out of those genes. The case for human freedom looks completely lost, unless you know a bit more about those genes.

Q: Explain to me first then how genes get passed from parents to their children.

A: Human beings carry 23 pairs of chromosomes – of which one pair is an "unmatched" pair in males (XY), but a "real" pair of sex chromosomes (XX) in females. All genes are located on these chromosomes, so they come in pairs as well. During conception, father and mother each contribute only a half set of their chromosomes, one of each pair, so their child ends up again with 23 pairs. Depending on whether the father passed on his X- or his Y-chromosome, the child will be male (XY) or female (XX).

These chromosomes hold all our genes. A decade ago, the general estimate for the number of human genes was thought to be well over 100,000, but turned out to be around 30,000 genes – that is only half again as many genes as a tiny roundworm needs to manufacture its utter simplicity. And we have only 300 unique genes not found in mice. No wonder that the president of Celera, a bio-corporation, said about this surprising finding "This tells me genes cannot possibly explain all of what makes us what we are." At least, we have a first indication here that genes are not as almighty as some tend to think.

Q: Yet, we often read about "a gene for intelligence," "a gene for pedophilia," "a gene for bullying," etc. What do these claims mean?

A: That is a great question: What does it mean when someone says there is "a gene for…"? Let me explain first what a gene is. Since the discovery of DNA, the boundaries of a gene have become rather fuzzy, but a classical definition has it that a gene is a unit of heredity that regulates a specific trait, feature, or characteristic of an organism. So there are genes that supposedly regulate our blood types, our eye colors, and what have you. A gene can carry several variants, called alleles. In short, all humans have the same genes, but not the same alleles.

Some genes work in one step; others need several steps to cause differences between people. There is, for instance, a gene that produces, in one step, a certain enzyme (*tyrosinase*) which creates the dark skin pigment melanin. This gene can also harbor mutated alleles that produce a non-functional enzyme, which then may lead to albinism (but there are also other kinds of albinism). This is a simple case of how a gene works. But most other genes require additional steps to take effect. The gene for the ABO blood type can hold an allele for antigen A or one for B; these alleles produce an enzyme that then creates the corresponding A- and B-antigens. That is a two-step process. Then there are genes that require many more steps, or they require the cooperation of many more genes in order to produce different end-results.

Whatever the actual path is, geneticists try to explain differences between people by differences in alleles of a specific gene. They are in search of a difference that makes a difference: a difference in *phenotype* associated with a difference in *genotype*. But is this connection also a *causal* relationship? That still remains to be seen.

Q: I would say there are some clear cases where different genotypes do cause different phenotypes.

A: Yes, in clear-cut *mono*-factorial cases, we do have plain evidence. Simple genetic disorders like albinism follow this rule.

Another case of a disease traceable to a single gene is muscular dystrophy. What these diseases have in common is that they follow a simplified formula: one gene can lead to one specific disease if it carries the "wrong" allele. That is where genetic determinism seems to have a case.

But most cases do not belong to this category. The vast majority of human diseases and other genetic traits are *multi*-factorial: They are influenced by many genes interacting with one another as well as by a vast array of signals from the environment of each cell (nutrient supply, hormones, electrical signals from other cells, etc.), and all of these together will reflect the external world of the organism as a whole (upbringing, learning, experience, culture, religion). Thus, the same mutation in a specific gene may produce very different results, depending on their surrounding background as well as their genetic background (all other interacting genes), as each human being has a background that is unique. No two persons are completely identical, not even when they have the same genes with the same alleles as in identical twins. Identical twins don't even have identical fingerprints! That is where genetic determinism is definitely on its way out.

Q: I still do not have an answer to my question: Is there a gene for cases such as pedophilia or alcoholism?

A: In order to answer your question, I must first get a bit more philosophical if you don't mind. In order to find a difference that makes a difference, we need to identify the difference to begin with. How do we identify similarities (or dissimilarities and differences for that matter)? That's easier said than done.

Since things can be "alike" in many ways, we need a unifying concept of similarity; things cannot be "alike" until their similarity has been identified first in a word or concept. We cannot lump carnivores together until we know of the concept "carnivore." Before we can "notice" a carnivore, we need the "notion" of a carnivore first. In other words, there is no re-cognition without cognition to begin with.

As a result, we cannot look for a difference that makes a difference until we have *identified* a relevant similarity or dissimilarity. Biologists, for instance, couldn't see the similarity in building blocks between animals and plants until the concept of a cell had been established; neither could they see the similarity between leprosy and tuberculosis until the concept of bacteria had become available. Seeing similarities has been the main driving force behind science.

But finding the right similarity is usually not an easy process. Often we happen to come up with similarities that do not hold upon further investigation; in such cases, the similarities we suggested were all found wanting; they turned out to be mere *inventions* but not *discoveries*. So we must keep searching for similarities that will hold. Someday, we may find out, for instance, what the fundamental similarity is behind all cases of Alzheimer's disease, or behind all cases of autism. Apparently, it can be very hard to procure a working hypothesis with a valid similarity. That is why science goes in leaps; it keeps searching and hopefully advancing – but not on immediate request.

Q: What do you mean when you say that not all inventions are discoveries?

A: Let me give you a very simple example. America was not discovered until the notion of "America" was invented; up till then, it was considered to be the "Indies." Did Columbus discover America? He did not as long as he was thinking he was in the Indies. That makes me say that the *invention* of "America" had to precede the *discovery* of America. Obviously, not all inventions lead to discoveries. The person who invented "Atlantis" did not discover Atlantis; it remains a legendary island until further notice.

The same in science: Discoveries always start as inventions – usually called *hypotheses* – but again, most inventions do not lead to discoveries. So do not ever claim that an invention is automatically a discovery; only research can tell. Yet many people, even some scientists, think they made a discovery when all they have in mind is an invention, a hypothesis. All inventions have to be tested first as to whether they also qualify as discoveries. Until such a time, we cannot claim we have discovered something. Claiming your invention qualifies as a discovery would at least be premature, no matter how enticing.

Q: Are you suggesting a similar problem with "a gene for..."? Are you saying it may be an invention without being a discovery?

A: Correct. It is so easy and tempting to come up with a similarity that makes a group of people differ from other groups. It happens all the time. Here is just a rather arbitrary collection of designations that lump certain people together: Attention Deficit Hyperactivity Disorder (ADHD), bi-sexuality, alcoholism, kleptomania, pedophilia – and all such syndromes as Hypothyroid Syndrome, Restless Leg Syndrome, Adrenal Fatigue Syndrome, Munchausen's Syndrome (which makes people fake diseases). And what should we say about ODD, Opposition Defiant Disorder? We love to invent specific similarities between people and then claim we have made a scientific discovery. We love to "categorize," without much to base it on.

I am not declaring all these inventions bogus, but most of them are still in the stage of invention and are awaiting the stage of discovery. And yet it remains tempting to claim a *genetic* difference for something that may not even exist. Perhaps alcoholism is not genetic but rather something acquired at home or in the womb or in a group of peers. Perhaps pedophilia is not genetic but a form of rape. Perhaps ADHD is just boyish behavior. Perhaps Munchausen's Syndrome is only a call for attention or sympathy. You might even say that I am beginning to develop a similarity to those who suffer from a "Syndrome Fatigue Syndrome" – but that idea is definitely my own invention.

Q: I don't think, though, you can deny that some of these so-called diseases are very real.

A: I am certainly not trying to put them all in the same category, but I just want to signal how often we get bombarded with a new "disease." First they invent a disease, then they invent the gene to explain such a disease – and then they sell us an elixir to cure it! We could very well be dealing with phantom diseases and phantom genes. There is even talk of Wilson's disease, also called Adrenal Fatigue Syndrome, which is a "disease" that would probably be better explained by chronic stress or by the fact that someone has lost sense and purpose in life. Or take again the Munchausen's Syndrome of people who fake their diseases; perhaps we shouldn't blame their genes but most likely their lack of receiving attention and sympathy in life. A better explanation for their "syndrome" might be found in childhood abuse, early deprivation, or whatever – but most likely not in their genes.

When we talk about things like the proverbial frugality of Scots, the typical efficiency of Germans, the notorious charm of Italians, the legendary literacy of Jews, or the American obsession with football, we shouldn't think genetics but culture, or actually stereotypes. In addition to differences in genetics, there are also personal and cultural variations. We often follow habits acquired at home, in school, through peers and friends, and through the society we live in – but that doesn't mean they are *genetic*. To put it differently, there certainly isn't a gene for everything. There's no "chip gene" for people with an addiction to chips, no "chocolate gene" for chocoholics, no "spending gene" for big spenders, etc. I could even come up with a gene that makes one believe in genetics!

Q: Yet, geneticists are in fact discovering genes for differences that you would consider fake...

A: Not too long ago, there was a lot of discussion about the detection of a gene for homosexuality. Let's take this as a test case for the kind of disputes we may be in for.

First of all, homosexuality would be many steps away from a specific gene. We know that the absence or presence of a Y-chromosome does lead to a sexual difference, but do not confuse a difference in *sex* with a difference in *gender*. A difference in gender entails much more than a difference in biological characteristics – namely also differences in behavioral traits, social roles, and cultural expectations that come with being a man or a woman. Very soon in our development, parents as well as society take on a molding role. As soon as parents know their child is a boy, they treat it as a boy, which makes the child consider himself as of the male gender. So the question is whether differences in gender are only the outcome of differences in sex, which in turn are supposedly based on differences in genes – or is there perhaps more going on?

Apparently, the distance between genotype and phenotype is a very long one here. There are also sex *hormones* involved; however, genes do not produce sex hormones, but rather the enzymes that in turn produce hormones – that is at least a *two*-step process. Even if you would argue that genes affect hormones, and that hormones affect the brain, and that the brain affects our behavior, then I would point out to you that this behavior, in turn, affects the brain again. A similar phenomenon is well known from sports, for instance: Strong muscles benefit those who play sports, but in turn, playing sports greatly benefits the development of the muscles.

However, it is not only the genes, the hormones, and the brains that shape our behavior, but everything that we see and hear around us, plus all the dreams, hopes, plans, and expectations we foster in our minds. All of these have an impact on the way we develop ourselves. What seems to be "in-born" may in fact very well be "in-printed" or even "self-taught." However, very often, or maybe even always, it is nearly impossible to tell what part is "nature" and what part is "nurture."

Q: Isn't there a way to peel "nature" and "nurture" apart?

A: Yes, there is. The best, and probably only, way is a *combination* of adoption research and twin research: identical twins split by adoption.

Adoption research on its own is not good enough. Although it is clear that relatives resemble each other more than strangers (because they have more alleles in common), parents do not only give alleles to their children but also parts of their environment. Even adopted children did, for at least nine months, share the surroundings of their mother's womb, including her voice, her hormones, her food, her moods, and even her medications. Plus adoption usually takes place in an environment that is very similar to the original one, often just around the block or with relatives or friends. So, we tend to easily *over*-estimate the impact genes have based on adoption research alone.

On the other hand, twin research, on its own, isn't good enough either. Identical twins have the same alleles, but their similarities aren't only the result of identical alleles but also of almost identical surroundings – the same womb, that is, often even the same placenta. Besides, their strong resemblances make it more likely that they are treated the same way later on in life, and that they even desire to be more like each other. So also in this case, we would *over*-estimate the impact of genes.

Another problem with this kind of research is that we need samples that are not biased but represent the total population accurately. I remember a case where scientists studied members of an organization of male homosexuals and found that these people came from families with a significantly higher percentage of male siblings – whatever that means. What they didn't realize, though, is that families with only female offspring were not represented in their sample at all, and thus they were under-represented in proportion to the percentage of female siblings in other families. Be aware, there is so much that can go wrong in this kind of research.

Q: How did homosexuality fare in this kind of genetic research?

A: Let me mention first that homosexuality is not a matter of sex (of producing either ova or sperm), but rather of gender, which suggests it is many steps away from the genotype, and hence, allows for many inroads from the environment. Yet, human geneticists keep looking for genetic determinants, and one of them, Dean Hamer, thinks he has found a genetic candidate on the X-chromosome. (By the way, he even had the audacity at one time to postulate the existence of a god-gene for religious experience!) I won't go into details as to how he did his research, but I do want to make some comments.

First, all we know based on his research is that there *might* be some gene involved, but we do not know what came from other genes and the environment. To find out how strong a gene's impact is, we would need research on adopted identical twins as well. We do know from identical twins that if one twin is homosexual, there is only a 50% chance the other one will be also. And adoption would probably give us some more information. In short, genes may have some impact but seldom a monopoly.

Second, Hamer's research had a statistical basis, so it can only detect associations, but not causality per se. Does the gene under consideration really *cause* homosexuality, or does it cause something that is related to it? Reasoning in terms of *Post hoc ergo propter hoc* (Latin for "after this, therefore because of this") is a logical fallacy that erroneously states, "Since that event followed this one, that event must have been caused by this one." We know this is certainly not always the case: When the barometer drops, we can expect rain, but the barometer does not cause the rain – it's the change in atmospheric pressure! Perhaps the hypothetical gene on the X-chromosome is not a "gay gene," but affects excessive maternal care instead. Didn't Hamer say that mothers give this gene to their homosexual sons? Well, could it be that mothers with this gene "create" homosexuals? Psychoanalysts might tend to think so. In other words, there isn't very strong evidence here at all. All too often similar hypothetical genes – for example, genes for schizophrenia, autism, and bipolar disorder – were claimed, and then had to be retracted. They were inventions that didn't lead to discoveries. You'd better get used to it: Hypothetical genes just come and go…

Third, I should also mention that if homosexuality were genetic, natural selection would weed it out – the same way it would eliminate celibacy if that were based on genes, since such genes could never reach the next generation and would therefore rapidly decline in frequency. Yet, homosexuality is on the rise, and hopefully celibacy also.

Q: But suppose they did or will find a gene for homosexuality, so what?

A: That's a good point. For some people, it wouldn't matter. They either keep calling homosexuality a genetic "deviant," or they keep describing it as a genetic "variant." On the other hand, some might reply, if you are born with it, it is not a free choice.

In contrast, some people like me might maintain that no one should be at the mercy of his or her genes; there are always choices involved, for genes do not have a monopoly. Children develop an identity in interaction with their parents. Parents are complementary to each other; some like to say men are from Mars and women are from Venus. Well, it is in this complementary environment that children develop their own identity.

That is where morality comes in as well. Biology is not about morality and cannot prescribe what is good and what is bad. Biology only gives us "facts," or what we take the facts to be at a particular point in time. However, there is no straight road from scientific facts to moral values. "Scientific maps," including maps of the human genome, tell us *how* to get somewhere, but they do not tell us *where* to go; hence, they do not contain moral directives. Destinations feature in the minds of the users of a "map," who can use their knowledge for any destinations – good or bad. That is the domain of morality. Science does not control morality, but morality should control science. We will get back to this issue in the next chapter.

Q: You keep speaking of *genes*, but hasn't the discovery of *DNA* changed the picture entirely?

A: Yes and no. My answer is Yes, for since the discovery of DNA in 1953, we have a better understanding as to how exactly genes operate. But my answer is also No, as the dogma of genetic determinism has become even more rampant since that discovery.

Let me start with the first part: How do genes operate? For a while, geneticists held on to what they literally called their "central dogma" that says: DNA makes RNA makes protein – a one-directional causal flow, with one item of code, a gene, ultimately making one item of substance, a protein (proteins include also enzymes), and all these proteins together making a body. However, this view has dramatically changed since. First, some DNA sections, so-called *introns*, get initially transcribed into mRNA but are then removed from the end-product by splicing. Due to alternative splicing, a single gene may code for several different proteins. That would partially explain why the number of genes can be much lower than we had initially expected.

Second, it turned out that protein-coding regions of genes can be interrupted by DNA segments that play more of a *regulatory* role by producing activator and repressor proteins that either activate or repress the activity of a "regular" gene. Some of these regulatory genes are actually very short and do not produce proteins at all but short strands of mRNA capable of blocking the mRNA of a "regular" gene from creating its protein; they are called micro-RNA-genes.

And then there was a third important development. Genes may be separated by long stretches of DNA that do not seem to be doing much – that is why they are often called "junk DNA," in spite of the fact that "non-coding," "neutral," or "silent" DNA would be a much safer term. Some of this "non-coding" DNA is repetitive DNA, often replicated from regular, coding DNA, and perhaps a rich source from which potentially useful new genes can emerge during evolution (see chapter four). Speaking of simple genetic inheritance, the story is getting more and more complicated.

Q: But I still see a lot of genetic determinism in all these scientific findings.

A: That depends on how you look at it. First of all, DNA can never do anything on its own. It is not even capable, as many still believe, of self-replication, for it is manufactured out of small molecular bits and pieces by an elaborate cell machinery that is made up of proteins. If DNA is put in the presence of all the pieces that will be assembled into new DNA, but without the protein machinery, nothing happens. It is actually the surrounding cellular machinery that makes sure that old DNA strands are replicated into new strands. This process is analogous to the production of copies of a document by an office copying machine, a process that would never be described as "self replication."

Second, DNA on its own does not produce anything, not even proteins! The role of DNA is to provide a specification as to how amino acids are to be strung together into proteins by some synthetic machinery. But this string of amino acids is not even yet a protein. To become a protein with physiological and structural functions, it must be folded into a three-dimensional configuration that is only partly based on its amino acid sequence, but is also determined by the cellular environment and by special processing proteins. Insulin for diabetics makes a case in point. Recently, the DNA coding sequence for human insulin has been inserted into bacteria, which are then grown in large fermenters until a protein with the amino acid sequence of human insulin can be extracted. But amino acid sequence does not determine the shape of a protein. The first proteins harvested through this process did have the correct sequence, but were physiologically inactive. Imagine what had happened: The bacterial cell had folded the protein incorrectly!

Q: Why are you so strongly opposed against the idea that human behavior and human diseases have a genetic cause or basis?

A: I am not against the thought that those *may* have a genetic cause, but that they *must* have a genetic cause. The latter claim stems from the tunnel-vision syndrome of some geneticists (which is probably also caused by a gene, I would quip). Let's widen our outlook, please. Like *spina bifida* turned out to be closer associated with a vitamin deficiency than with a gene, so could ADHD very well be more connected with the use of food additives than with genes. Fatigue syndromes are perhaps more a matter of "spiritual dehydration" than of genes. Perhaps addictions can be healed better by religious conversion than by medication. Perhaps child abuse can be better cured with self-discipline than with sedatives. Perhaps sexual abuse of children is not based on a pedophilia gene but on sinful behavior – another form of rape that requires self-discipline rather than genetic manipulation. It could very well be that a guilt complex – another name for a syndrome – doesn't require a shrink session but the therapy of the confessional.

In short, many scientists tend to reduce sinfulness to sickness, so they can get rid of its moral and religious dimension. Be aware, though, that this is basically another form of nothing-buttery by not seeing the forest for the trees. We need to constantly remind ourselves that there is more to life than genes. Genes do not provide us easy alibis. Not only do we "have" a body with genes but also a soul with a mind.

Q: But all you are saying here doesn't make determinism, whether it is genetic or not, *wrong*!

A: I think it does. For one, it is *scientifically* wrong: Never could we compute an organism since an organism doesn't compute itself from its genes, so we found out earlier. But it is also *morally* wrong: If determinism – in any form – is in fact true, then our whole conception of morality is a pointless illusion. If everything in existence is the result of necessary and pre-determined causes – whether it is from genes or whatever – then even something like murder can be considered a normal act, just a matter-of-fact issue.

Determinism fails to take into account human freedom. I know that most of us would choose not to kill or to be killed, but determinists would also claim that our choice to be killed or not to kill is itself already a predetermined effect. In essence, the acceptance of determinism makes each one of us into a mechanical and non-autonomous entity without the power to deliberate or change our direction in life. As a consequence, we wouldn't be responsible for anything we do.

The alternative to determinism is free will: Make free choices and decisions in life based on *rationality* and *morality*. Go for a version of yourself, not someone else's – which is called self-determination. To be self-determined, you cannot be fully pre-determined!

Q: Who is the one to make such choices and decisions?

A: It is *I* who makes rational and moral decisions. We saw in the previous chapter that we have a fascinating situation here: I-as-a-subject (I-now) can reflect on I-as-an-object (I-past). As a subject, I may investigate I-as-an-object and then realize, for instance, that I-as-an-object made a mistake. Call it *self-examination*, if you want. Because I-now is always a pace ahead of I-past, I can never blame my "glands" or my animal ancestry for what I did wrong. All decisions are *my* decisions – whether they are rational and moral, or irrational and immoral. Whenever I reflect on myself as an object, I determine who I want to be in life.

Because "I-now" is always a pace ahead of "I-past" – thus leaving open what the next step of "I-now" will be – my past is part of my future, but it doesn't determine who I am now or will be in the future. That is why I am also responsible for my future – including all the rational and moral decisions I am about to make.

Perhaps I need to clarify this point better. The more we are aware of our constraints, the more we are actually free. That is what players do on the golf course or on the pool table: They use the laws of physics for a specific goal that they have in mind. Although we cannot violate the laws of nature, we can still transcend them; we cannot go against them, but beyond them.

So as to be free, "Know Yourself," says that old inscription in Delphi – for that is the way mind can rule over matter. "By free will one shapes one's own life" (CCC 1731). The best we can do to reach this point is praying to God, "Lord, teach me about myself." In other words, self-reflection, self-examination, and self-determination allow me to make free choices and decisions based upon *rationality* and *morality*. Hence, we have a rational and moral responsibility for our own future. "The *right to the exercise of freedom*, especially in moral and religious matters, is an inalienable requirement of the dignity of the human person" (CCC 1738).

Q: I take it that genetic determinism is at odds with having responsibilities in life, right?

A: It certainly is. You could even make the case that genetic determinism is one giant alibi for human responsibility. Once we declare ourselves no longer responsible for our moral decisions, we think we are off the moral hook. If you wish to be innocent, you must find a way to make the claim that you cannot be held morally responsible. And some have found a way! All you have to do is "geneticize" or "medicalize" bad moral behavior: The victimizer is no longer a *person* but a disease or pathology caused by genes. All of a sudden, we find ourselves suffering from some "they-all-do-it" or "something-caused-it" syndrome – a "disease" supposedly beyond our moral control. Once we have made ourselves victims, we feel released from moral responsibility, since victims are, by definition, not responsible for their conditions, but can point instead to something else as the culprit – genes, hormones, diseases, syndromes, and pathologies.

Unfortunately, that is what is happening when people *ignore* that their lives should be under the guidance of rationality and morality. When we say that people are held justly responsible for a crime, or that they deserve praise or reward for a heroic act of self-sacrifice, we mean that they were the author and cause of that act in such fashion that they had it in their power *not* to perform the act. Human freedom is "the basis of praise or blame, merit or reproach" (CCC 1732). Our modern society tends to downplay human responsibilities by suggesting that extraneous causes make us do what we do. That is a dangerous ideology. Make no mistake, saints are made, not born.

Q: You are suggesting that, if we were fully predetermined by our genes, there would not be any human dignity left, right?

A: The idea of human dignity requires freedom. It is basically and originally a Judeo-Christian concept. But I wonder how long it can stay afloat in a post-Christian society when the bottom is taken out. It is our Catholic religion that tells us that the dignity of human life is grounded, not in our genes, but in the fact that human beings are made in the image and likeness of God. Human rights are not *man*-made *entitlements* but *God*-given *rights* that we cannot invent on our own.

Human dignity was given to Adam and Eve by God, but due to the Fall, they lost their original dignity, so it needs to be restored to its original state. There is a strong tension here: We were given human dignity, yet it is not fully realized yet, because we lost it. The Catechism expresses this tension very clearly with a quotation from Pope Leo the Great: "Christian, recognize your dignity and, now that you share in God's own nature, do not return to your former base condition by sinning" (1691). In other words, our human dignity has to be guarded very carefully. Though it was given to us in creation, God has to restore in us the original dignity we had lost. None of this is a matter of genes.

Q: As a Catholic, I wonder how all this gene stuff you mentioned fits into God's creation.

A: Nature follows the laws God has bestowed on His creation in its cosmic design. As Vatican II says, "By the very nature of creation, material being is endowed with its own stability, truth and excellence, its own order and laws" (GS 36, 1). And no doubt those laws do include the laws of genetics. Francis Collins, the longtime leader of the Human Genome Project, even called DNA "God's language."

Laws like these are, in the words of the Catechism, "the sign and pledge of the unshaken-able faithfulness of God's covenant" (346). But this doesn't mean the world was made by God as by a watch-maker who makes a watch, and then abandons it to itself. Quite the opposite, the Creator of this world is a *loving* God who has a *plan* for His creation, a plan for all that He creates, including you and me. Thus, His creation is "'in a state of journeying' toward an ultimate perfection yet to be attained" (CCC 302). The way God guides his creation toward this ultimate perfection is called "divine providence." God's creation is not perfect yet, but it is on its way... And we are invited to be God's co-workers, participants in His Creation.

Q: Well, how determined are we then?

A: No doubt, we are to some extent predetermined by our genes and our surroundings, for we just do not start from scratch. So, how *pre*-determined are we? We found out that there is a lot of flexibility in our genes, and that many of our characteristics do not even come from a gene. That is one side of the story. In addition, we have much self-determination – a strong desire to shape ourselves in the image and likeness of God. Each one of us should be very determined to be self-determined!

How *self*-determined are we then? It is our calling to become more and more like God in Jesus, the New Adam. We won't reach perfection until we arrive in Heaven, but we must keep striving. Like creation is "in a state of journeying toward an ultimate perfection" (CCC 302), each one of us is in a state of journeying as well. Our "feet" may be shackled in genes, but our "wings" are geared for Heaven. Let's be determined to be more *self*-determined and less *pre*-determined. The more we are aware of our constraints, the more we are actually free – free to do what God wants us to do with our genes, our abilities as well as our disabilities, our gifts as well as our limitations. Not only do you and I "have" a body with genes, but also a soul with a mind, which is our compass to the future.

7

The Roots of Morality

Is Morality in Decline?

Morality has come under attack from many sides these days – probably more so than ever before in history. It seems to be a slow-motion form of moral decline, yet it is a persistent process. I realize, of course, that morality has *always* been under attack – actually from the very moment Adam and Eve caved in to the first attack in history.

But nowadays, there is more going on than just human weakness. Many cultural, philosophical, and even scientific efforts are being made to undermine the very foundation of morality. What they all seem to have in common is the idea that our moral values are undergoing constant change, and are therefore subject to various cultural and historical fluctuations. If this were true, morality would just be a matter of emotions, personal preferences, cultural trends, and majority votes. That explains why we seem to be living in a world of disposable moral values.

This chapter wants to go to a deeper level, though, in order to unearth the religious foundation that has been upholding morality since the beginning of humanity. It was written for "moral dummies." I hope and pray that this chapter will again open the eyes of those who have become morally blind.

A *skeptical* moralist (S) in discussion with
a *religious* moralist (R)

S: I always hear that morality is about what is right and wrong. Where does this idea of "right and wrong" come from?

R: I can see why this is confusing, especially so for people who have a scientific background. Science only gives us "facts," or what we take the facts to be at a particular point in time. So where do those moral values suddenly come from? They do not seem to be facts, for there is no straight path from scientific facts to moral values. "Scientific maps," including maps of the human genome, tell us *how* to get somewhere, but they do not tell us *where* to go; they do not contain moral directives. If science is all you believe in, then there is no discussion anymore in terms of "right and wrong."

Yet, it is hard to deny that people do consider certain actions morally right or wrong. Even children know what is fair and unfair when they play. The fact that we have "standards" for judging human actions seems to be an undeniable fact. Not only do we *notice* things, we also *evaluate* them. I realize this doesn't mean that those standards are therefore valid and correct, but that is an altogether different issue (soon to come, so bear with me).

When we evaluate things, we discern a specific feature or property that turns them into something valuable – which is called a *value*. Although there are several kinds of values (moral, aesthetic, and religious values), the *moral* values are the ones best known; those are the subject of this chapter. Moral values summon us to action, to what *ought to be done*, no matter what. As the prophet Isaiah said, "Woe to those who call evil good and good evil" (Is. 5:20)

S: I wonder what it is then that turns actions into something valuable. In other words, what does it mean for something to be called "good" or "wrong"?

R: I think we need to make an important distinction first. Something can be called "good" in relation to a given goal or objective. Medical rules and medical procedures, for instance, are "good" for the purpose of medical care. I would rather call them rules, norms, or standards – but not values in the strict sense. Some people, though, like to call them *instrumental* values. That is fine with me. But what remains true is that these values are always *relative* values because they tell us what we need to do in order to attain something *else*. Cardiopulmonary resuscitation (CPR), for instance, is a "good" procedure in order to manually preserve intact brain function. It is "instrumentally" good to attain something else – the preservation of human life.

If anyone ever wonders why a certain act is "good" in this instrumental sense, we can provide an explanation in terms of its objective: Does the act meet its objective, yes or no? If it does, it is considered "good." And every action that does *not* meet the objective is consequently "wrong." But I must emphasize this doesn't mean that those actions are also right or wrong in a *moral* sense. Abortion may sometimes be medically right, but that does not make it also morally right.

S: Isn't that exactly, though, what moral values achieve as well? I would say moral values are "good" because they achieve some important objective.

R: I don't think so. In a *moral* context, "good" has a very different meaning. Whatever is called "good" in a moral sense tells us what we *ought* to do – no matter what, whether we like it or not, whether we feel it or not. Only in this case would we speak of *moral* values. CPR, for instance, is instrumental to attaining something else, but that objective is no longer an instrumental value but a moral value – the preservation of human life. The moral value of preserving human life is a goal in itself, and no longer instrumental to anything else. That is why morality is a very demanding issue – it demands absolute authority.

Consequently, moral values are *absolute*, because they tell us what we ought to do as human beings, irrespective of any other objective; hence they are often called *intrinsic* values. They make for universal, absolute, objective, and binding prescriptions; they are ends-in-themselves – and not, like instrumental rules, means-to-other-ends. CPR is a means to another end – the preservation of human life. But the preservation of human life is an absolute moral value that *ought* to be respected, even when we didn't know yet about CPR. Be aware, though, good ends never justify bad means; means as well as ends must be moral (CCC 1753). In the old Hippocratic Oath, a physician swears to the absolute and intrinsic moral rule of preserving human life, but all the other medical rules in the Oath are relative rules instrumental to this one absolute moral rule.

All I am trying to say here is that there's nothing "useful" about moral values. If anyone ever wonders why a certain act is "good" in a moral sense, we have no explanation to offer and cannot refer to other ends; all we can say is "It's evidently right to do so." It is a matter of self-evidence. The moral value of human life is self-evident, whereas the technique of CPR is only right if and as long as it works to reach its objective, a moral end. The "moral eye" sees values in life, just like the "physical eye" sees colors in nature. Moral values are definitely real, but not so in a physical sense.

S: How on earth can moral values be *evident*? My guess is that they only *seem* to be evident because our genes tell us that they are.

R: If you were right, we wouldn't be morally *obligated*, but we would only *feel* obligated; our genetic make-up would only have us *believe* that our moral obligations rest on an objective foundation – which makes for a collective illusion, so to speak, foisted on us by our genes. But such a foundation is as fragile as the genetic material it is said to be made of – DNA. You are talking here "genetic determinism" again; we discussed this issue extensively in the previous chapter.

If you were right, morality would not have the universality that is supposed to transcend differences in culture, era, genetic make-up, and personal preferences. If you were right, moral values would indeed look as if they were evident, but would in fact be worth nothing. They would be resting on molecular quicksand. Their *intrinsic* value would be like what some call the "intrinsic value" of gold; gold has no value in itself, but it gets its value from those who value it highly.

In return, I would ask you this question: What makes you think morality is a matter of genetics? You got this idea probably from scientists who think that science can explain everything under the sun, including morality. As a matter of fact, some biologists, the hard-core evolutionists, want us to believe that evolutionary biology can actually explain how humanity acquired its morality. Their magic wand is the theory of natural selection, which we discussed in chapter four. Take the example of incest (CCC 2388). There is an almost universal human taboo on incest – described as intimate relations between relatives or in-laws within a degree that prohibits marriage between them (Lev. 18:7-20). Well, these biologists would point out that inbreeding between close relatives tends to bring out recessive lethal traits and other afflictions that lessen the offspring's reproductive success. So they argue that natural selection has been promoting a genetic basis for behavioral avoidance of intercourse with close relatives. And that would be the only valid explanation as to where this moral value "really" comes from.

Or take moral laws such as "You shall not kill" (the 5th commandment) or "You shall not commit adultery" (the 6th commandment). Some biologists have made the case that humans must be monogamous "by nature" (just like animals such as swans), since that would give the offspring a better protection, thus giving a selective advantage to monogamy – and that would be the biological basis of the 6th commandment. Others have made the claim that killing members of the same species would undermine the persistence of the species and was consequently selected against by the process of natural selection. They even consider the moral value of paternal care for children to be a product of natural selection; their reasoning is that fathers who do not feel an "instinctive" responsibility towards their underage children would reduce their offspring's reproductive success.

What all these cases have in common is that morality is allegedly based on genes promoted by natural selection. They tell us that moral values are just inborn, and that is all there is to it!

S: I must say those arguments sound very compelling to me. I see no other explanation as to where moral values could come from.

R: I think that there is a strong flaw in all these arguments. My fundamental rebuttal is as follows: Why would we need an articulated *moral* rule to reinforce what by *nature* we would or would not desire to do anyway? If we were really moral by nature, we wouldn't need any articulated moral rules anyway, for our genes would take care of everything.

However, reality tells us that far too many people are willing to break a moral rule when they can get away with it! Too many parents ignore their so-called "natural" responsibility. Too many spouses violate the 6th commandment "You shall not commit adultery." Too many also violate the 5th commandment "You shall not kill." Are they really going against their genes? Apparently, there is something else going on...

Therefore, my conclusion is that moral laws tell us to do what our genes do *not* make us do "by nature." Morality is about something that is outside the scope of biology, far beyond the reach of science. My slogan in life is: Be well in a physical sense, so you can do good in a moral sense. The question remains, of course, where morality does come from then, if it is not rooted in our biology, our physiology, our genes, or our DNA. If we are not moral "by nature," there must be something else that makes us moral beings, right?

S: I do not give biology away that easily. There are some biologists, called socio-biologists, who have even found, in the animal world, examples of *altruism* – a real moral issue I would say. The pressing question in socio-biology is the following: How can altruistic behavior in the animal world still be advantageous to its agent? I would say socio-biologists have come up with some interesting answers.

R: True, the animal world does have cases of animals helping one another; just think of sterile worker bees "unselfishly" helping the queen raise her own progeny. Socio-biologists would explain such bio-altruism as a form of helping one's close relatives, because those carry alleles very similar to one's own; so in an indirect way, they are still promoting their own kind of alleles. And that is exactly what bees accomplish. If you want to know how, read the following technical explanation. Because these bees have a very peculiar sexual system, females are more closely related to sisters (sharing 75% of their genetic material) than to daughters (sharing only 50%). So sterile females actually increase their own reproductive success by 25% in an *indirect* way – by helping rear their queen-sister's progeny (75%) rather than their own (50%).

There are even stronger cases of altruism as a form of hidden self-interest. The geneticist J.B.S. Haldane once said, "I will lay down my life for two brothers or eight cousins." His calculation of costs and benefits was based on the fact that, in a regular sexual system, siblings share ½ of their genetic material, whereas cousins only share 1/8. By helping close relatives, one is somehow promoting dispersal of one's own genetic material, but in an *indirect* way through relatives – for instance, through 2 brothers ($2 \times 1/2 = 1$), or 8 cousins ($8 \times 1/8 = 1$).

Then there is altruism based on the principle of helping those who *return* the help; divided you may fall, but united you may conquer says a famous politicians' motto; "I give so you give." This happens, for example, when two or more chimpanzees band together; in helping others, they help themselves. Socio-biologists have studied this phenomenon with what they call "game theory," and they have been rather successful doing so. I grant them their victory as far as biology is concerned.

S: I think sociobiology has achieved such a huge victory that the issue of altruism in morality is on its way out!

R: Not really. We should make some important distinctions here:

- *Bio*-altruism is behavior with the *effect* that one's own offspring is diminished but compensated for by helping relatives. That is where biology feels at home.

- *Socio*-altruism is behavior with the *motive* of helping others, but limited to those who return the help. In helping others, one helps oneself (according to the old Roman motto of *Do Ut Des*).

- *Moral*-altruism, in contrast, is behavior for the sake of the *value* of serving others, without expecting any advantage. This is what we really and rightly call "unselfish altruism."

165

This is absolutely not a biological issue but a moral issue.

In other words, what you ought to achieve (which is a *value*) is not necessarily what you want to achieve (which is a *motive*), and what you want to achieve is not always what you actually do achieve (which is an *effect*). Please, let's remain clear-headed and not mix up these very different concepts.

Sociobiology may be about effects and motives, but values do not occur in its vocabulary. It may have solved bio- and socio-altruism, but moral-altruism stays untouched; it remains outside science's reach. Think of that mother who says to the person who attacks her and her son, "Take me instead of my son," or a priest such as Fr. Kolbe who said "Take me instead of that married man," or Jesus Christ who said "Take me instead of all others." Did their genes really make them say this, or was this in fact a heroic act of self-sacrifice?

Genuine moral-altruism is done out of love. Love is the reason why Jesus Christ died on the cross for us. No wonder that moral-altruism is central to the teachings of Jesus, especially in the *Sermon on the Mount* and the *Sermon on the Plain*. This is the kind of altruism we find in Saints such as Mother Theresa of Calcutta, or Father Kolbe, the Saint of Auschwitz, or Saint Gianna (Beretta Molla), who was willing to give up her life for the life of her baby. The list could go on and on. Such saints follow in the footsteps of their Savior, who carried His Cross to Golgotha to suffer for all our sins. And this is also true of all of us who are willing to follow Him in carrying our own crosses for the redemption of others – something that is certainly not the outcome of natural selection. In chapter 9, we will go much deeper into the problem of suffering.

S: If biology cannot explain such altruistic behavior, what else can?

R: For sure, many have tried to base morality and its values on something else, on something non-moral. Genetic determinism is one of those trials, but I hope I defused it. Another popular move is utilitarianism; it considers something morally right depending on its effects – that is, if it leads to "the greater happiness of a greater number of people." The problem here is that we treat moral values – which are *intrinsic* values as I said earlier – as if they were *instrumental* values – that is, relative values which tell us what we need to do in order to attain something else. Once we consider morally right anything that leads to "the greater happiness of a greater number of people," we are making those acts instrumental to some kind of happiness.

However, moral values are *absolute*, because they tell us what we ought to do as human beings, irrespective of any other objective – whether we like it or not, whether we feel it or not. They make for universal, absolute, objective, and binding prescriptions; they are *ends-in-themselves* – and not, like instrumental rules, means-to-other-ends. Do not make morality a matter of politics, ruled by majority votes, let alone special interest groups.

Let me explain this point with an example used by our former president Abraham Lincoln, of all people. It seems to me that Abe put things better than I ever could when he was talking about slavery. In his own, rather technical words, "If A. can prove, however conclusively, that he may, of right, enslave B.—why may not B. snatch the same argument, and prove equally, that he may enslave A.?—You say A. is white, and B. is black. It is color, then; the lighter, having the right to enslave the darker? Take care. By this rule, you are to be slave to the first man you meet, with a fairer skin than your own. You mean the whites are intellectually the superiors of the blacks; and, therefore have the right to enslave them? Take care again. By this rule, you are to be slave to the first man you meet, with an intellect superior to your own."

President Lincoln's point is clear: All the answers you might come up with to defend your *moral* claim use criteria that are morally irrelevant, such as a darker skin color or a lower intelligence. Because those criteria are *relative*, someone with a lighter skin or higher intelligence would have the "moral right" to enslave you. And the same holds for the value of human life. This value cannot be based on biological standards, since those are per definition morally irrelevant and relative besides.

In contrast, moral values are absolute ends-in-themselves – not disposable means-to-other-ends. So in no way would "a greater good" ever permit "minor evils," for one cannot do evil so that good may come. In morality, there's no "Thou shall not…, *unless…*"

If actions are either morally right or morally wrong, you cannot further divide the morally wrong ones into right and wrong again. In other words, new wrongs cannot erase previous wrongs, but can only *add* to them by making things worse.

S: What do you mean when you speak of criteria that are morally irrelevant?

R: Let me explain what the British philosopher G.E. Moore used to call the *naturalistic fallacy*. It consists in erroneously reducing a *moral* property (being good or right) to a *natural* property (being natural, functional, genetic, more evolved, better for the majority, or whatever). Therefore, it would be a fallacy to define moral notions in non-moral terms. Let me give you some examples.

Science discovers the way things are, not the way they ought to be. The fact that something *is* this way doesn't mean that it *ought* to be this way. The fact that something *is* natural doesn't imply that it is also a moral value that *ought* to be enforced. The fact that human beings are genetically different doesn't imply that we ought to *value* them differently. The fact that natural selection is "natural" doesn't mean that it also should be put into action as a *moral* duty. Or reversed: If slavery, murder, prostitution, or what have you, helps us fit into our environment – in line with the dogma of "survival of the fittest" – there wouldn't be anything morally wrong with it. But we all know better, or at least should know better. The moral "order" is not a take-off from the biological "law of the jungle," for such a substitution would be morally wrong. If some behavior is functional or natural, it does not follow from it that we have the moral duty to put it into operation. Science should not control morality, but morality should control science instead, in the same way as rationality should control science. Morality cannot be derived from something non-moral and cannot be reduced to something non-moral.

S: Are you trying to tell me that *natural* properties and *moral* properties are basically incommensurable?

R: Yes, that is the right word you are using there. Morality can never be based on morally irrelevant principles in terms of a useful or beneficial outcome. Such entities are incommensurables, similar to the two options robbers threaten their victims with when they yell "Your money or your life." There is no comparison – they differ even more than apples and oranges.

So we must come to the conclusion that morality cannot be based on anything non-moral. It is not rooted in our genes, it is not the product of natural selection, it is not the result of any legislation, it is not a scientific conclusion, and it is not based on anything useful or beneficial such as "the greater happiness of a greater number of people." All of these substitutes are relative and morally irrelevant, since morality includes a new dimension that only morality has access to. Because of its *absolute* values, morality cannot be based on anything that is *relative* or non-moral by nature. In short, there is just nothing "useful" about morality. We do not live in a world of moral values that are disposable when no longer useful. A moral law is universally valid, "it obliges each and everyone, always and everywhere" (CCC 2261).

S: If you are right, that would have quite some consequences for the way we make moral decisions.

R: Indeed, we ought to fight the timeless temptation of reducing *moral* properties to *natural* properties. Take, for instance, the abortion debate. The value of human life has often been based on the use of biological criteria, such as the extent of cerebral activity. This kind of "moral argument" goes along the following lines: The more cerebral activity there is, the more value a human life has, and therefore, the more protection it deserves. For others, viability is the criterion that determines the humanity of an unborn child. However, the biological criteria adduced here are, again, relative and morally irrelevant. The moral quality of human life cannot be quantified; it does not depend on the level of cerebral activity. We cannot use *relative* standards of intelligence, viability, maturity, health, fitness, and the like to measure or judge the *absolute* value of human life.

Instead, we need the moral, absolute standard of old that says whatever is born of human beings is human life and deserves absolute protection – irrespective of its extent of cerebral activity, its level of intelligence, or the number of its "defects." The Catechism puts it unmistakably: "*Human life is sacred* because from its beginning it involves the creative action of God" (2258). This viewpoint would imply that all human life deserves moral protection – from womb to tomb, from conception to natural death, from orphanages to mental institutions, and at all stages of its development. Just like no one can be halfway pregnant, no one can be halfway human or half a human being. Each human being bears the image of God – which is a gift, not an accomplishment that would come through maturation.

This also explains why a movement such as eugenics – the study and practice of selective breeding applied to humans – is morally wrong. If humans were solely animals, why couldn't we *breed* them like we breed animals? The answer is simple: the fact that natural selection is "natural" doesn't entail that it also should be put into action as a *moral* duty – no matter what eugenics claims. Whatever is called "biological" or "functional" does not have to be evaluated as "morally good" at the same time. Yet, the founder of *Planned Parenthood*, Margaret Sanger, declared once that "Birth control must lead ultimately to a cleaner race" (1922) and that "Eugenic sterilization is an urgent need" (1933). Nowadays someone like the Princeton microbiologist Lee M. Silver is still looking forward to "a genetically engineered modern-day hereditary class of genetic aristocrats." One of the two co-discoverers of DNA, James Watson, even has the audacity to ask, "If *we* don't play God, who will?" These people have the nerve to claim that there are some human lives unworthy of life.

Apparently, eugenics places the final end of human beings solely in their biological worth, but the Catholic teaching places it in eternal life. Only God can "play" God. Anything that is biologically true may very well be morally wrong. Biology only talks in biological terms of "winners" and "losers," but "good" and "bad" are actually *moral* terms, entirely outside its scope. Just think of clergy and other celibate people who may withhold many "good genes" from future generations, but unlike animals, have so many immaterial goods to offer to humanity.

S: I do not think Pope Benedict XVI would agree with your distinction between "is" and "ought." In his address to the German Parliament (Sept. 22, 2011), he rejected this distinction!

R: I think I need to clarify better what the Pope did reject. He rejects an ideology based upon an artificially narrow concept of reason that treats any certain knowledge about right and wrong as impossible. He traces this ideology back to a positivist interpretation of "is" in which nature is viewed as an aggregate of *objective* and scientific data linked together in terms of cause and effect, making everything else a *subjective* matter, including the moral realm of "ought." Then he continues, "A positivist conception of nature as purely functional, as the natural sciences consider it to be, is incapable of producing any bridge to ethics and law, but once again yields only functional answers. The same also applies to reason, according to the positivist understanding that is widely held to be the only genuinely scientific one. Anything that is not verifiable or falsifiable, according to this understanding, does not belong to the realm of reason strictly understood. Hence ethics and religion must be assigned to the subjective field, and they remain extraneous to the realm of reason in the strict sense of the word." In contrast, Christianity has always, in his words, "pointed to nature and reason as the true sources of law" (that is, both natural law and positivist law).

In other words, what Pope Benedict is stressing here is the power of reason that goes far beyond the power of biology and other sciences. The sciences of what "is" are just a very specific part of reason – "that we may not dispense with," according to the Pope – but that part should not banish other parts of realities, including the moral realm of "ought." Then he poses the question "How can reason rediscover its true greatness, without being sidetracked into irrationality?" His answer is "Man does not create himself. He is intellect and will, but he is also nature, and his will is rightly ordered if he respects his nature, listens to it and accepts himself for who he is, as one who did not create himself."

What I have called so far the "self-evident truths" of morality would be dubbed by Pope Benedict as "rational insights." Let me quote him again, "The conviction that there is a Creator God is what gave rise to the idea of human rights, the idea of equality of all people before the law, the recognition of the inviolability of human dignity in every single person and the awareness of people's responsibility for their actions. Our cultural memory is shaped by these *rational insights*" (italics are mine).

S: Sounds nice, but moral values keep changing over time and between cultures. So I would say that ends their absolute claim. Your "rational insights" have become very volatile!

R: I do not agree with you that it is the moral values themselves that change over time, but you are right in the sense that our moral *evaluations* may change. Moral evaluations are our personal feelings or discernments regarding values. Evaluations concern someone's personal attitude toward moral values, causing some to think that morality is merely a matter of evaluations determined by special interest groups or a majority vote. However, the value itself ("being a value") should be distinguished from human attitudes toward values ("being valued"). Morality is not a matter of *political* correctness but of *moral* correctness.

Nonetheless, many people think that "having value" is the same as "being valued." In so doing, they believe that in making *evaluations*, we create *values* in accordance with these evaluations. So when evaluations change, the moral values and laws are believed to change as well. If that were true, evaluations – and thus values – would be a matter of utter relativity, depending on the era, culture, and location of the person who makes these evaluations. That makes some people believe that morality is a matter of politics. I consider that a real mix-up! Think of this comparison: We shouldn't confuse our current understanding of physical laws with the way those laws really are as we may find out some day. In a similar vein, do not confuse our current moral evaluations with the way the moral laws really are.

S: But how could we ever have access to objective values if our subjective evaluations keep changing?

R: Your line of thinking leads to what they call "moral relativism," which asserts that values are subject to change during the course of human history – ruled by a majority vote, so to speak. This viewpoint is held by *relativists*; their stance amounts to an absolute claim stating that there are no absolutes (except for this absolute claim itself, of course). Relativists reject any authority but they want to be the new authority by proclaiming the dogma that there are no dogmas. And anyone who disagrees with them must be misinformed. Relativists have lost all "common sense," because they proclaim we have nothing in common.

As a result, relativists consider themselves in charge of the moral terminology we use and they manipulate it according to their needs. They replace, for instance, the old term "abortion" with the new term "selective reproduction." They determine what the term "human" means by demarcating whoever qualifies for this predicate: perhaps only Arians, only the biologically fit, only those who were not aborted, only those who have left the womb, or those who have not become a burden to society. From then on, everything becomes relative to the criteria relativists invent on the spot, all by themselves. They plainly adjust their moral vocabulary to make it sound politically correct.

The Church wants us to take the side of moral *absolutists* who emphasize that evaluations are merely a reflection of the way we discern moral values at the current time and react to them – in other words, evaluations may change but values won't. Absolutists want to stress that moral values and laws are eternal, objective, and absolute. Whereas relativists wouldn't acknowledge the possibility of making moral mistakes, absolutists certainly would, because there are absolute and eternal standards by which to judge our actions.

Such an absolutist view is not as bizarre as you might think. It is in fact a standard attitude in science: Our understanding of scientific laws did need, does need, and will need revision until we reach a correct understanding of those laws the way they really are;

just keep searching for the correct laws. Like moralists, scientists are basically absolutists: They are ultimately in search of absolute, objective laws of nature, but they realize they may not be there yet. In morality, we should strive for something similar. Just as we may be oblivious to laws of nature that we didn't know yet, we may violate moral laws we are not aware of.

It is the Church's task to make us aware of those moral laws. First of all, there is what is called the "natural law," which finds its biblical roots in St. Paul's reference to pagans "who never heard of the Law but are led by reason to do what the Law commands" (Rom. 2:14). This is something like a "moral common sense." St. Thomas Aquinas describes the natural law as "the light of understanding placed in us by God; through it we know what we must do and what we must avoid. God has given this light or law at the creation" (CCC 1955). Then there are also revealed laws: "The Law of Moses expresses many truths naturally accessible to reason" (CCC 1961) as well as the law of the Gospel, "the perfection here on earth of the divine law, natural and revealed" (CCC 1965). The Ten Commandments come to us from the outside and complete the interior knowledge of the natural law that has become obscured (see the next chapter).

S: Well, how do we justify those moral laws and values then?

R: Again, the only apt answer is "They are (self-) *evident*," based on *rational* insights, but also on special revelations. Some among us are able to clearly discern certain values and evaluate them properly, whereas others are not. Anyone who does not see their evidence is "blind." Just as there are color-blind people, there are also value-blind people. Just as science has its geniuses, morality has its sages – think of people such as Jesus Christ, Moses, Prophets, and Saints.

Let me illustrate this point a little further. A few centuries ago, slavery was not evaluated as morally wrong, but nowadays it is by most people. Did our moral values change? No, they did not; but our evaluations certainly did. Only a few people in the past – Saint Anselm being one of the first and then Pope Eugene IV (in his 1435

Bull *Sicut Dudum*) as well as Pope Paul III (in his 1537 Bull against slavery, entitled *Sublimis Deus*) – were able to discern the objective and universal value of personal freedom and human rights (versus slavery), whereas most of their contemporaries were blind for this value. The latter were value-blind, because they didn't "see" that one is obliged to be "color-blind" when it comes to racial issues. They could and should have known better! The 7th Commandment forbids acts that lead "to the *enslavement of human beings*, to their being bought, sold and exchanged like merchandise, in disregard for their personal dignity" (CCC 2414). No wonder, St. Paul directed a Christian master to treat his Christian slave "no longer as a slave but more than a slave, as a beloved brother, […] both in the flesh and in the Lord" (Philem. 1:16).

Something similar holds for the value of monogamy; many people in the past were blind for this value (and some still are). The way we discover moral laws is comparable to the way scientists discover scientific laws: It often requires the "genius" of especially gifted people, such as Moses, the prophets, and Church authorities – and ultimately Jesus, the Son of God. As Jesus would say, "You have heard that it was said […] But I say to you […]" – which means, whether you "see" it or not, this is the way it ought to be in this world, for this is the way this world was created and designed.

S: That sounds to me like "I see, I see what you don't see."

R: In a way, that is true. Sometimes, we ought to say to someone who is value-blind that something is "evidently" and even "rationally" wrong. There is none so blind as those who will not see. Apparently, there are many forms of blindness – not only physical blindness, but also spiritual blindness, and even moral blindness. As the dictum in the United States Supreme Court on pornography put it, "You know it when you see it" – that is how evident it is. This may not be a very precise criterion, but I wouldn't know of a better way.

Let's consider a different case. Nowadays, many people have become blind for the value that all human life, including the life of the unborn baby, deserves protection; only some discern very clearly the *absolute* value of all human life – which makes abortion a wrongful act (perhaps medically right, but morally wrong). Does this mean their opponents are blinded and shrouded? People who have a clear discernment of the value of human life would say so – and the Church would definitely join them. Yet, many people still need an ultrasound to see that abortion is wrong.

Let's face it: How often were the best people who had the clearest discernment of moral values persecuted by the mass of blind people! And yet, the advancement of humanity often depended on these very people who had a sharper and better discernment of moral values. As we are very grateful for those anti-slavery activists of the past, perhaps some day, most of us will also be very grateful to the anti-abortion activists, including the unwavering moral voice of the Church. It is not the values that change but our evaluations – that is, our subjective attitudes toward these objective and universal values. The Church is our moral compass. As G.K. Chesterton put it, "I don't need a church to tell me I am wrong where I already know I'm wrong; I need a Church to tell me I am wrong where I think I'm right."

S: Well, I keep repeating my question: Where do those absolute moral values come from then?

R: There is only one answer: They come directly from God, our Creator. Moral values are God-given, or in Catholic terms, "natural" – that is, rooted in nature as a *natural moral law*, engraved in our conscience, to be detected by a sound reason. As I said earlier, moral values have an added dimension and therefore must be derived from a different realm – from the Kingdom of Heaven, that is – and, as a result, ought to be "done on earth as it is in Heaven." Moral values do not change but our evaluations may – that is, our subjective attitudes here on earth toward these objective and universal values in Heaven.

Let me say it one more time, morality is not rooted in our genes, it is not the product of natural selection, it is not the result of any legislation, it is not a scientific conclusion, and it is not based on anything useful or beneficial such as "the greater happiness of a greater number of people." All of these substitutes are morally irrelevant, since morality includes a new dimension that only morality has access to. And that is where we need "divine help." Why? Nature can only contain norms, if a Will had put them there – which fact presupposes a Creator God whose Will has entered into nature. Hence, morality must be from "Above." It is "the work of divine Wisdom" (CCC 1950). How could there be moral laws if there were no moral Lawgiver? Morality is written in our hearts and minds, guiding us to make the right choices in life. As the prophet Isaiah (5:20) keeps stressing, "Woe to those who call evil good and good evil."

Q: But I know of people who act in a moral way. And yet do not believe in God. How would that be possible?

A: Those people certainly *can* act morally, but they do not know why they *should* act that way. They just do not know because, without God, there can be no absolute or objective standard of right and wrong, as there is no eternal Heaven that would make values objective and universal. Let me give you just one example. Nowadays, many people fight for social justice, yet they do not believe in God. They forget that social justice is ultimately based on the fact that we are God's children and that God has given all of them human dignity. They forget that social justice is deeply rooted in Christian faith – otherwise it is a baseless and hollow claim. Think of this comparison: If we would detach cancer treatment from its scientific roots, it would soon perish. Well, once we detach social justice from its Christian roots, it will soon expire as well. If justice were just a human invention, it could mean whatever we want it to mean – literally anything. Instead, social justice is a law from Heaven and is rooted in Heaven. Moral laws are not the monopoly of special interest groups, but they are God's monopoly.

It was Friedrich Nietzsche, of all philosophers, who clearly understood how devastating the decline of Christianity has been to society. If we are only the fortuitous effects of physical causes, we have no other moral measures but ourselves. That is why Nietzsche could say that humanism and other "moral" ideologies shelter themselves in caves and venerate shadows of the God they once believed in; they are holding on to something they cannot provide themselves – mere shadows of the past. Even the non-religious German philosopher Jürgen Habermas expressed as his conviction that the ideas of freedom and social co-existence are based on the Jewish notion of justice and the Christian ethics of love.

Pope Benedict XVI expressed a similar thought when he said to the world religious leaders gathered in Assisi on October 27, 2011: "The horrors of the concentration camps reveal with utter clarity the consequences of God's absence." And in his address to the German Parliament on September 22, 2011 he quoted Saint Augustine, "Without justice – what else is the State but a great band of robbers?"

S: I find it dangerous to declare morality as being so closely related to God and religion.

R: Quite the opposite! Because there is a Creator, we have not only a *rational* Lawgiver – who guarantees order, intelligibility, and predictability – but also a *moral* Lawgiver – who guarantees decency, integrity, responsibility, justice, and human rights. The writer Fyodor Dostoyevsky was ultimately right when he showed us in his book *The Brothers Karamazov* that, without God, all things are permissible; without God's eternal "Beyond," there wouldn't be eternal moral laws and we would be mere animals. Let me make clear that Dostoyevsky is not claiming that without God there would be no moral rules, for even in atheist societies there are moral rules. What he does claim, through Ivan, is that nothing would be *always* and *everywhere* wrong for the simple reason that everything would be, at least at some point and under some circumstances, permitted. Without God, moral absolutism becomes moral relativism. In other words, if God is dead, Ivan himself must take ultimate responsibility for the moral order of the world. When God is absent, Ivan would become the moral commander-in-chief, all by himself.

Something similar is stated by Jean-Paul Sartre: If atheism is true, there can be no absolute or objective standard of right and wrong, for there is no eternal heaven that would make values objective and universal. Without God, there wouldn't be any objective moral standards. The tree of knowledge of good and bad in paradise was planted by God Himself. As Vatican II puts it, "in the depths of his conscience, man detects a law which he does not impose upon himself, but which holds him to obedience" (*Gaudium et Spes*, 16).

But there is more! Without God, we wouldn't even have any moral *rights*. The US *Declaration of Independence* states very clearly that our human rights are *God*-given rights – otherwise we wouldn't have any: "We hold these truths to be self-evident, that all men are created equal, that they are endowed by their Creator with certain unalienable Rights, that among these are Life, Liberty and the pursuit of Happiness." These are divine birthrights. Without God, we would have no *right* to claim any rights. If rights really came from men, and not God, men could take them away anytime – and they certainly have tried and will try again.

Since we received our rights from *God*, let no one, and certainly not the government, decide how to exercise those rights. And let no one tell you that the *State* gave you those rights and can therefore decide how to exercise them. It is a self-evident truth that all men are endowed by their Creator with certain unalienable rights, and that among these are Life, Liberty, including Religious Freedom, and the pursuit of Happiness.

S: It seems to me that it is basically our *judicial* laws that take care of those moral rights.

R: I do not think we can equate *legal* laws with *moral* laws as easily as you think. Even if something is legal, it may still be immoral, for what we call legal is not necessarily based on moral values, but rather on moral evaluations. Slavery, for instance, was legally right at one point, and now abortion is in many countries, but that doesn't make them morally right. Laws that subordinate the rights of one person to those of other people are always unjust.

In his 1963 *Letter from Birmingham Jail*, Martin Luther King Jr. could not have put it better: "there are just and there are unjust laws." And then he goes on, "I would agree with Saint Augustine that 'An unjust law is no law at all.' […] A just law is a man-made code that squares with the moral law or the law of God. An unjust law is a code that is out of harmony with the moral law. To put it in the terms of Saint Thomas Aquinas, an unjust law is a human law that is not rooted in eternal and natural law."

Obviously, the relationship between morality and legality is rather intricate. When *moral* consensus fades – as it did, for instance, in St. Thomas More's time, and as it does now in ours – we usually turn to law. But when morality is no longer widely shared, legal laws begin to falter as well, making society and culture teeter on the brink of chaos. In other words, legal laws cannot be divorced from morality – and morality cannot be divorced from religion, so we found out. As a consequence, law, morality, and religion are strongly intertwined. When religion begins to fade in society, a cascade of effects sets in and starts a dangerous domino effect.

Q: But aren't our human rights a direct consequence of what they call our *human dignity*?

A: The idea of human dignity is not a new concept, but is basically and fundamentally a Judeo-Christian concept. It did get a fresh look, though, after World War II when the first photographs of inhumane atrocities in the Nazi concentration camps appeared. So in 1948, the UN affirmed in the *Universal Declaration of Human Rights* that "all human beings are born free and equal in dignity and rights."

However, the UN assumed a generally shared understanding of "human dignity," going back to its Judeo-Christian roots, but failed to define it. As a result, the declaration of human rights was put at the mercy of special interest groups. New sexual and reproductive "rights," such as abortion, were included, and so were the new "rights" of scientists to experiment with human embryos, as well as another invention, the "last civil right" to die.

Obviously, the concept of human dignity had become what Adam Schulman called "a placeholder for whatever it is about human beings that entitles them to basic human rights and freedoms." It became a placeholder for a man-made morality. Just think of how abortion was renamed as a reproductive right, but I wonder how a "reproductive right" could ever allow for abortion after the reproduction has already taken place. At the moment we start to call abortion and abortive contraceptives *"health* care" issues, we find ourselves in a terminological jumble, for none of this has anything to do with the health of the mother, let alone the health of the aborted unborn baby.

The ultimate source of this mix-up is that rights are being confused with entitlements. A right is a moral concept based on a moral law, whereas an entitlement is a legal (and not necessarily moral) notion based on a legal law. There are no minority rights or sexual and reproductive rights; these are, at most, entitlements. Rights are God-given, whereas entitlements are man-made. Once we fail to differentiate between them, we get ourselves into trouble. Always say what you mean and mean what you say!

S: Why do moral rights have to be God-given?

R: People tend to think that our moral rights spring from our human dignity. But where does that dignity really come from? It certainly is not based on our position in the animal world. We didn't earn human dignity in the process of *evolution*. From a biological point of view, humans are failures, fitted with eyes of a poor quality, olfactory organs of hardly any account, an inferior sense of hearing, a lack of any natural weapons such as claws and jaws. No, our dignity was bestowed on us in the process of *creation*, when our humanity took on divinity – and that's where our moral rights stem from. They are God's gift of creation.

No wonder then there is so much more to moral rights than you might think. Take the discussion of all those various forms of in-vitro-fertilization (IVF). I couldn't express this point better than it was done on several occasions by the priest and neuroscientist Fr. Tad Pacholczyk from the *National Catholic Bioethics Center* in Philadelphia. He morally argues against IVF by claiming that our children have the *right* to be procreated, not produced; our children are gifts, not choices (CCC 2378). They have the *right* to come into the world in the personal, love-giving marital embrace of their parents, not in the cold and impersonal glass world of a test tube or Petri dish. They have the *right* to be uniquely, exclusively, and directly related to the mother and father who bring them into the world. As a matter of fact, in-vitro-fertilization ignores and violates all these moral *rights* of the child – and therefore IVF is morally unacceptable (CCC 2376).

Something similar is going on in the mainstream infertility world. It directs infertile couples to *bypass* their reproductive systems in order to achieve pregnancy. In contrast, morality would direct us differently: Why not *fix* the reproductive system instead? As a matter of fact, there are alternatives available, such as *NaPro Technology*, which cooperates with the reproductive cycle to identify the fertility problem and then corrects it – instead of bypassing it and turning human procreation into inhuman production. Our future children have the *right* to be received in a waiting womb. Each human life is a journey, and journeys just do not start half-way. We have rights because we are all God's children; but entitlements we only have because we belong to a certain society. Go for what is morally correct, not for what is politically correct.

S: I keep wondering, though, how we can make moral mistakes if we are supposed to have direct access to those natural laws that you believe God has cemented in His Creation.

R: Indeed, how can humans, made in God's image, be blind for what is right? How can our moral evaluations be out of line with the eternal and absolute natural law? That is the tantalizing question. The answer to this question is to be found in the beginning of the Book of Genesis, where we are told that Adam and Eve decided, in their free will, to follow their own version of morality, inspired by Satan. Instead of the light of God that enlightens us, they let in satanic forces that blind people as to what is good and right. Ever since, our *sense* of morality has been under attack. That is why the Catechism (1960) says: "The precepts of natural law are not perceived by everyone clearly and immediately. In the present situation sinful man needs grace and revelation so moral and religious truth may be known." Although the Ten Commandments are accessible to reason alone, sinful humanity needed a special revelation, "a privileged expression of the natural law" (CCC 2070-2071).

Because of the Fall, we are permanently "under the influence" – under the influence, that is, of good Spirits and bad Spirits. We live under constant attention of both God and Satan – and Satan never sleeps. Strong spiritual forces are battling each other to either *guide* our morality, by encouraging the human will, or to *deceive* our morality, by crippling the human will. Whereas good Spirits strengthen our virtues (such as faith, hope, and charity), bad Spirits incite our vices (such as lust, doubt, despair, violence). It is the bad Spirits that want us to "right" what is wrong. When calling certain people "misguided," that is exactly what we mean – they literally are mis-guided. They in fact sold their souls to God's enemies, to God's fallen Angels.

S: Isn't the Fall in fact a consequence of what we call "freedom"?

R: Indeed, the Catechism tells us that "God created man a rational being, conferring on him the dignity of a person who can initiate and control his own actions" (CCC 1730). That is the source of our human freedom – the power to act or not to act, to make right or wrong decision s. However, as long as freedom "has not bound itself definitively to its ultimate good which is God, there is the possibility of choosing between good and evil, and thus of growing in perfection or of failing and sinning" (CCC 1732). Amazingly enough, we become free and truly ourselves only when we open up to God.

Blessed Cardinal Newman was very emphatic in warning us not to make the mistake of separating intellect and virtue – or mind and will. We tend to think that intellect is the key thing – that if we *know* what is right, we will pursue it. But this fails to account for weakness of will – that is, when we know what is right but fail to do it. The Bible makes no bones about it: "He who says 'I know him' but disobeys his commandments is a liar" (1 John 2:4). All efforts of the intellect also require efforts of virtue. That is why having a free will does not guarantee that we do the right thing. By cultivating virtue, we prepare the ground for the work of the intellect.

Obviously, our freedom does not bestow on us the right to say or do whatever we want to do or say. The more we do what is good, the freer we become. Freedom needs to be guided by a *conscience*. The Catechism calls our conscience "man's most secret core and his sanctuary. There he is alone with God whose voice echoes in his depths" (CCC 1776). It is in this sanctuary that human freedom makes right or wrong moral decisions. That is why a good conscience needs to be nurtured in prayer, so that our moral decisions will be guided by *universal* moral values that transcend differences in culture, era, and personal interests. Otherwise, a person's conscience can easily become numb or callous.

S: Tell me more about this "conscience." Isn't following your conscience all there is to it?

R: Ironically, even moral relativists hold on to at least one moral absolute that says "never disobey your own conscience." So we should ask them the question as to where the absolute authority of a human conscience comes from. Do my genes, or other natural factors, have the right to demand absolute obedience from me? Of course not! Does society have the right to demand my absolute obedience? Certainly not! Does any person, including myself, have the right to demand my absolute obedience? None of the above! The only authority that can obligate me is something – or rather Someone – infinitely superior to me; no one else has the right to demand my absolute obedience. In other words, a moral conscience is explainable only as the voice of God in our souls. The absolute authority of our conscience comes from Above (CCC 1776). Do not turn the one who is supposed to follow the law into the lawgiver by placing the now sovereign individual in the place of God and His Church. That would be a form of idolatry.

I am sure this is not the kind of conscience moral relativists are referring to when they make it their absolute authority. The Catholic Church tells us very clearly that conscience can be understood only in relation to the individual's duty to obey the divine law – not to give people the freedom to live as they please. Man's conscience is a sanctuary where he is alone with God "whose voice *echoes* in his depths" (CCC 1776; italics are mine). Man's conscience participates in God's knowing. In other words, the individual's conscience does not speak on its own but it merely *reflects* the law spoken by God. It is not the place for the *creation* of moral values – like relativists believe it is – but it is simply the place for *appropriation* of the natural law; it does not create moral values but merely receives them. That is the reason why we cannot take our conscience as an entirely private issue that we form at our own discretion. A "dialogue" with oneself would only amount to a mere monologue that isolates and alienates us from God, our moral Lawgiver. Therefore, one's moral judgment doesn't become true by the mere fact that it has its origin in conscience, because a conscience needs to be truthfully formed first so as to *echo* the natural law (*Veritatis Splendor,* 54).

Our conscience is like an alarm that alerts us before we sin; when it goes off, we must not ignore it. When a red warning light in your car lights up, have the problem fixed – not by disconnecting the light but by fixing what causes it to light up. It is the same with your conscience: Do not silence it. However, when "the alarm" does *not* go off, that doesn't mean there is an "all clear" sign, but we may have intentionally lowered its "volume" or ignored its upkeep. That is how we can manipulate or even damage our conscience. A gas gauge in the car that does no longer go down is broken, yet the tank may be almost empty. Have it fixed! When it comes to your conscience, have it "calibrated" again.

As a consequence, moral disagreements can never be settled on the level of a person's private and personal conscience, for that means there would be a tie, for instance, between the conscience of a pro-choice pregnant mother and the conscience of her pro-life obstetrician. Each "private" conscience must ultimately be under the authority of the "natural law" of morality (CCC 1776-1778). In other words, a good conscience needs to be taught and nurtured – and that is done through what is called the "natural law," passed on to us by the teaching authority of the Church. Hence, it shouldn't surprise us that the "education of the conscience is a lifelong task" (CCC 1784). At the XXIV World Day for Peace, Pope John Paul II spoke of "the grave duty to form [one's] conscience." It is the natural law that is our ultimate moral authority and compass, not our conscience per se or on its own.

S: But if our conscience echoes the divine law, how come that we do not hear all the same voice?

R: The answer to this question must sound familiar by now.

Because our conscience is dependent upon human reason, it is also subject to all of the weaknesses to which human reason is prone, as it is damaged by sin. Because of this tendency to error, we cannot treat our conscience as an infallible guide to truth. As a result of original sin, there is a permanent need for the correct formation of conscience. It is just a naïve understanding of conscience to think that following your conscience is all there is to it.

Humans do have the freedom to not only make rational decisions but also moral decisions; yet, they have a history of making the wrong decisions. Many Christian writers have stressed this scandal. The Catholic French philosopher Blaise Pascal once put it this way, "It is dangerous to show man in how many respects he resembles the lower animals, without pointing out his grandeur. It is also dangerous to direct his attention to his grandeur, without keeping him aware of his degradation" (taken from his *Thoughts* or *Pensées*).

In other words, there is the grandeur as well as the degradation of human nature. Each day, we must choose between the glory and the scandal. In spite of our human degradation, there is still our original human grandeur, but we have to work much harder to make it come true. And make no mistake, it can only be given back to us through the New Adam, Jesus Christ, our Savior, who died for the sins we committed and keep committing. Like He cleansed the leper of his leprosy, He cleanses us of the leprosy of sin.

In order to help us regain our original identity, God has become very concrete and fully immanent in Jesus Christ, when He became flesh of our flesh, "the new Adam," a "servant," and yet our "Savior." Jesus was God and Man in one person, so that God and Man might be happy together again. In the words of John Paul II, Jesus Christ is "the human face of God and the divine face of Man." It is the "Man on the Cross" who shows us how much God loved the world when He gave His one and only Son (John 3:16). Ever since those "crucial" events took place in Palestine, we know that our true identity is no longer the "old Adam," the Adam from after the Fall, but the "new Adam," the Adam from after the Incarnation. What was given to us at creation, when humanity took on divinity, had to be given back to us during the Incarnation, when Divinity took on humanity.

S: I cannot believe, though, the scandal of the Fall has also affected our innocent children.

R: You have in fact philosophers such as John Locke and Jean-Jacques Rousseau on your side. They tried very hard to make us believe that humans are born good, that a child is just a blank slate, uncorrupted and free of any predispositions. But I would point out that, without morality, life would just bring out the cruel, selfish, and bullying parts of our inborn animal nature. Just look around to see how these philosophers are deceiving us. Every parent who has raised kids knows that they are not born good but need to learn manners and discipline; they need to be taught and nurtured in rationality and morality.

True, humans were *created* good, but that doesn't mean they were also *born* good. First, moral goodness is not a matter of genes. And second, as a result of the Original Sin, our sense of morality has been corrupted. The Fall shows us that Adam and Eve didn't like God's Commands, because they didn't want to be commanded. Ever since that disastrous moment, humans have lost their original innocence, for in their desire to rule their own lives, they rejected being dependent on God and being subject to God's laws of nature and God's natural law. Because they passed this on to their offspring, we are certainly not "born good."

To paraphrase G.K. Chesterton, as far as sin is concerned, there are two kinds of people: not, as you might think, those who sin and those who do not sin, but those who know they are sinners and those who do not know they are sinners. Not only is there so much good in the worst of us, but also so much bad in the best of us. Mother Mary, pray for us sinners.

Q: Isn't this what they call the *original sin*? I don't like that concept, though. I can see that we pass on our genes to the next generation, but how can we pass on sinfulness?

A: Without any doubt, there is genetic heredity, but in addition, there is something like spiritual and moral heredity. When a pregnant mother takes drugs, her baby is born an addict; that is basically *original sin* – spiritual and moral heredity. There is this biblical principle that the sins of the fathers are visited onto the children to the third and fourth generations (Ex. 20:5; 34:6-7; Num. 14:18; Deut 5:9). Well, what we have here is basically an issue of spiritual and moral heredity. If you come from a dysfunctional family, chances are you will start another dysfunctional family. I don't think there is a better word to capture this than *original sin*. C. S. Lewis even argued that the existence of original sin is perhaps one of the most obvious facts of human life, even to non-believers.

So where does the original sin come from? The answer is: from the *Fall* in Paradise, when the first humans decided with their free will that they wanted to follow their own commandments, not God's – and thereby they introduced moral evil, actually a cascade of evils that keeps going on an on. Because God is a free, reasonable, and loving Being Himself, He to a certain extent set aside His will when He created the human will also to be reasonable, a free offshoot of His will. As a consequence, human beings are so free that they can set themselves against God. God allows human free-will to the limits of sin. Isn't it striking how our weak human will can withstand an Almighty God? And that is how we ended up *"in a fallen state"* (CCC 404).

The Catechism explains this further by telling us that Adam "has transmitted to us a sin with which we are all born afflicted" (403). Not only is sinfulness hereditary but it is also contagious, and can be passed on like we pass on leprosy. Because of the unity of the human race "all men are implicated in Adam's sin, as all are implicated in Christ's justice. [...] By yielding to the tempter, Adam and Eve committed a *personal sin*, but this sin affected *the human nature* that they would then transmit *in a fallen state*. [...] And that is why original sin is called 'sin' only in an analogical sense: it is a sin 'contracted' and not 'committed' – a state and not an act" (404).

Do we have to call this evil? For some people, evil belongs to a superseded and superstitious world of black and white. They think we don't *do* anything wrong, but things just *go* wrong (due to our genes, hormones, etc.). They consider evil some kind of disease located somewhere in a gene or temporal lobe or whatever. They even tell us that we can evade moral responsibility by saying that our glands made us act that way. We discussed all of this in chapter six. However, morality is about choices you and I constantly make based on moral values and laws. As a consequence, evil is often the outcome of a corrupted morality. At the very moment that we let self-interest become the driving force behind all our human actions, moral-altruism is on its way out – and evil will take over and control us. Without the compass of morality, we would head down a dangerous blind alley. It would be a world without good and bad, right and wrong, good and evil.

S: I think I need more specific cases in order to understand what all of this entails for our daily lives. What about abortion?

R: That is a good example you mention there! In the abortion debate, morality leaves us no room for "pro-choice." A child is a gift, not a choice (CCC 2378); if you doubt that obvious fact, just ask parents who cannot have their own children (CCC 2379). Morality does not allow us to choose between pro-life and pro-abortion, or between pro-freedom and pro-slavery for that matter. The sanctity of life and the sanctity of human freedom are moral, God-given rights that no one can take away from us. They are based on the natural law that God has cemented in His creation and therefore should be anchored in our conscience.

Morality is not about the choices we have but about the choices that are right; it obliges us to go for pro-life and pro-freedom, otherwise we would make a moral mistake. But some are so "blind" for this absolute value that they need an ultra-sound to "see" with their own eyes the evidence of what is morally wrong with abortion. Does this mean that abortion is *never* permissible? Couldn't there be situations where abortion would be the best solution of several alternatives? My first response would be: There are no gradations in good and evil; there is no "lesser evil" or "greater good." New wrongs cannot erase previous wrongs, but can only *add* to them by making things worse. Evil is evil, no matter how you look at it. How could "a greater good" ever permit "minor evils," for how could good ever originate from evil? Even eugenics could be defended this way as being for "the greater good." Apparently, in morality, there is no "greater" versus "minor," because morality is not about

189

relative criteria, but about absolute standards.

Applied to abortion, the good of saving a mother's life can never offset the evil of killing a human life (abortion). Never give up God's gift of life – no matter whether it is through abortion, euthanasia, or suicide – even if medical rules suggest differently. As I said earlier, medical rules are instrumental rules, whereas moral rules are intrinsic rules that can never be overruled by instrumental rules. *Medical* rules should always comply with the *moral* rule of preserving life, for morality is not a calculus of consequences, depending on circumstances or the end in view.

S: What about a case where the mother has a disease or illness that would be "burdened" by her carrying an unborn baby. Shouldn't we choose the health of the mother over the life of the unborn baby?

R: It looks like you are using *biological* criteria again to make a *moral* decision – something like "the adult is more important than the unborn baby," or "independent human life outweighs dependent human life," or "a full-grown person is worth more than a growing fetus," "a full-grown brain is worth more than a brain in development," and so on. As I stressed earlier, moral decisions can never be justified by non-moral, relative, biological criteria.

Therefore, all human life – that is, from womb to tomb, from orphanages to mental institutions, and at all stages of its development – shares in the sanctity of human life. The Bible tells us "Before I formed you in the womb I knew you, and before you were born I consecrated you" (Jer. 1:5) and "thou didst form my inward parts, thou didst knit me together in my mother's womb" (Ps. 139:13). Remember that billboard in Manhattan? It said: The most dangerous place for African-Americans is in the womb. They count for 60% of the city's abortions. Some may defuse this as a racist remark, but it is as little racist as the factual statement that 1 in 12 African-Americans carry the genetic trait for sickle cell anemia. It is just a matter of fact that the womb is the most dangerous place for African Americans in New York City. We should ask them and ourselves: Would there be any sanctuary left if even the womb of a pregnant mother is no longer a safe hiding place?

S: And yet there are situations where we have good and bad effects combined.

R: When a certain act has two effects, one good and one bad, we have a case where the moral *principle of double effect* comes into action. This principle relies on the distinction between a good effect one intends and an evil effect one does not intend (like in the case of self-defense: the double effect of the intended preservation of one's own life and the not-intended killing of the aggressor; CCC 2263).

According to this principle, it may be morally permissible to perform an act with double effect, but only if all of the following criteria are fulfilled:

- the act is not morally wrong;
- the good effect is directly intended;
- the bad effect is only indirectly intended;
- the bad effect is not the means for attaining the good effect;
- and there is a proportionally serious reason for tolerating the bad effect.

Actions that would result in the death of an unborn baby would never be permissible unless all of the aforementioned conditions have been fulfilled. At the moment of conception, human life starts its journey – for journeys never start half-way. That is why every obstetrician should always take care of *two* patients.

Let me give you a less abstract example of the principle of double effect: a woman who has a proportionately serious pathological condition during her pregnancy. Operations, treatments, and medications that will result in the death of the unborn baby may be morally permissible if-and-only-if they have as their direct purpose to cure the pregnant woman, and if they cannot be safely postponed until the unborn baby is viable. In other words, actions that might result in the death of an unborn baby might be morally permitted, but only if all of the following conditions are met:

- treatment is directly therapeutic in response to a serious pathology of the mother or child;
- the good effect of curing the disease is intended;

- the bad effect is foreseen but unintended;
- the death of the unborn baby is not the means by which the good effect is achieved;
- the good of curing the disease is proportionate to the risk of the bad effect.

S: How come we have lost these insights? In other words, why is morality in decline, as you asked in the subtitle of this chapter?

R: First of all, morality has been in decline since Adam and Eve entered the world scene. Second, there was a further decline when we replaced morality with "the greater good of a greater number of people" based on some kind of majority vote. Then morality experienced a further relapse when we began to justify moral decisions with biological criteria that are per definition non-moral or morally irrelevant. And it went even further downhill when morality became subject to historical changes, cultural trends, majority votes, and demographic diversity. It is telling that some politicians nowadays no longer speak of *moral* issues but refer to them as *social* or *political* issues instead. They only go for what is politically correct, not what is morally correct.

What I have been trying to emphasize in this chapter is that morality is on its way out at the very moment we try to detach it from religion and the eternal Heaven that makes moral values objective and universal. When we lose religion, we also lose the foundation of morality, and from there on, it just goes farther downhill, as our moral compass no longer works in a proper way. Satan keeps encouraging us to eat from the "tree of good and evil," by making our own moral laws. "God knows that when you eat of it your eyes will be opened, and you will be like God, knowing good and evil" (Gen. 3:5).

Can morality stay afloat once its bottom has been taken out? I refer to Dostoyevsky again, when he said that without God all things are permissible. Fortunately, God gave us the Ten Commandments, for He loves the sinner, but not the sin. So let's see in the next chapter what those ten moral laws entail.

8

God's Perscription
for Happiness

Two Tablets a Day

Our society is obsessed with the search for happiness; there seems to be so little of it. The other day, I found a brochure for nutrients in my mail box that featured in big letters: *instant happiness delivered at home*. We all know better, I hope. Happiness is not for sale!

God has a much better prescription for happiness: *two tablets a day* – that is, the two tablets holding the Ten Commandments or Decalogue. They are not ten suggestions, not even ten options, but *Ten Commandments*. They are not nutritional supplements but "nutritional essentials." Well, those vital Ten Commandments have lost their prominent position, not only on the walls of our court houses, but even – what is much worse – "on the walls" of our conscience. That is why our happiness is in trouble, more so than ever.

They are more than "Ten Words of Wisdom"; they are "Ten Laws of Life" – one for each finger. We have got our hands full with these laws. Let's find out in this chapter how we can get our health and happiness back with the right "diet."

The table below shows three different traditions of numbering the Ten Commandments or Decalogue: Talmudic (T); Orthodox and Calvinists (P); St. Augustine, Catholics, and Lutherans (C). There are two versions of the Decalogue in the Bible: Exodus 20 and Deuteronomy 5. All traditions use the version given in the Book of Exodus.

T	O	C	Exodus 20
1	1	1	2 I am the LORD your God, who brought you out of the land of Egypt, out of the house of slavery;
2			3 you shall have no other gods before me.
	2		4 You shall not make for yourself a carved image, whether in the form of anything that is in heaven above, or that is on the earth beneath, or that is in the water under the earth. 5 You shall not bow down to them or worship them [...]
3	3	2	7 You shall not make wrongful use of the name of the LORD your God, for the LORD will not acquit anyone who misuses his name.
4	4	3	8 Remember the Sabbath day, and keep it holy. 9 Six days you shall labor and do all your work. 10 But the seventh day is a Sabbath to the LORD your God; you shall not do any work [...]
5	5	4	12 Honor your father and your mother, so that your days may be long in the land that the LORD your God is giving you.
6	6	5	13 You shall not murder.
7	7	6	14 You shall not commit adultery.
8	8	7	15 You shall not steal.
9	9	8	16 You shall not bear false witness against your neighbor.
	10	9	17 You shall not covet your neighbor's wife...
			...you shall not covet your neighbor's house... ...or male or female slave, or ox, or donkey, or anything that belongs to your neighbor.

Q: Why do we have Commandments anyway?

A: The Catechism describes the Decalogue – literally the "ten words" – as "the gift of God himself and his holy will. In making his will known, God reveals himself to his people." (2059). God's Revelation tells us who He *is* and what He *wants*. These two are thoroughly intertwined with each other: What He *wants* of us is related to the Person He *is*, a God of Love who fell in love with us. Not only is God all-powerful, all-knowing, and all-present, but also all-loving – with a love that surpasses all the kinds of love we know. The love God talks about is surely not the love we know.

The Ten Commandments are, in themselves, the covenant between God and his people, something like a spousal relationship. They were kept and carried around in the Ark of the Covenant. They are the terms and conditions and guidelines of a covenant (CCC 2058) – or more specifically, of a "spousal" relationship. "I will be your God; you shall be my people" — and here is how we will treat each other. Thus, it is within the context of a *Covenant* that the Ten Commandments take on their full meaning.

Q: Why are there *two* tablets instead of one?

A: Jews place five Commandments on each tablet or table, as if they represent the five fingers on each hand, whereas Catholics follow St. Augustine who has three Commandments on the first tablet and seven on the second one (CCC 2066). Either split is based on the idea that the first tablet has "love God" commands, and the second one "love neighbor" commands.

That is a nice thought, as long as we do not loose sight of the fact that all ten commands are simultaneously ten ways to love God and ten ways to love our neighbor. They go hand in hand: "The two tables shed light on one another; they form an organic unity […] One cannot honor another person without blessing God his Creator. One cannot adore God without loving all men, his creatures" (CCC 2069).

St. Paul also stresses their unity in Romans 13:8–10: "Owe no one anything, except to love one another; for he who loves his neighbor has fulfilled the law. The commandments, 'You shall not commit adultery, You shall not kill, You shall not steal, You shall not covet,' and any other commandment, are summed up in this sentence, 'You shall love your neighbor as yourself.' Love does no wrong to a neighbor; therefore love is the fulfilling of the law." Love is apparently the key word of God's Covenant with us. After all, He is an all-loving God.

Loving your neighbor is ultimately based on loving God; it begins with loving God before we can love our neighbor. Notice how the *Our Father*, like the Ten Commandments, begins also by establishing the primacy of *God* in its first half, which then leads naturally to finding the right way of being *human*. As Pope Benedict puts it in his book *Jesus of Nazareth* (Part I, 134), "The first thing we must do is step outside ourselves and open ourselves to God. Nothing can turn out right if our relation to God is not rightly ordered." The rest flows from there.

Q: Shouldn't we think of the Decalogue then as being on *one* tablet?

A: Interestingly enough, Rabbi Gamaliel, who was the Jewish Law teacher of St. Paul, does mention that "the Sages say ten on one tablet and ten on the other." That may have very well been the case, because the Commandments establish a covenant between God and His people; so it is possible that both tablets were complete replicas – one for each party in the Covenant. This can be compared to diplomatic treaties of Ancient Egypt, in which a copy was made for each party. In a love relationship, like in a covenant, there are duties and rights; it is give and take, in good days and bad.

So we could say that it is our *duty*, as an act of love, to make God the only one (Commandment #1); but it is equally true to say that God has a *right* to sit on that divine throne in our lives. Next, it is also equally true to say that God alone has the *right* to give and take human life and that people have a *duty* to respect that right. The Decalogue brings to light the duties and rights inherent in the nature of a covenant. There are always two sides to the story, as long as we realize it is a covenant of *love*. So it doesn't really matter whether we were given one or two tablets.

Q: You speak of rights and duties, but the Ten Commandments seem to be more about duties than rights.

A: Yes, eight of them begin with "You shall *not*..." No wonder that many people think the Catholic Church is the church of "No." Cardinal Seán O'Malley likes to tell this story about one of his community members who wrote a book on moral theology and was teased by one of the friars with the question "350 pages just to say no?" And then Cardinal Seán often mentions those five stained-glass windows in a church on Martha's Vineyard which had on each window one of the words "Go and sin no more." On hot summer days, only the fourth window could be opened, so parishioners would read the challenging words "Go and sin more." No one ever complained about that window! People must have thought "Finally, a church without NO."

The message is clear: We think the Church is saying NO to numerous moral issues: no abortion, no euthanasia, no divorce, no blasphemy, no perjury... But in fact, the Church is really about saying YES to God, YES to love, YES to life, and YES to other people.

Q: So your point is that "Love God" and "Love your neighbor" go actually hand in hand.

A: Yes, the fact that my God is the Creator of all people is also good for my neighbor, since we are all neighbors of each other, brothers and sisters from the same Father. As a consequence, the Commandment that I must not kill my neighbor is also good for God, because He is the giver of my neighbor's life as well, which makes every single human life precious in God's eyes. Put differently, we cannot honor other people without blessing their Creator, and we cannot adore God without loving all His people (CCC 2069).

When thinking in terms of rights and duties, we often do so in the sense of *a favor for a favor*. Not so in the Scriptures. The Bible does not teach that "*if* [the big *if*] you keep the Commandments, I will be your God and deliver you from bondage." No, the redemption from Egypt and the adoption as God's chosen people happen by *grace*, by God's initiative, out of love – that is, *before* the law is given. The law's primary function is to outline how to stay free and live out the life of love and justice in relationship with each other and with God in response to His love. The Catechism makes it very clear: "God has loved us first. [...] The Commandments then make explicit the response of love that man is called to give to his God" (2083). So living a moral life in accordance with the Ten Commandments is a *response* to the Lord's loving initiative (CCC 2062).

No wonder then the Decalogue is in fact a *dialogue* between God ("I") and Man ("You"). All Commandments are stated in the first person – "*I* am the Lord..." – and addressed by God to another person – "*You* shall..." God makes His will known to each person individually, so that each person can respond to His love. Therefore, it is only through each individual person that God speaks to the whole people (CCC 2063). So, in essence, the Decalogue brings our *religious* and *social* lives into unity, as the Catechism puts it. The Decalogue stands for the "ten words" that connect God to humans and humans to God. They are "Ten Words of Wisdom" – a manual of how to treat one another as one people under God. This was well put by Pope Benedict XVI in his book *Jesus of Nazareth* (Part I, 146) when he says, "that we give God his just due and, in so doing, discover the criterion for what is justly due among men."

Q: Where did these Ten Commandments come from?

A: The best and shortest answer is: directly from God. But as to *how* they got to us, the Bible is more ambivalent. According to Deuteronomy, it was God who personally wrote them on the two tablets of stone, with His own finger and in a special handwriting (Dt. 5:22; 10:2-4). The Book of Exodus, however, has a different, more down-to-earth version: It was Moses himself who wrote down on the two tablets of stone everything God had told him on the mountain (Ex. 24:4; 34:27). Jeremiah goes even one step farther when he says that God will write His law upon the hearts of people, rather than on tablets of stone. But no matter how they got to us, they do come from God.

Together with the Beatitudes, they are, in the words of the Catechism, "the paths that lead to the Kingdom of Heaven.

Sustained by the grace of the Holy Spirit, we tread them, step by step, by everyday acts" (1724). They teach us that true happiness is not found in riches or well-being, in human fame or power, or in any human achievement, but in God alone.

Q: Is that the reason why any violation of the Ten Commandments is called a *sin*?

A: The Church calls them actually *mortal* sins; they are like a "spiritual death penalty"; yet they are not a penalty coming from *God*, but a "lethal" consequence of *sin* itself. That is why they are called mortal. Think about these "ten laws" as if they were traffic signs. The sign *"Wrong Way. Do Not Enter"* can obviously be ignored, but if you do ignore it, you will most likely experience a "mortal penalty." What kills the violator is not this traffic law or the maker of this law, but the law was made by lawmakers to prevent actions that are by nature potentially deadly; that is the reason why the act was made illegal. The Church takes sinful acts as "mortal" because they "kill" our relationship with God. It is not God withdrawing from us, but the sinner pulling away from God.

Needless to say that some sins are not "mortal" but "venial"; they "wound" but do not "kill." They rather resemble traffic rules such as *"10 minutes parking limit."* Violating this kind of regulations is illegal but does not kill. Examples would be: petty theft, lies of convenience, mild laziness, etc. St. Thomas Aquinas considers a mortal sin to be *"against* the law," whereas a venial sin is considered to be *"out of step* with the law."

Q: I would like to echo the question some young man posed to Jesus: "Teacher, what good deed must I do, to have eternal life?" (Mt. 19:16).

A: And what did Jesus reply? He answered him with these simple words, "keep the Commandments." The man said to him, "Which ones?" And Jesus answered, "You shall not murder, you shall not commit adultery, you shall not steal, you shall not bear false witness, Honor your father and mother, and, you shall love your neighbor as yourself."

These Commandments keep us on the right path, from which so many people tend to deviate. They are vital for our society, although the Supreme Court has ruled that it is illegal to display them in public schools. (Imagine, children might be religiously influenced, or might even obey them!) Yet, the Ten Commandments are chiseled into the facade of the Supreme Court building, at the very place where this ruling was made!

I think it is best now to just look at the individual Commandments and discuss what each one entails, so as to know what we must do. Please follow me on this path of discovery...

Q: #1 says: *I am the Lord your God: you shall not have strange gods before me.*

A: What this Commandment says is basically the following: Do not honor or revere creatures in place of their Creator. Away with any human being, any object, any deity before God! Do not bow to anything and do not shudder before anything. Do not believe that anything in the world has the power to heal you or ruin you. Why not? God answers that question very directly: "For I am the Lord your God."

In the light of God's countenance, all entities that call themselves god, or deem themselves to be a god, fade away and shrivel up. Their masks are torn off. Just look at what some call the mysterious power of Mother Nature – it turns out to be a tiny piece of God's creation for the mere use of human beings. Watch the lights of Sun and Moon and Stars – they are merely lamps created to give people light and to show them what time it is. Take King and Government – they are nothing but a human institution curbed by human limitations; their assignment is temporary and their power transitory. Don't ever bow for them!

But there are so many other idols and deities that we venerate more than God. Think of "the god of pleasure" – pleasure in its many forms, from sex to alcohol, from sports to gambling. Its worshippers are "lovers of pleasure rather than lovers of God" (2 Tim. 3:4). Think of "the god of materialism." The worshippers of material possessions "cannot serve God and mammon" (Mt. 6:24), because "the love of money is the root of all evils" (1 Tim. 6:10) Take "the god of appetite" who lures us into over-eating and binge-drinking. Or take "the god of self-worship" venerated by people who idolize themselves and their Ego, because of their talents, education, title, or career. They venerate "I, me, and myself," and choose to live in splendid isolation, even isolated from God.

The Catechism states: "Idolatry not only refers to false pagan worship... Man commits idolatry whenever he honors and reveres a creature in place of God, whether this be gods or demons (for example satanism), power, pleasure, race, ancestors, the state, money, etc." (2113). The Catechism also mentions various forms of divination: the use of horoscopes, astrology, palm reading, clairvoyance, mediums, etc. (2116). If you thought these were gods, you must not be in your right mind! A coin may hold the emperor's image, but you and I carry God's image. Thank God, the Bible has cleared the sky of all those fake and misleading deities who like to put us in bondage. They only enslave and degrade us. They are extremely addictive.

The things that imprison us can easily deceive us. St. John of the Cross put it this way: "A bird can be held by a chain or by a thread, still it cannot fly." Even those tiny threads can hold us earthbound; they may hold us as firmly as if they were made of steel. No matter what, we end up being shackled. With our very own eyes, we notice how people prostrate themselves before these gods and how these gods bind our world hand and foot to their relentless and gruesome tyranny.

Q: So let the real God stand up then!

A: No doubt, Baal is dead, Jupiter is dead, the Pharaohs and the Caesars are dead. But what about Israel's God, the God of Jesus? Many people ask this question nowadays. They have lost even God in various forms of atheism as we discussed them in chapter one – which is quite painful, isn't it? Are we really on our way to live without God? Having no God means the sea has been drunk dry, the fourth dimension has been taken out of our lives, the bottom has fallen out, and our sixth sense is gone. Everything is just the way it is, they say – only a matter of historical facts and laws of nature. They can no longer look beyond the natural to see the supernatural, beyond the physical to see the metaphysical, beyond the visible to see the invisible, beyond the present to see the eternal.

Having no God means that our horizon has been wiped out; there is no more direction and perspective, no other future and destination than the things we have created on our own. There is no more sense or purpose in life. There is no light to help us make a judgment, a choice, or a decision. There is no light to shine on our paths, thus leaving us no choice but to grope blindly and march obediently. Thank God, we still have our God – He who brought us out of the land of Egypt, out of the house of bondage. It is He who sets us free. Never forget his appeal "*I am* the Lord your God."

Q: Why do certain churches have a different version of this important 1st Commandment?

A: What St. Augustine and Catholics combine into one Commandment – "You shall not have strange gods before me" – other traditions split into two separate commandments: "You shall have no other gods" and "You shall not make an idol." The reason for combining them is that idols easily become "strange gods" that tend to take over God's place in our minds. So what is it then that makes those idols so dangerous?

First of all, what are idols? The Bible is in a constant battle with "idols." An idol in itself can do nothing; left alone, it will deteriorate, rust, rot, or chip. Scripture calls idols literally "nothings" when it says "For all the gods of the peoples are idols" (Ps. 96:5). So where does their power come from then?

Well, the idol itself is nothing, but every idol has a demon associated with it. Demons are the spiritual agents acting in all idolatry. We can find these demons all over the Bible: "They sacrificed their sons and their daughters to the demons" (Ps. 106:37) and "They sacrificed to demons which were no gods" (Deut. 32:17).

Do not think idols are something from the past, remnants of a pagan past! Idols may be nothings, but we still keep idol-izing them. We idolize our movie-stars, our sports-heroes, our deities on

TV, even our role-models in *American Idol*. But we forget so easily that, in fact, they are idols, nothings. So often, these idols tend to take over God's place in our minds. In addition, there are other, seemingly harmless idols that we need to fight – I am thinking of superstition in magical practices, against divinizing what is not God, against buying or selling spiritual things. There is nothing wrong with using religious objects to enhance our faith, but the danger lies in losing focus – when they pull our attention away from God. When Catholics "pray to statues," they pray actually to God, albeit through the intercession of the Saint behind the statue. The only way to keep our faith from sliding into superstition and idolatry is to remember that spiritual blessings come not from created matter, such as statues, but from the Creator of all matter.

Because God alone is the Creator of all matter, no one else can take His place – not even human beings. Secularism and humanism may make us believe that we are fully self-made. They declare humanity as the measure of all things by pronouncing that all our problems can be entirely solved by using the right human knowledge, technology, reasoning, and judgment. They even believe that we can make our own moral values and rules. This is a pseudo religion, the religion of "I, me, and myself." Why is this idolatry? Because we are venerating ourselves as if we were gods! Because we endow ourselves with the power of our Maker, with the authority of our rational and moral Lawgiver! We are actually putting ourselves in the place of God. However, like all idols, we will deteriorate and decay when left alone. Have you ever seen a piece of clay telling the potter what to make? Well, we are the clay and He is the potter, our Maker!

And then there is the worst idol of them all, atheism. Atheists like to occupy God's throne that they had declared vacant. All idols, including the idol of atheism, keep doing what they used to do in the past. They are still trying to put clouds between the living God and us, to alienate us from God, from one another, and from ourselves. Perhaps we should reconsider and take these gods seriously again; and yet we should take them for what they really are: nothings! No wonder the Catholic Church combines "other gods" and "idols" into one single Commandment, for they all try to take God's place, but they are actually "nothings"! Once we belong to God, everything else loses the allure of divinity.

Q: What about those religions that worship a different God?

A: Some people say all religions worship the same God – no matter whether they call God by the name of Allah, Brahman, Vishnu, or you name it. In support, they often use the story of those legendary blind people who felt each a different part of an elephant, thinking an elephant to be all trunk, all tail, or whatever. Each one had part of the truth, but they all shared somehow in the same truth – something like "one faith but many beliefs." Nevertheless the Catholic Church would counter that all of them were *blind* people, not able to "see" the real thing, an elephant.

This is not to say that we shouldn't respect other religions, for these often reflect a ray of truth which enlightens all people. The Catechism puts it this way: "All men are bound to seek the truth – which is a duty that derives from the very dignity of the human person" (2104). So all of us have the right to religious freedom, but this is neither a moral license to adhere to error, nor a supposed right to error, but rather a natural right of the human person to civil liberty from external constraint in religious matters by political authorities (CCC 2108).

Yet, we were taught that there is no salvation outside the Church. How should we take this? What about the millions who have a different religion? As the document *Lumen Gentium* from Vatican II puts it, "Those who, through no fault of their own, do not know the Gospel of Christ or his Church, but who nevertheless seek God with a sincere heart, and, moved by grace, try in their actions to do his will as they know it through the dictates of their conscience – those too may achieve eternal salvation."

In Pope Benedict's encyclical *Caritas in Veritate* ("Charity in Truth"), it is well articulated that the aim of any dialogue between religions is *truth*. The aim for both sides should be to come to the truth, but through respect and love. We can and should agree to agreeably disagree. So the 1ˢᵗ Commandment remains standing: "You shall not have strange Gods before me."

Q: #2 says: *You shall not take the name of the Lord your God in vain.*

A: Every once in a while, you may read the following words on a highway billboard: "Speak out about God, but do not abuse His holy name." It makes many of us think of the 2ⁿᵈ Commandment, which supposedly has something to do with swearing. I do admit swearing is a very annoying habit. If the names of God and Jesus mean anything, one wouldn't use them in and out of season. However, the previous answer seems to miss the cue of the 2ⁿᵈ Commandment – if only because our manner of swearing hadn't been invented yet when Moses was around.

There is much more serious stuff at stake in the 2ⁿᵈ Commandment. Let me put it this way: Doesn't the Bible tell us that God made the divine Name known to us. Well, God has been introduced to us! God has divulged His deepest secret to us! God has given us the right to use His name, so He is no longer a stranger to us. God wants to associate with us. What a name that is: I am; I am the I-am; I am who I am; I am present as I am. We all know how important a name is; even when someone misspells your name, you feel personally offended. So imagine, we may call Him by His Holy Name, as if He were our partner; we are allowed to claim that God is with us – Emmanuel! We know His Name, and He knows the name of each one of us: He has written your name in the palm of His hands (Is. 49:16).

That is why we shouldn't use God's name for shallow and deceitful purposes. Don't pull God down by name. Don't cause harm to God's concern – that is, God's dedication to people and their well-being – by abusing the holy Name. Words like slander and fraud come to mind. Those are the issues that the 2ⁿᵈ Commandment is really about. As Pope Benedict XVI worded it in his book *Jesus of Nazareth* (Part I, 145), "Do I take care that God's companionship with us will draw us up into his purity and sanctity, instead of dragging him down into the filth?"

Sure enough, human history is one long-winded, miserable story of all the things we have done and not done – supposedly in God's name and with God's support, turning *our* concerns into *God*'s concerns. At one time, someone was even sentenced to death, to death on a cross – and again, it was done in God's Name. People thought these horrors were the right thing to do, in God's Name. They forgot that when Joshua drew his sword and asked God's angel, "Are you for us, or for our adversaries?" the angel answered, "Neither!" (Joshua 5:13).

And yet, we have to keep using His Name, calling upon His Name – without abusing His Name. We do have to keep praying to Him, so our relationship doesn't get damaged, or even broken, by negligence. We have a Covenant, remember?

Q: I would say we have reason now to pray, in the *Our Father*, "Hallowed be thy Name."

A: The Bible says several things about calling upon God's Name when we pray to Him.

First, by using His Name, we are permitted to be familiar with God, who is always eager to listen. God is only a prayer away. On the other hand, how rotten can such a relationship be if I look only after myself and my personal interests, if I talk without listening? What is the use of prayer if we plan to live our own lives anyway? In other words, what is the use of prayer if it doesn't change us? Prayer is meant to change *us*, not *God*. Prayer is not sending a to-do-list to God. He is not a cosmic vending machine. Imagine that you would pray for patience and demand it right now.

Second, since God confides his Holy Name to those who believe in him, the gift of a name belongs to the order of trust and intimacy. So, in our own talk and prayers, we should never use His Name except to bless, praise, and glorify Him. Therefore never abuse God's Name:

- In blasphemy: uttering against God words of hatred, reproach, and defiance (CCC 2148).
- In false oaths: calling on God to be witness to a lie (CCC 2149).

- In perjury: making a promise under oath with no intention of keeping it (CCC 2476).

The third thing about God's Name is that others should believe in God as well. The Holy Name should become known among people, for His Name is not something you keep to yourself. His stories should be passed on – which is a precarious undertaking. It is in His Name, that people go to the sick, to lepers, to the poor, and even to the ones in prison. But times are changing; nowadays, it may be even more of a concern whether God's Name will still be used at all and whether present-day people will ever have a chance to hear from others how beautiful it still is to have faith in God, to be part of His Church. "Hallowed be Thy Name" is a cry that comes from a deep hunger of the human race. It should never be silenced…

In our highly secularized society, there seems to be a new 2nd Commandment: "You shall not use the Name of God, *unless* you do so in vain." Somehow, we have lost the reverence for God's Name. His Name has become a forbidden word in many circles, politically incorrect. But even if there were no one left crying out His Name, "the very stones would cry out" (Lk. 19:40).

When God gave us His Name, He took the risk that we may abuse His Name, may neglect or even reject His Name. As a matter of fact, many people nowadays live in a vacuum that was once filled by faith in God. This has left a "God-shaped *hole*" inside of them that only God can fill – nothing else. In his *Pensées*, Pascal describes what man does with this hole: "This he tries in vain to fill with everything around him, seeking in things that are not there the help he cannot find in those that are, though none can help, since this infinite abyss can be filled only with an infinite and immutable object; in other words by God himself." And then we are back again at the 1st Commandment: You shall not have strange gods before Me, for *I am the Lord your God*. Hallowed be that Name!

Q: #3 says: *Remember to keep holy the Lord's Day.*

A: This one particular "day off" that the 3rd Commandment speaks about, this one holi-day per week, is really a great invention. It is a gift from the God of the Bible, which has been given, through Israel, to all people who didn't have a holiday at the end of a seven-day week. The Sabbath was the completion of the old creation, but for us, Christians, a new day has dawned: the day of Christ's Resurrection. The eight day begins the new creation (CCC 349 + 2174). That is the day when humanity was re-created in Jesus Christ.

It used to be that people labored seven days of the week – each day was exactly the same. There was no stopping, for "such was life." Life was laboring until death came. It was slavery for everyone. That is how most people lived their lives for centuries, not knowing any better. Living is laboring, right? For what else could it be? Until a voice said something to this effect: "One day is Mine – and I want to give this day to you too. It is meant to be a pleasant day. It is a reminder of our Covenant. On that day, you do not need to work; and what is more, on that day, I do not allow you to work, because I want you to rest, to find yourself, and to discover what I gave you. Plus, I want you to share this day with others, your personnel, your cattle." Isn't that a miracle!

Q: I don't think many people consider Sunday a gift anymore, let alone a miracle.

A: I wonder myself. Picture this fictitious scenario: One day, Congress decided to install Sunday in all schools of the US. After many years, when nobody remembers anymore who and what started all of this, people begin to wonder. May one read a book on that day? No, that's English. Take a walk? No, that's gymnastics. Do handicrafts? No, that's art. Do puzzles? No, that's math. Sunday was no longer taken as a gift. Well, this story really happened! The Gospels mention several debates concerning the Sabbath. In Christian circles, many quarrels were to follow. Protestants took their puritanical views to America, to enact rigorous "blue laws" governing conduct on Sundays. How sad!

It is actually quite strange that nowhere in the Bible are we ordered to work hard. Instead, the Bible says we should be able to *stop* working; it asks us what we have experienced from God's creation by the time we die. Did we notice God? Did we have a taste of life? We just keep running, but God tells us to stop and think. Let's give our God, ourselves, and our fellow people a moment's thought and prayer. The Catechism calls it "a day of protest against the servitude of work and the worship of money" (2172). To put it in a nutshell, being the richest person in the cemetery shouldn't be our main concern.

Q: What *should* we do on Sunday then?

A: We should rest with the Lord and thank Him for the six days of creation He gave us. The best way to do this is by celebrating the Holy Eucharist (CCC 2177), as a testimony of belonging and of being faithful to Christ and his Church (CCC 2182). In so doing, we proclaim that all there is belongs to God through Jesus. Humans do not live to work, but they work in order to enjoy the gift of life – or in Jesus' words, "The sabbath was made for man, not man for the sabbath" (Mk 2:27). Put differently, do not mingle this one holiday of the week with other weekdays.

A day of rest doesn't mean we should lie in bed, sit on the couch, or walk the golf course all day. This day off was given to all of us together, as each one of us needs such a day equally badly. That is why Sunday is also a day of service to others – to those who do not have anything to live for, those who are drowning in their work and in their worries, those who are unemployed because of social or personal circumstances, those for whom Sunday is the most difficult day of the week because they have no one, or because they have only painful memories. That is why the 3rd Commandment wants *everyone* to have a Sunday, not only you and me (CCC 2186).

Q: Is that the reason why Jesus heals the sick on this very day of rest?

A: Right! Seeing the Bible in this light, we may better understand those gospel stories in which Jesus, on the Sabbath of all days, does several things that are forbidden, or at least seem unnecessary. Luke 13:10-17, for instance, tells us that Jesus healed a woman severely stricken with rheumatism. He "happens" to heal her on the Sabbath. Couldn't Jesus have waited one more day? Why this act of provocation? Was it meant to get a rise out of the religious hairsplitters? Was it meant to show people how open-minded and broad-minded He is? Was it meant to demonstrate how *in*significant the Sabbath is?

No, none of the above! Jesus did what He did for none of these reasons. Rather, He did it out of respect for the Sabbath and for the God of the Sabbath. Here was a woman for whom it was never Sabbath; all her days were painful; all her days were drab. Jesus gave the Sabbath back to her when He healed and liberated her. At last, she could enjoy the day that everyone deserves. Finally, there was a Sun-day in her life! That is the crowning glory of God's creation.

Q: Isn't the Sabbath the core of the Jewish social order, and isn't the Sunday the core of the Christian social order?

A: In his book *Jesus of Nazareth* (Part I, 108), Pope Benedict XVI dwells extensively on this issue. He stresses that the Sabbath is indeed, for Judaism, the core of its social order. One is supposed to rest on that day, and resting means: re-forming one day a week the circle of family and household, everyone at home and in place.

But things begin to change when Jesus comes around. Pope Benedict brings to our attention that the verses immediately preceding the Sabbath narrative read as follows: "Come to me, all who labor and are heavy laden, and *I* will give you *rest*" (Mt. 11:28; italics mine). The rest that is intended here has to do with Jesus, so the Son of Man has now become Israel's Sabbath. No wonder that around 100 AD Ignatius of Antioch wrote already that Christians had given up keeping the Sabbath and now ordered their lives by the Lord's Day instead.

Does this mean that the Sabbath has lost its great social function of holding Israel together? Doesn't centering upon Jesus break open this sacred structure? In a way it does, for the community of disciples has become the *new* Israel. Wasn't it risky, one might ask, to break up Israel's sacred order for the sake of a community of disciples that is defined, as it were, solely in terms of the figure of Jesus? The answer is no, for the Church as the emerging community of disciples transferred the social function of the Sabbath to the Lord's Day. Sunday became a day of freedom and rest within a legal system that was now shaped on Christian principles. So Jesus did not abolish the social order but created a new and broader context for it. He gave the third commandment a wider meaning.

Q: #4 says: *Honor your father and your mother.*

A: This Commandment looks very straightforward – something like this: You shall not give up those parents of yours, who spent their whole life toiling for you. Although they may no longer be able to do anything and may have become useless and needless, you shall not treat them like dirt; you shall not throw them on the dumpster of life; you shall take care of them as they have taken care of you, in a godlike manner. You shall honor and value them as any human being deserves to be honored and valued, to the very end.

Not so in these days, of course, you might counter. Haven't we wrapped our folks in comfortable cotton? They have their pension plans, their social security benefits, and so on. They have their elderly homes and nursing homes. What more could they wish for? Yet, we should ask ourselves whether an honorable place is still left in our midst for them to live. Do they still feel that they are a part of everything, that they are worthwhile and have some say in what is going on? Instead, we spare them and boss them around; but that is about it.

Of course, there must be much more to this Commandment! Actually much more! Following St. Augustine, we place this Commandment on the 2nd tablet, the "love neighbor" section, whereas other traditions think it belongs on the 1st tablet – "love God." There is some profound truth to this latter position: Parents are our lifeline to God. They were (or should be) the first ones to tell us about God and about all we know about Him. The Catechism stresses this very clearly: "we should honor our parents to whom we owe life and who have handed on to us the knowledge of God" (2197). In short, the family is the *original cell of social life* [...] an initiation into life in society" (CCC 2207). Since parents are our lifeline to God, loving them is an expression of our loving God. So through them, we love the One they gave to us.

What our parents hand on to us is the rich tradition of the

Catholic Church. Tradition means literally: something we "pass or hand on." Unfortunately, our culture doesn't appreciate what has been handed on, because it is often considered second-hand. Indeed, the material things that we pass on usually deteriorate with age. But the tradition that the 4th Commandment refers to doesn't deteriorate; it is more like gold that doesn't tarnish; it is definitely first-hand – directly from God. It came to us through our parents.

Q: Are you telling me that being our lifeline with God makes our parents worthy of reverence?

A: Honoring our parents means to give them the weight they have received from God; not the weight they have given themselves! So the real issue is this: What does it mean to be a parent, as far as the Bible is concerned? Parents are the ones to pass on the sacred stories to the next generation – stories about salvation, about the Good News, stories about "things that we have heard and known, that our fathers have told us. We will not hide them from their children, but tell to the coming generation the glorious deeds of the LORD, and his might, and the wonders which he has wrought." (Ps. 78:3-4). The Catechism calls parents the "first heralds" for their children (2225).

Although this commandment is addressed expressly to children in their relationship to their father and mother, it covers in fact a much wider range: We should respect all those whom God, for our good, has vested with His authority (CCC 2197). "This commandment includes and presupposes the duties of parents, instructors, teachers, leaders, magistrates, those who govern, all who exercise authority over others or over a community of persons" (CCC 2199). But we should also stress that this is a two-way street: we owe respect to those who earn respect.

So what is essentially at stake in this Commandment is the continuation of God's cause, of God's concern for humanity. Parents and others with authority are like people on a mission; actually an important mission. Their concern is to ensure that God's history with His people continues. That is the mission the Bible talks about. Hence, we can call them God's representatives. In time, children will be representatives for the new generation. Therefore, you just cannot leave current and previous generations out; they deserve reverence, because they are part of a continuing chain. Do not think the world began with you! However, the opposite side of the coin is this: Those before you should also be *worthy* of reverence!

Q: What if our parents didn't earn respect and failed in their mission?

A: Indeed, some parents failed because they never passed on much of God's story; but fortunately, God's reliance on parents is a relative one. And then there are parents who think they failed because their children didn't accept the "tradition" they handed on to them. There may be many reasons. Sometimes, evil forces from outside the family took over. Sometimes, parents just failed to be there for their kids. At times, the black shadows of their views darkened the lives of their children. At other times, they stood in someone else's way. Didn't they pass on the Original Sin to us? And yet, they tried to make sure the Good News had a sequel. You may not be able to *respect* your parents, but you are asked to *honor* them by loving them, even though they may have failed.

That is also the reason why the Church of all ages established All Saints' Day and All Souls' Day, on which all those gone before us – our parents and ancestors who contributed to our lives, all the faithful throughout history, saintly or not – are commemorated. We commemorate them because God had called them to pass on the stories about divine greatness. We are connected with them. We commemorate them because God carried them, as God carries us. We commemorate them with love, reverence, clemency, and gratefulness. Many of them deserve to be our role models, because they did earn our respect.

Q: The Fourth Commandment may have been the backbone of Jewish social life, but didn't it lose its importance for Christians?

A: In his book *Jesus of Nazareth* (Part I, 113), Pope Benedict XVI dwells extensively on this issue. He stresses that this Commandment does strengthen the relationship between generations and the community of the family as an order both willed and protected by God. It glorifies the cohesion of the family tree, if you will.

However, it is also this very connection between the land, as the place for the people to live, and the basic order of the family that Jesus calls into question. When Jesus is told that His mother and brothers are waiting outside, He questions who His mother and brothers are and declares that anyone who does the will of His Father in heaven is His brother, sister, and mother (Mt. 12: 46-50). By doing so, Jesus definitely affects the entire scope of the social structure of the people of Israel, for from now on it is the community of disciples that forms the origin and center of the new Israel.

But isn't this the dissolution of the family? Was it right to set aside the social order of the "eternal Israel"? Yes it was, for Israel no longer exists simply for itself but as a light for all the nations. Jesus has brought this universality to *all* nations over and above the bonds of descent according to the flesh. The vehicle of this universalization is a new family in communion with Jesus. Pope Benedict calls this "a yes to the fourth commandment on a new level, the highest level. It is entry into the family of those who call God Father." It is this new family that will soon be called Church. So Jesus did not abolish the family but created a new and broader context for it. He gave the fourth commandment a deeper, more universal meaning.

Q: #5 says: *You shall not kill.*

A: Even those who do not know what to make of the Ten Commandments assume there is one clear and obvious rule: You shall not murder. It seems to be an evident rule. But is it really?

In the Bible, murder and manslaughter are more than knocking someone's brains out. Murder can actually happen much sooner – at the moment one doesn't acknowledge that someone else is equally worthwhile. When Cain shouted "Am I my brother's keeper?" (Gen. 4:9), the Bible responds very clearly: "Yes, you are! What else would you be?" Essentially, that is the point at issue in the 5th Commandment. Because we all have one Father in Heaven, we *all* are His children on earth and are equally worthwhile. That is the very basis of the principle of human dignity. Once we step out of the closed circle of "I" and surrender ourselves to communion with the other children of God, we truly become "children of God."

Jesus of Nazareth was the incarnation of this "rule of life." Life was always flowing from Him. To the hungry, He was bread; to the sick, health; to the enslaved, liberation; to the convicted, forgiveness; to the downtrodden, justice. God's NO to manslaughter is not some kind of law designed to protect the abstract entity "life." Saying NO to manslaughter is God's way of saying YES to tangible people. We can never say kill all Jews, all Blacks, or all Christians, as each one of them is as much a child of God as we are. "Hatred of the neighbor is a sin when one deliberately wishes him evil" (CCC 2303). Instead, "To love is to will the good of another" (CCC 1766) – which is certainly more than not killing another.

Q: You seem to be expressing very clearly that this commandment means saying YES to *everyone*.

A: Taking the words "You shall not murder" seriously means we have no good word to say about someone's inconsiderate attitude toward any form of human life – no matter whether abortion, euthanasia, reckless driving, or the arms race is the issue. The growing aggression against life around us is horrible. Having an abortion when one pleases is horrible. The feeling that people should be discarded once they are regarded as past hope is horrible. The use of weapons in Northern Ireland, in the Sudan, and in any "holy war" is horrible.

This world of ours has become murderous – it is becoming more and more people-unfriendly, less and less loving. Radio, TV, and newspapers keep bombarding us with violations of the 5th Commandment. We are exposed to such news for "24/7." The lives of individual human beings seem to have lost their value. All these horrible news reports and TV images have almost made us tone-death and eye-blinded for the reality behind murders and killings. They make it sound and look like these things come with human nature. They make us forget that we have the moral duty to obey the 5th Commandment – but we also have the freedom to reject it. Being in the image of God, you and I possess "the dignity of a person, who is not just something, but someone" (CCC 357).

I admit hospitals do fight an admirable battle for a patient's life; just think of the transplantations performed, the expensive devices applied, the number of doctors standing at the same bed! On the other hand, there are millions killed by abortion, euthanasia, traffic accidents, road-rage, famine, poverty, and war. Is life still worth living? Would there be any sanctuary left if even the womb of a pregnant mother is no longer a safe hiding place? Life was given to us by God; we cannot just take it away or refuse it. The message of peace cannot be spread by the sword.

Does this mean killing is never legitimate? Although there are no exceptions to the prohibition of murder, sometimes murder can have a double effect: the preservation of one's own life and the killing of the aggressor – one intended, the other not (CCC 2263). Therefore, *self-defense* is legitimate "since one is bound to take more care of one's own life than of another's" according to St. Thomas Aquinas. This even holds for governments, as they have "the right of lawful self-defense, once all peace efforts have failed" (CCC 2308).

Q: What about doctor-assisted suicide? Isn't that a good kind of killing, done out of mercy?

A: Isn't it amazing how some people manage to "massage" their language with a misleading and seductive terminology. "Suicide" becomes "aid in dying" and "doctor-assisted" is supposed to stand for "with merciful medical compassion." Suddenly, assisted suicide is considered no longer as a form of killing. How deceptive words can be! Even the term "eu-thanasia" is part of a misleading vocabulary, for there is nothing "good" (*eu-*) about this kind of death. Why not?

First of all, doctor-*assisted* suicide is in fact doctor-*prescribed* death. It actually compromises the age-old practice of medicine. The Hippocratic Oath has guided physicians for more than two thousand years with the words "I will not give a lethal drug to anyone if I am asked, nor will I advise such a plan." The refusal to assist in *killing* is part of an ancient moral code – for killing it is.

Abandoning this code takes us on a slippery moral slope. Doctors in in my home country of the Netherlands once limited euthanasia to terminally ill patients; now they provide lethal drugs to people with chronic illnesses, disabilities, mental illnesses, and even depression. It is death on request, and someday perhaps on command...

Second, we can never really help people by killing them. We are called to comfort the sick, not to help them take their own lives. Our society will be judged by how we treat those who are ill or disabled. They need our care and protection, not our lethal drugs. As Christians, we should be imitators of Christ, who stretches out His hand in compassion toward the sick and disabled. We should certainly not give them the feeling that they will be better served by being dead – that would be a dubious premise indeed!

Third, any kind of suicide is a violation of the 5th Commandment. The Catechism (2280-2281) says, "Everyone is responsible for his life before God who has given it to him. It is God who remains the sovereign Master of life. [...] We are stewards, not owners, of the life God has entrusted to us. It is not ours to dispose of. Suicide contradicts the natural inclination of the human being to preserve and perpetuate his life. It is gravely contrary to the just love of self." So the bottom-line remains: You shall not kill.

Q: #6 says: *You shall not commit adultery.*

A: In the 6th Commandment, marriage is the issue – not only marriage, but actually the entire gamut of sexual morality. Marriage isn't easy. No matter how much we love our spouses, we will have our differences. They may be as minor as where to squeeze the toothpaste or as serious as having different religious convictions. Marriage isn't easy and has never been easy, but times have changed. Since made easier by civil law, the number of divorces has been increasing. It used to be rather common for parents to have four or more children; nowadays it is rather common for children to have four or more parents.

That makes me appreciate even more what this older, long-married man used to say to people he introduced his wife to: "Did you ever meet my first wife?" She was and ever would be his first and last wife. How true, there is nothing more nourishing than love.

No wonder the Gospel is a love story, in which everything revolves around love. Nothing else shows the beauty of a human being so clearly and gives meaning to life so deeply as love does. God who created us out of love also calls us to love – the fundamental and innate vocation of every human being (CCC 1604).

However, love is a two way street. On the one hand, it means "Someone is there for you." On the other hand, it also means "You are there for someone else." The very essence of love demands that we give it away, for love cannot exist in the same space as possessiveness and selfishness.

Q: Yet nothing is more precarious than love.

A: Indeed, this very same love – or is it lust? – makes people leave their families and neglect their duties. Love can create the deepest problems and practically incurable wounds when it is refused, trampled upon, or just not returned. Love is like a beautiful river that turns into a menacing torrent once it exceeds its bounds. Yet, this very love urges people to make one of the most important decisions in life: the decision to marry, to take another's side for good, to share every part of life from now on with someone else. In fact, love is the only valid reason to do so. Otherwise, having the other person always around will gradually become more and more of a nuisance.

The Church makes it very clear that the husband and wife are the ministers of the sacrament of marriage to each other. The ceremony itself does not bring about a sacrament, but the full and free consent of a man and a woman; the priest is only the official witness. However, if the gift of self is not given, no sacrament takes place. That is the reason why a marriage can be annulled. An annulment does not destroy the indissoluble bond of marriage, but that bond may have never taken place if, at the time of the vows, there was something either present or absent that made the consent invalid.

What a valuable gift this sacramental bond can be! What a valuable gift it is to have someone beside you, in good days and bad! Didn't Genesis 2:18 say about Adam, "I will make him a helper fit for him"? A more accurate translation would be: "I will make him a helper, his opposite." Both a helper and an opposite, in one person! A person who gives you an answer and makes you answer. It is always a two-way street! Love is not meant to be kept to oneself, but has to be given away.

Q: How do we make such a marriage work?

A: Obviously, the Bible doesn't offer us recipes as to how to make a marriage successful. The Bible has only one story to tell, not in one or some of its sections, but in all of them, from Genesis 1 to Revelation 21. It is the story about the covenant between God and God's people. A covenant is like a marriage, according to the Bible. Indeed, a marriage is a reflection of the Great Covenant between God and us. It is a covenant between two people who have accepted the call to give to each other the gift that God gives to all human beings – happiness, nurture, and support. "God himself is the author of marriage" (CCC 1603).

If that is the case, the word *love* is no longer sufficient in itself; another word is needed, namely the word *fidelity*. These two words mark the covenant. However, fidelity means more than what we usually think it does; it expresses constancy in keeping one's given word (CCC 2365). Most people believe in the idea of a "soul mate," someone who is always there for them, ready to meet their every need. But many forget there is another side: They should also be there for their soul mate as well – not "as long as we both shall *love*" but "as long as we both shall *live*." Fidelity is a gift, not a choice. God allows infidelity but wills fidelity.

All of this is closely connected to *chastity*. The Catechism explains that "Chastity means the successful integration of sexuality within the person and thus the inner unity of man in his bodily and spiritual being" (2337). It tolerates neither a double life nor duplicity in speech. It matures through self-mastery, which is a form of training in human freedom by ridding oneself of all slavery to unruly passions (CCC 2339). Make no mistake, chastity applies to each and every human being, whether a spouse, a widow, or a virgin.

Q: Can anything break a covenant of fidelity?

A: Many things can cause a breach of this covenant. First of all, there are many ways one can commit an offense against chastity. The Catechism mentions several: lust, masturbation, fornication, pornography, prostitution, and rape (2351-2356).

Then there are seemingly minor things, although they can have life-lasting effects. Attachment to our jobs or our hobbies is one of them, as are our ingrained opinions, our unwillingness to listen to that other person, our persistent selfishness, our apathy and lethargy when our marriage needs work. The list could go on and on: exploiting one another, letting one another wither, tearing one another's heart out, tying up one another, overlooking one another. These are the silent kinds of infidelity, which may last throughout a marriage. They make for a marriage that is everything but a covenant. That is where the 6th Commandment calls us to order.

But I also need to mention that we tend to put so much emphasis on being married that singles might get the impression they are not quite normal, that they are only half a person. Do singles have any place left to go to, or any person left to call on, without the risk of being merely endured? I believe we should just say out loud that marriage is not the only way to function as a human being. It is better to refuse a marriage than to enter a bad one. Besides, there are so many other ways to be "productive." The Church has a high esteem for all those celibates in priesthood and religious life, and all those singles, widows, and widowers in regular life; they have so many immaterial goods to offer to humanity, and to the Church in particular. Just think of those who forgo marriage in order to care for their parents or brothers or sisters, to give themselves more completely to a profession, or to serve other honorable ends; they "can contribute greatly to the good of the human family" (CCC 2231).

Q: #7 says: *You shall not steal.*

A: I admit that hearing about armored trucks and ingenious tricks to break into bank safes makes for fascinating stories. However, stealing may be annoying, especially when we ourselves are the targets, but it is usually not all that dramatic. It is only about money, made of paper or metal. Even the Bible doesn't make much of a fuss about such kind of stealing. Somehow offenses involving someone else's property are not taken too seriously in the Bible. There is no question of cutting off hands as punishment, as is still done in some societies. According to the Bible, all one is expected to do, in cases like these, is to pay compensation, albeit manifold (Ex. 22:1-4). Although we do have property rights (CCC 2401), it is apparently not true that our properties are utterly inviolable. Jesus blesses Zacchaeus for his pledge: "if I have defrauded any one of anything, I restore it fourfold" (Lk. 19:8).

Let us be clear, though, that there is nothing wrong with having property or even being wealthy either. St. Francis de Sales used to make a big difference between having poison and being poisoned. Pharmacists, for instance, deal with lots of poison without being poisoned themselves – as long as the poison is in their stores, not their bodies. The same with wealth: If you have wealth, make sure it is in your wallet and home, not in your heart. What we possess shouldn't possess us.

But there is another dimension to the 7th Commandment. The Catechism places it in a much wider and more proper context: "The right to private property, acquired by work or received from others by inheritance or gift, does not do away with the original gift of the earth to the whole of mankind" (2403). Apparently, there is more at stake here than protecting our properties from violation by others.

Q: This seems to imply that we shouldn't steal from the whole of mankind, right?

A: The answer to your question lies in the well-known story about that well-known person called Adam, the "gardener" in the Garden of Eden. That story is still being enacted today: This earth belongs to God; therefore, everything belongs to us together; what we have has been given to us as stewards; we should use it the way God has intended us to use it. The person who claims to be the boss, who keeps everything for himself or herself, is actually taking things away from God's purpose, keeping them away from God.

Such a person is breaking away from God, refusing to be under God. Such a person is said to be a thief. In *Fiddler on the Roof*, this thought was used for a great joke: If the rich who do not want to die could hire the poor to do so for them, the poor could make a nice living. Well put...

Now, I should be able to rephrase the 7th Commandment as follows: "You shall not steal" means "You shall not keep everything for yourself, but give each person what is badly needed, so that all people can make a living on God's earth." It shouldn't surprise us that the Catholic Church has always been very involved with charity in its double sense – "love to our neighbor" and "aid to our neighbor." Whereas thieves seem to think "what's yours is mine," Christians tend to reverse things: "What's mine is also yours."

Interestingly enough, Jesus doesn't pray in the Our Father for bread in the singular – give *me* my daily bread today – but in the plural: "Give *us* this day our daily bread." We pray for *our* bread – and that means we also pray for bread for others. From this comes the social teaching of the Church on "superfluous goods," those things of which there is more than is needed for our personal welfare. The seventh Commandment does require respect for the right to private property (CCC 2401), and yet a person is not entirely free with regard to his or her personal possessions. At a certain stage of ownership, we lose the right to property even with regard to things which are unquestionably ours. Once a priest was visiting a rich factory owner who was known to have exploited her workers; he opened one of her cupboards and cried, "Everything here is crying out for its rightful owner."

Q: But aren't there also more hidden forms of stealing, especially in our modern society?

A: You are probably referring to the many forms corruption has taken on in this world of ours. We hear about pinching at schools, manipulating declarations, defrauding the tax system, faking damage claims, abusing welfare, withholding lost items, lifting company goods, and swindling others. Actions like these seem to have become utterly normal. Isn't everyone involved in these "mild" kinds of stealing? Aren't these just "light" offenses of the 7th Commandment?

Saint Augustine warns us: "If you take them for light when you weigh them, tremble when you count them." Suddenly, we find ourselves on a very slippery slope. When it comes to making money and making a profit, how does one manage to remain a person of integrity, living in a world of greed? As St. Thomas More showed us, integrity is for *all* seasons – not something to put on or take off when the desire suits us.

At times, though, one wonders whether one looks like an idiot when trying to be honest. There's no doubt, the dollar knows no bounds. Money has become the end to justify any means. But nothing corrupts more than money; it is an idol without equal. The Worship of Money, Mammon, is the only religion that doesn't have to cope with apostasy. Not only is money called the root of all evil, but credit cards are next, as some consider them the devil's vehicle to the End Times. More than ever do we need the 7th Commandment, for being the richest person in the cemetery shouldn't be our main concern!

Therefore, it shouldn't surprise us that the 7th Commandment refers not only to material properties but also the people behind them. It requires respect for persons *and* their goods. Therefore, it also forbids acts that lead "to the *enslavement of human beings, to their being bought, sold and exchanged like merchandise, in disregard for their personal dignity*" (CCC 2414). Do not think slavery is something from the past. A modern-day form of slavery is human trafficking – the illegal and immoral trade of human beings for the purposes of reproductive slavery, commercial sexual exploitation, or forced labor. It shows us again how timeless the 7th Commandment is.

Q: #8 says: *You shall not bear false witness against your neighbor.*

A: The 8th Commandment touches on issues that are much more exciting than always telling the truth. It says: "You shall not give false testimony against your neighbor." A more literal translation would be: "Regarding your neighbor, you shall not respond as a false witness."

The central question is this: Do we realize that someone's honor, well-being, and happiness may depend on what we say, or fail to say? Do we realize that our words have the power to make or break one another? It does not matter how and where we hurt others with our words – whether we do so behind someone's back or right in their face; in court, in the family room, at work; in the newspaper, on radio, or on TV. That it does happen is enough in itself, and in violation of the 8th Commandment.

The damage inflicted by malicious words can be as painful and as long-lasting as any physical wound. The victims usually cannot even combat a nasty lie; the louder they protest, the more people are likely to believe the falsehood. The only thing that may help them is to remember that actions speak louder than words, especially false words.

In his letter, St. James puts it very harshly (3:5-6): The tongue is a small part of the body, yet the most dangerous. We seem to be able to discipline every part of our bodies, but what about our tongues? We use the tongue to praise the Lord, and we use the same tongue to curse the people created after God's image. The tongue is like a two-edged sword.

Q: Amazing what such a tiny organ like the tongue can do...

A: Although it is a tiny organ, it is proportionately the strongest muscle of the body. Isn't it disgusting to see how this tiny but strong organ can be used, in secret and in public, for gossiping, twisting the truth, for nonsense talk and empty talk, for hollow phrases and false rumors, for vicious gossip and black lies, for shallow opinions about others, for commercials and propaganda? It is a cascade of words, hollow words, dangerous words... We hear lies all day – on radio and TV, on the internet, you name it. I always worry about our new generation: When you grow up listening to lie after lie in commercials and broadcasting, twenty-four-seven, you must think this world revolves around lies and half-truths. Bombarded with lies, we do not know anymore what truth is like; sadly enough, truth has become a relative and pliable commodity.

One single lie, or even a half-truth, can ruin someone else's life forever: Think of a politician who is being *falsely* accused of sexually harassing a staff member, or a Priest who is being *falsely* accused of touching a minor. Sometimes it is done out of revenge or hate, sometimes for political reasons, sometimes out of self-interest. Whether it is true or not, the harm has been done and the blemish will never leave the victims. St. Aquinas put it well: "Men could not live with one another if there were not mutual confidence that they were being truthful to one another. [...] one man owes it to another to manifest the truth." No wonder, Jesus teaches us the unconditional love of truth: "Let what you say be simply 'Yes' or 'No'; anything more than this comes from evil" (Mt. 5:37).

Q: Does this mean we *always* have to tell the truth?

A: Some people take great pride in always "talking straight from the hip," or "calling a spade a spade," or "saying things to someone's face" – even to someone on a death bed. They want the real truth, nothing but the truth, the bare truth, the cold truth – in plain terms, that is. Is that really the message of the 8th Commandment? Not really. Has anyone given us the right to always say the truth to someone else's face? Who is being served by our words – that is the fundamental question.

In other words, the right to hear the truth and the duty to tell the truth are not unconditional. The Gospel precept of fraternal love requires us in concrete situations to judge whether or not it is appropriate to reveal the truth to someone who asks for it (CCC 2488). The Catechism uses here the term "discreet language," because "No one is bound to reveal the truth to someone who does not have the right to know it (CCC 2489).

The Greek word for truth is *aletheia*, which means disclosure and exposure. The Hebrew word for truth, however, is *emeth*, which means fidelity, reliability, and respect. What a world of difference between these two words! The 8th Commandment is not about *aletheia* but about *emeth*. There are times when "the truth" – whatever that may be – should not be disclosed, because fidelity or respect is at stake. The real truth can resound only in love; otherwise it makes a false sound. "Speak your mind" is not a biblical motto; "Love one another" is what the Bible wants us to do instead.

Q: Sometimes, a lie can be well-intentioned, though. The famous example is "the Gestapo at your door," asking you whether you are hiding Jews. Or the people who exposed the actions of Planned Parenthood by falsely portraying themselves as being in need of help.

A: You seem to have the Bible at your side when it comes to well-intentioned lies. Abraham, for instance, lies when he tells people that Sarah is his sister (Gen. 20:1). Jacob lies when he tells his father that he is Esau (Gen. 27:19). The Egyptian midwives, when asked by Pharaoh to kill the Hebrew boys on the delivery table, lie when they tell Pharaoh that Hebrew mothers are more vigorous than Egyptian women and will give birth before the midwives arrive (Ex. 1:15-19). Moses lies when he tells Pharaoh that he intends merely to celebrate a festival to honor the Lord of Israel in the desert (Ex. 5:1). Rahab has to lie while keeping the Israelite spies hidden (Josh. 6:17). Samuel lies when he announces that he is going to Bethlehem to make a sacrifice, instead of to anoint David king (1 Sam. 16). Jonathan lies when he tells his father that David is absent because of a family celebration (1 Sam. 20:6; 20:28). St. Paul lies, or at least tells a half-truth, when he tells the Sanhedrin that he is standing trial because of his hope in the resurrection of the dead (Acts 23:6). All these "lies" seem to be well-intentioned lies. Shouldn't we be proud of those priests in the Vatican, I might add, who gave false passports to Jews during W.W. II?

Nevertheless, I still wonder whether one should lie in these cases by intentionally leading someone else into error, by thinking that good may come out of something intrinsically bad. The fact that lies are reported in the Bible doesn't mean they are sanctioned by the Bible; the Bible contains actually a lengthy record of sinful acts, which doesn't mean they received approval. You may not have the duty to tell the *truth*, but that doesn't give you the right to tell a *lie*. Once we allow bad things "for the greater good," every lie can be legitimized as a "truth." But the day will come when that lie catches up on us. Mark Twain put this in very practical terms, "Tell the truth. Then you do not have to remember what you said." In other words, do not lie but make sure that your hiding place for Jews is well hidden. You shouldn't lie, but you may have to withhold the truth from people who have no right to hear the truth. Withholding the truth is very different from distorting the truth.

This is the radical interpretation of the Ten Commandments in Christianity, fully in line with Jesus' instruction "Let what you say be simply 'Yes' or 'No'" (Mt. 5:37). Both St. Augustine and St. Thomas Aquinas further elaborated this radical interpretation. The Catechism says it very harshly, lying is "speaking a falsehood with the intention of deceiving" (2482) and it is "the most direct offense against the truth" (2483). If we do lie, we in fact take the side of Satan, who is the "father of all lies." Is lying a *crime*? Sometimes it is, but that is a legal issue. Is lying a *sin*? Always, but that is a moral issue. No wonder, the Catechism considers lying destructive to society by undermining trust among people and tearing apart the fabric of social relationships (2486). There is no way around it, although there may still be room left for so-called half-truths, because someone may not have the right to hear the whole truth.

This brings us to another aspect of not telling the truth. Sometimes, even withholding the truth does amount to a lie. We are called by God to be witnesses to the truth. When we fail to defend people whom we know with the good things we know about them, we are, in fact, betraying them. In the same vein, when we fail to defend our deep convictions and our dearly held beliefs, we are, in fact, denying what we believe in, which may be a direct offense toward God. Martyrs actually died for not withholding the truth, but instead spreading the truth (CCC 2473). So to keep silent is sometimes, in effect, to live a lie.

Q: #9 says: *You shall not covet your neighbor's wife.*

A: St. Augustine split the last Commandment of Exodus 20 into two separate Commandments, as it is done in Deuteronomy 5. First of all, he didn't want to place the neighbor's *spouse* on the same line as the neighbor's *goods* – a spouse is not a property! Second, Augustine knew how destructive sexuality can be, so he made sure there is a 9th Commandment, separate from the 10th. Perhaps, this gave the Catholic Church the blemish of being mostly – or even only – focused on *sexual* sins. As a kid, I knew of a priest whose sermons dealt mainly with the 6th and the 9th Commandments; he seemed "obsessed" by these two, so we called him "six by nine."

Isn't it rather common to stress certain Commandments, while turning a blind eye to others! Yet they all deserve equal attention and observation, for violation of any of the Ten Commandments disrupts our relationship with God. Nonetheless, each era may tend to focus on those issues society happens to be blind for at that particular time. Once it was murder, later sexuality, and perhaps today the value of life again.

Nowadays, the society we live in seems to be more than ever obsessed with sexuality, or rather sex. It is the main ingredient of books, magazines, TV shows, movies, and the internet. We get bombarded with pornography – the explicit portrayal of sexuality for the purposes of sexual arousal and erotic satisfaction. A multi-billion dollar pornography industry pours garbage into our homes every day through the Web and other media. Not only is it highly addictive, but it also detaches the body from the soul and thus poisons the human heart, imagination, and soul. It distorts the image of sexuality and demeans the person, whether it is a man, a woman, or a child, by making them pure objects of lust and pleasure. It changes sex into a deity that wants to be idolized – in defiance of the 1st Commandment besides. The Catechism describes it as "removing real or simulated sexual acts from the intimacy of the partners, in order to display them deliberately to third parties" (2354).

Archbishop Charles Chaput of Philadelphia worded it this way: "Pornography is never 'innocent entertainment,' no matter how private it might seem. It turns human beings into objects. It coarsens our appetites. It darkens our ability to see real human beauty. It creates impossible expectations about sexual intimacy. It kills enduring romance and friendship between the sexes. And ultimately it is a lie and a cheat. Pornography is a cheap, quick, empty copy of the real thing — the real joy of sexual intimacy shared by a man and woman who have joined their lives in a loving marriage. [...] Pornography is poison. It should be controlled like any other toxic waste."

Q: But don't we all have sexual feelings?

A: Since Sigmund Freud, we know how strong our sexual feelings can be; Freud didn't really discover them but probably strengthened them. As a consequence, we have become a culture ruled by Viagra, pornography, sexual abuse, and rape. They call this nicely the "sexual revolution," but it is time for a counterrevolution based on the 9th Commandment. We need to confirm once again that sex belongs to the domain of marriage, monogamy, and fidelity; that sex is for life, not just for fun; that the taming of the sex drive and harnessing it to the family are a necessary condition for social stability and long-term human happiness.

What we need is sexual virtue again. The one word for sexual virtue is *chastity*. It doesn't mean abstinence of sexual intercourse but it includes it. It means *purity*: pure sex, right sex, not twisted sex. Since we are often tempted to kinky sex, chastity requires self-control, self-mastery. The heart is the seat where our feelings and acts originate: "For out of the heart come evil thoughts, murder, adultery, fornication, theft, false witness, slander." (Mt. 15:19). We need to become masters of our feelings and emotions again.

The Catechism calls this "The Battle for Purity" (2520). Purity of heart brings freedom from widespread eroticism and avoids entertainment inclined to voyeurism and illusion (2525). It is based on *modesty*, which guides how one looks at others and behaves toward them in conformity with the dignity of persons and their solidarity (2521); it protects the mystery of persons and their love (2522). Each one of us has to fight this battle for purity, and hopefully win. When the Catechism speaks of *passions*, it says that they are neither good nor evil, but they are "morally good when they contribute to a good action, evil in the opposite case" (1768). Sexuality is one of those passions; it needs to be curbed by rationality and morality. That is our decision!

Q: Purity of heart would probably also make a good remedy against divorce.

A: True, very often the reason for a divorce is not located inside the marriage but inside the person – the lust of the flesh, the lust of the eyes, which leads to coveting a neighbor's spouse and thus disrupting and harming at least *two* marriages and *two* families. Lust is disordered desire for sexual pleasure, when it is sought for itself, isolated from its natural purposes inside the marriage. Societies have survived with very bad political systems and very bad economies, but not without strong families.

Families are to society what cells are to a body. The family is the only place where most of us learn life's most important lesson: unselfish love and lifelong commitment, chastity and self-control, purity and modesty. None of these are inborn; they must be taught and nurtured! Young people in particular need to learn sexual responsibilities – a lesson that starts at home. Not only should they learn to say NO to drugs, but also NO to sex. The so-called "sexual revolution" has only led to growing numbers of children who are sexually abused and of women who are beaten, abandoned, or raped by men who do not want to hear about self-control. That is when the 9th Commandment resonates: Do not covet anyone.

Q: #10 says: *You shall not covet your neighbor's goods.*

A: Like the 9th Commandment, the 10th one also seems to deal with things residing *inside* of us: Again it says you shall not *covet*. Well, coveting has something to do with your heart, doesn't it? We can keep our hands off and we can swallow our words, but a covetous heart is much harder to control. Envy comes upon you, whether you like it or not. It makes you desire to have what some other person has, or possibly more. Envy can poison you inside, by spoiling your enjoyment of what you do have at home, including a loving spouse. Who isn't familiar with such feelings? Can we really curb or stop them, as we can stop ourselves from killing, stealing, and lying?

Yet, the 10th Commandment refers more to our doings than to our feelings; at least it refers to what we *do* with our feelings. Loving is something we do with our hands, so to speak. It is not an emotion word but an action word. The same thing applies to coveting; coveting is something we do with our hands. Of course, what we do relates to what we feel, and that what we do with our hands reveals what we feel in our hearts. Just as the 9th Commandment added an *internal* dimension to the 6th (on adultery), the 10th Commandment adds internal depth to the 7th (on stealing).

Do not take this the wrong way. Nowhere has the Bible ever banned desire for things we do not yet have – a good house, a nice job, good friends, things that make life pleasant, and money to spend on fun things. Desire is an important drive; we work to achieve our desires. God wants to be part of the nice things in life as well as the more serious and profound aspects of life.

Coveting, on the other hand, means that you have set your heart on what belongs to someone else. Never shall you put your hands on it. Those who covet what someone else owns become ugly as sin, both on the inside and the outside. Complete households can get ruined. Intrigues become part of the life-threatening race to keep up with others or to get ahead of them, by fighting one's way up and letting no one stand in one's way. It is a rat race, a satanic drive. Of course, this causes accidents and may even cost lives!

Q: This shows again that change must come first from *within* – not from politics.

A: How true: "there is nothing outside a man which by going into him can defile him; but the things which come out of a man are what defile him" (Mk. 7:15). Once we are set free from the tiring need to look with jealousy at the things others possess, we can begin a new life. Others do perhaps possess a little more, or even much more, than we do – but so what! Their possessions may do them good. "Rejoice in your brother's progress" says St. John Chrysostom. My own calling and my own chances are enough to handle. It would be a "sin" to miss out on all I do have.

What the 10th Commandment forbids instead is greed, envy, and materialism; it doesn't want us to be possessed by possessions. How true it is that he who loves money never has money enough (CCC 2536). Envy can lead to the worst crimes. St. Augustine considered envy "*the* diabolical sin," for "through the devil's envy death entered the world" (Wis. 2:24).

In contrast, the 10th Commandment teaches us to be grateful for our own lives and to be pleased that someone else has different circumstances and may actually have a few more or even many more possessions. Let's live our own lives, as unique individuals, as people of God. After all, it is not a question of the things we *own* but of the persons we *are*. As St. Augustine says, "The more one loves, the less one covets."

Q: We seem to be coming to an end...

A: Not yet. I want to stress once more that the Ten Words are a life-saving beacon in our lives and in our societies. They contain the moral values that should guide and shape our moral evaluations. But often they don't. The Commandments often go against what the surrounding culture prescribes. The prohibition of polygamy is as countercultural in Africa as the prohibition of divorce is in America. As G.K. Chesterton put it, "I don't need a church to tell me I am wrong where I already know I'm wrong; I need a Church to tell me I am wrong where I think I'm right." Sometimes we know so much that isn't so.

Why do we need Ten Commandments? God gave us commandments that we should obey. But we cannot obey the moral laws of nature the way we obey other laws of nature, such as the law of gravity. Natural laws you cannot help but obey, but moral laws you can ignore if you want to. Morality is not anchored in your genes, but is guided by your conscience. We do need such rules because God, according to St. Augustine, *"wrote on the tables of law what men did not read in their hearts."* Since we are not moral by nature, morality has to be taught and nurtured, above all by the Scriptures and the teaching authority of the Church.

And yet, we don't need rules, only love. St. Paul explains it as follows: Commandments are needed for those who break the law, not for those who keep it. That same St. Augustine we quoted already several times had this famous motto "Love God and [then] do what you will." If I love someone, then I shall quite certainly never steal anything from them or say bad things about them. In other words, if you truly love God and His will, then doing what you will, will, in fact, be doing what God wills. But the grand question is: Do we have that love already? Perhaps the Commandments will help us to come closer to that love, closer to

God's Heart. God's prescription for happiness is definitely "two tablets a day."

So what happens when we sin against God's Law? All those who violate any of the Ten Commandments – no matter which one – disrupt their relationship with God. Is that forever? For Catholics, there is no "forever," as long as there is a Sacrament of Confession. When G.K. Chesterton was asked "Why did you join the Church of Rome?" he answered that question in his autobiography as follows: "'To get rid of my sins.' For there is no other religious system that does really profess to get rid of people's sins." How right he was; the Catholic Church is unquestionably a "hospital for sinners."

9

How Evil Is Suffering?

Our Tears Are God's Tears

The problem can be stated very simply: How does an all-powerful God get away with the evil in the world? If God is not able to take evil away, God cannot be all-powerful. And how does an all-powerful God deal with human freedom? If God is almighty, human beings must be powerless....

In this chapter, we will find out how the Catholic Church deals with this dilemma. If suffering came through sin, it is evil. Like Jesus, we have to fight evil with all we have, including medical care. But we also have to battle the way we perceive suffering. Like Jesus, we may discover there is redemptive power in carrying our cross. Through the Cross on Golgotha, Christians have come to see God's human face: an afflicted and crucified God, who does not cause our afflictions, nor does He sanction them, but He makes our tears His tears.

Jesus came, not to abolish, but to sanctify suffering with His presence. Even in suffering – or particularly in suffering – we can find the Glory of God. But there is a long road in between. Let's find out how we can get to God's answer.

Q: I don't think there is a bigger problem for religion than the problem of suffering and evil. How can religion ever come to terms with this immense problem?

A: You have the entire history of the Judeo-Christian tradition standing right behind you. The Bible starts with the problem of evil in the Book of Genesis and it ends with the problem of evil in the Book of Revelation; then there is the Book of Job which focuses entirely on the problem of suffering; and so does the New Testament. There is no institution more concerned with understanding suffering, its causes, meaning and significance, and how it can be remedied, than religion – and Christianity in particular.

All through the ages, people have blamed Heaven for suffering and evil in the world, have even lost their faith because of this, wondering why God has become their enemy. No wonder the Catechism puts it this way: "The world we live in often seems very far from the one promised us by faith. Our experiences of evil and suffering, injustice and death seem to contradict the Good News" (CCC 164).

Q: Why is suffering such a problem for religion?

A: The reason for this is pretty simple when you look from a logical perspective: If God is so good, why is His world so bad? If an all-good, all-wise, all-loving, all-just, and all-powerful God is running the show, why does He seem to be doing such a miserable job of it? Religion – and Christianity in particular – is obligated to address these crucial questions.

Then we have the problem that afflictions are so *unpredictably* distributed: They strike the just as well as the unjust, believers as well as unbelievers, the good and the bad alike. There is no pattern! We all seem to have the same chances to be stricken by evil and suffering; no one is exempt; one's religion doesn't seem to make a difference.

In addition, we have the problem that afflictions are so *unequally* distributed: Some people have to stomach so much more than others; some receive one blow after another, whereas others are apportioned poorly. At times, you meet people who remain erect in the hurricane of misery; then again, you come across people who lament endlessly about trifles. We were created equal, but surely not as far as misery is concerned.

Anyone eager to build a system explaining all of this will eventually be buried under a collapsing house of cards. Nothing fits, nothing makes sense. And yet, religion is the only place where we could search for an answer.

Q: Isn't religion per definition disqualified to give us an answer? It tells us there is an all-good and all-powerful God, and yet we live in a world of evil and suffering. How does an all-powerful God get away with the evil in the world? If God is not able to take evil away, God cannot be all-powerful. And how does an all-powerful God deal with human freedom? If God is almighty, human beings must be powerless…

A: Let me start with the last part of your question first: How can there be human freedom if God is all-powerful? This is indeed a very serious question; it basically turned the French philosopher Jean-Paul Sartre into a zealous atheist. He saw a clear dilemma here and worded it in the following way: An almighty God doesn't leave room for free human beings, whereas free human beings do not leave room for an almighty God. In this dilemma, God and Man seem to be in a power battle. Sartre opted in favor of human freedom over divine omnipotence, and thus became an atheist. The poor man felt he had no other choice.

I would say instead that there *is* a way out. Sartre's dilemma puts God and Man on the same level, but they are not! God is not one of the persons among other persons, just as He is not a cause among other causes. Therefore, submitting ourselves to God, the Maker of Heaven and Earth, is not like submitting ourselves to a dictator, who is just another person in our midst. On the contrary, the more we become like God, the more we become like ourselves, for we were made in His image. The Catechism words this as follows: "to acknowledge God is in no way to oppose the dignity of man, since such dignity is grounded and brought to perfection in God" (CCC 2126). Because of sin, we tend to think that our freedom is compromised by God's will. Pope Benedict XVI says in his book *Jesus of Nazareth* (Part II, 160) about this sinful man: "He regards consenting to God's will, not as his opportunity to become fully himself, but as a threat to his freedom against which he rebels."

So we should really question the statement that God and Man are supposed to be in a power battle. God's power is not a blind brute force like the forces we are familiar with, but a loving, intentional power far beyond our comprehension. Not only is He an all-powerful, all-knowing, and all-present God, but also, or even first of all, He is an all-loving God. In everything that happens, we can discern God's "hand" – not a hand that *causes* all the good and bad things that we read about in the newspapers, but a hand that *holds* all these things together by saving them for a better purpose and destination.

And yet, God wanted us humans to be "participants" and "co-workers" in His creation, in accordance with His image, because creation did not spring forth complete from the hands of the Creator (CCC 302). The Catechism puts it this way: "God grants his creatures not only their existence, but also the dignity of acting on their own, of beings causes and principles for each other, and thus of cooperating in the accomplishment of his plan" (306). So God enables us "to be intelligent and free causes in order to complete the work of creation" (CCC 307). God could perhaps have chosen to eliminate the possibility of evil and evil-doing, but then God would have also taken away the possibility of good and doing-good.

Q: Do you really think your answer solves the problem of an all-powerful God?

A: Yes, there can definitely be human freedom under an all-powerful God. God lets the actors on the world stage be free actors, who may not act the way the Author of the play would like them to act. Dictators may take human freedom away, but God made us in His image and thus He created us, not as marionettes, but as beings endowed with freedom. Such is the biblical message according to a quote of St. Irenaeus: "Man is rational and therefore like God; he is created with free will and is master over his acts" (CCC 1730). And it is for that very reason – because not all that happens on earth is in accordance with God's will – that we must pray daily, "Your will be done on earth as it is in heaven."

In other words, human freedom is a great *good* that may lead to much *evil*, for we can abuse our freedom at any time. Freedom is always a two-way street, leading us either *toward* God or *away* from God. Human freedom doesn't force us at all to make a choice between human freedom and divine omnipotence. Being all-powerful doesn't mean being able to do what is logically contradictory – namely, giving freedom without the potentiality for sin. God gave us the grace to choose, which in turn allows us to make good as well as bad choices in life. We can therefore go astray and cause much evil. God does not will evil, but He does allow it.

Q: Did God really have to accept the evil consequences of our freedom?

A: In a way, He did. How could He give us freedom without accepting its consequences up to the point of us freely choosing the wrong outcome, away from God? If you love a person, you accept that he or she doesn't return the love. C. S. Lewis could not have expressed this better when he said: "We can, perhaps, conceive of a world in which God corrected the results of this abuse of free will by His creatures at every moment: so that a wooden beam became soft as grass when it was used as a weapon […]. But such a world would be one in which wrong actions were impossible, and in which, therefore, freedom of the will would be void; nay, if the principle were carried out to its logical conclusion, evil thoughts would be impossible, for the cerebral matter which we use in thinking would refuse its task when we attempted to frame them."

If such a scenario were the case, wouldn't that be the end of human freedom? Absolutely! Instead, God made us free "participants" and "co-workers" in His ongoing creation of the world (CCC 307). "*God has freely chosen to associate man with the work of his grace*" (CCC 2008). We should feel very much honored. God took us seriously, with all the consequences that come with it. Evil is not something that God wills, but that He does allow.

Q: I would say God took a big risk by giving His authority away, didn't He?

A: He certainly did! Lewis is absolutely right when he states that if our world were fully preordained by God, our brains would automatically refuse to enforce what our free minds would like to do. That would be a travesty of human freedom. Fortunately, God takes His creatures seriously, so they can make the wrong decisions. And that they did and keep doing, including you and me.

God respects our freedom so much that somehow He even needed Mary's "fiat" to have His Son be born as our Savior; her "Yes" counteracted Eve's "No" and allowed her to become the Mother of God. Thank God, He didn't make us robots entirely at His mercy – but as a consequence, we will be at His mercy at the final judgment. St. Faustina has us pray "Have mercy on us and on the whole world."

So I hope I have convinced you that humans do not have to be powerless if there is an almighty God. Sartre was wrong on that issue and created a false dilemma: No longer do we have to question God's existence if there is human freedom. The fact that we do have freedom actually points to a Creator after whose image we were made: How could there be human freedom if there were no God who freely created us after His image?

Q: You answered the first part of my question – how does an all-powerful God deal with human freedom. But how about the second part – how does an all-good and all-loving God get away with the evil in the world?

A: Instead of questioning *God* again, we should examine first what *evil* is. That latter question is not as easy as you might think. I warn you, we need "reason" again, for Catholics must be reasonable in their faith as much so as they must be faithful in their reasoning.

First of all, we have to state that evil is not a *thing* like a tree or a black hole. Yet, most people tend to picture evil as a thing – a dark cloud or a dangerous storm or a faulty gene, for instance – but in fact, it isn't a thing, or entity, or being. St. Augustine says that evil exists only in the sense that it subtracts from the good. So, evil is not a thing but a wrong choice, or the damage done by a wrong choice. When we do something evil, we damage God's creation. That is what happened in Auschwitz, in the Gulag Archipelago, in Southern Sudan, on Ground Zero – murder, genocide, and destruction. Again, murder is not a thing – just as an amputation is not a thing, but rather a *lack* of something ("that subtracts from the good").

Q: Are you suggesting that evil is not a reality then?

A: No, I am not. Although evil is not a thing, it is not an illusion either; there are things that *are* definitely evil. St. Thomas Aquinas has some great thoughts on this in one of his last books (*De Malo*). He says there that no-thing is evil in itself or by nature, as every-thing is good. Then he repeats: No being (*essentia*) is evil in itself, for evil is not a thing (*ens* or *res*), not even a reality (*realitas*). Aquinas often compares this with blindness: Being blind is not a thing, but whoever happens to be blind is something real; evil is not some-thing on its own, but it can be seen in relation to some-thing good. Or take amputation again: It is not a thing, but lack thereof. Evil exists just like amputation does. In other words, evil only exists in the sense that it subtracts from the good, as St. Augustine had said earlier.

Why are these heavy reflections so important? The answer is that Aquinas wants to stress that God didn't *create* evil. The Creator is a being, and so is every-thing created by Him. Every-thing God created is good, according to Genesis, but evil is not some-thing, let alone some-thing that God created. Therefore, God created good things, but He did not create evil, as it is not a thing that was created. Was St. Thomas nitpicking here? I don't think so.

Q: I can accept your reasoning when it comes to any kind of evil that humans cause themselves. But what about all the evil humans didn't cause on their own?

A: True, the problem of evil is easier when talking about what is often called *moral* evil. But there is also *physical* evil, which is not caused by human beings – evils such as natural death, famine, diseases, earthquakes, tsunamis, and other catastrophes. So your question is what the cause of *physical* evil is. Could it be caused by God? I think what St. Thomas Aquinas said about evil is even more important when it comes to physical evil.

When Jesus is asked this question, He says "there will be great earthquakes, and in various places famines and pestilences; and there will be terrors and great signs from heaven" (Lk. 21: 11). Jesus seems to suggest that these events shouldn't surprise us; they are part of life on earth. But He explicitly mentions that this is not the end of the story, for God is not done with it yet – in his own words, "do not be terrified; for this must first take place, but the end will not be at once" (Lk. 21: 9).

The Catechism places physical evil in a wider context: "God permits evil in order to draw forth some greater good" (CCC 412). Most of this teaching is based on what Aquinas inherited from St. Augustine who argued that God could not have created evil in the world, as it was created good, and that evil only exists in the sense that it subtracts from the good. This leads both of them to the idea that evil is the *absence* of the good that should have been (*absentia boni debiti*). Aquinas explains this by using the example of the lion that couldn't live without killing its prey. What may be evil for the individual, the prey, is good for the larger picture, the universe. Consequently, if there were no evil, such a fact would diminish the good of the universe. In other words, Aquinas would apply this explanation to both moral and physical evil.

Q: I find it hard to follow, let alone accept, all these philosophical hair-splitting subtleties.

A: I think the main point both Augustine and Aquinas want to bring across is that God did not *create* evil – certainly not moral evil, but not even physical evil. Evil is not like the things that the Creator created. God does not will evil, but He does allow it. Yet the question remains: Where does evil come from then?

As to moral evil, the Catholic Church would teach us, in line with the Book of Genesis, that this kind of evil is a consequence of the Fall in Paradise. After God gave the first humans rationality and morality, they fell for His adversary. They wanted to be "like God" in the sense of "next to God," but not "under God"; they wanted to be creators, not creatures; they wanted to be their own commanders-in-chief. The Fall shows us that Adam and Eve didn't like God's Commands, because they didn't want to be commanded.

Ever since that disastrous moment, humans have lost their original innocence; they rejected being dependent on God and being subject to God's laws of nature and God's natural law. The Catechism says, "After that first sin, the world is virtually inundated by sin," and then it speaks of "the universal corruption which follows in the wake of sin" and the *universality of sin in man's history*" (401). All of a sudden, moral evil had entered the scene. And this evil they passed on to their offspring – which is called the *original sin*, as we explained in chapter six.

In other words, *sin* can no longer be explained "as merely a developmental flaw, a psychological weakness, a mistake, or the necessary consequence of an inadequate social structure, etc. Only in the knowledge of God's plan for man can we grasp that sin is *an abuse of the freedom* that God gives to created persons so that they are capable of loving him and loving one another" (CCC 387; italics are mine).

It is because of the original sin that we are out of alignment with the will of God. We are permanently "under the influence" – under the influence, that is, of good Spirits and bad Spirits. We live under constant attention of both God and Satan – and Satan never sleeps. Whereas good Spirits strengthen our virtues (such as faith, hope, and love), bad Spirits incite our vices (such as lust, doubt, despair, violence) – and the latter ones could lead to *eternal* evil.

Q: Let me interrupt you before touching on physical evil. What do you mean by *eternal* evil? Are you saying there is something like an eternal *hell*?

A: Because we are free human beings, we will be held accountable for our choices in life. Evil is a matter of bad choices; and bad choices not only affect our own lives but also those of others. That is where a final judgment comes in. If there is no *instant* repayment for good or bad actions and choices, there must be a *final* repayment (2 Mac. 6:26; 7; 44:46; Wisd. of Sol. 2:16-20; 5:4-5; 5:14-16). If there is salvation, there must also be damnation. We need and deserve to be judged, for God is also a *just* God: Good actions are rewarded with Heaven, bad ones with Hell. As Pope Benedict XVI put it in his book *Jesus of Nazareth* (Part II, 133), "'unconditional forgiveness' would be that 'cheap grace' to which Dietrich Bonhoeffer rightly objected in the face of the appalling evil encountered in his day."

An eternal Hell is the ultimate consequence of freedom. As Peter Kreeft says, "We freely choose hell for ourselves; God does not cast anyone into hell against his will. No sane person wants hell to exist. No sane person wants evil to exist. But hell is just evil eternalized. If there is evil and if there is eternity, there can be hell." The Catechism confirms this very clearly: "Mortal sin is a radical possibility of human freedom [...] it causes [...] *the eternal death of hell*, for our freedom has the power to make choices for ever, with no turning back" (1861; italics are mine). In other words, hell is a state of "definitive *self*-exclusion from communion with God" (CCC 1033; italics are mine). People who commit grave injustices actually condemn themselves. As St. Augustine put it, God "did not will to save us without us."

Jesus speaks about hell more than anyone else in the Gospel, in the Book of the *Good* News. He told His disciples that weeds will be in the field of the world until the end of time, but then the King of Justice will throw those weeds "into the fiery furnace," so grave injustices will not go unaddressed. The Catechism puts it this way: "The Last Judgment will reveal that God's justice triumphs over all the injustices committed by his creatures" (1040).

Q: Do we really need a final judgment?

A: A final judgment is the answer to many questions we might have had in life. What about all those people who have experienced so little joy in their lives? What about all those victims of genocide, gas chambers, torture chambers, wars? What about all those people who cannot be called back to life again to receive a bit more warmth and love? What about those left behind by their spouses or their parents? So many people had hoped for something good but received so much evil and suffering instead. What are we to do with all these people?

Put differently, there are too many debit accounts that still need to be settled. I am not talking about those little accounts that you might like to settle with your neighbors, but about those enormous accounts that caused sorrow, tears, afflictions, and disasters to millions of people. If there were no final judgment, those accounts would remain unsettled. In a Godless world, there is no hope those issues will ever be addressed. Yet, the earth is crying out for justice! Thank God, we have a loving God who is also a *just* God. That is why we need judgment. There is a particular judgment at the end of each one's life, and there is a final or last judgment at the end of time (CCC 1021). The last judgment takes place when Christ returns in His glory to "pronounce the final word on all history" (CCC 1040). In His presence, "the truth of each man's relationship with God will be laid bare" (CCC 1039).

Q: Then my next question is: Where does purgatory fit in here?

A: Purgatory is a place or condition of temporal punishment for those who depart this life in God's grace. The Catechism says about purgatory: "All who die in God's grace and friendship, but still imperfectly purified, […] undergo purification, so as to achieve the holiness necessary to enter the joy of heaven" (1030).

I think this is best explained by an example the legendary Mother Angelica of EWTN uses: If a prostitute had a profound conversion and decides to enter Mother Angelica's convent, a one-day transition would definitely be too short a period for such a person to make the transition – a massive shock actually – in spite of all her good intentions. Indeed, for most of us, the transition from a life on earth to a life in Heaven would be so dramatic that we would need some extra preparation time, as nothing unclean can enter the presence of God in heaven (Rev. 21:27). No wonder, the Catholic Church has always stressed the importance of a purgatory where we can see in all clarity who we were and where we came from before we can enter the eternal glory of God. Fr Benedict Groeschel has expressed this well, "Purgatory is not a temporary hell, but a preliminary heaven." Holiness is certainly not an over-night thing.

Q: Isn't purgatory a Catholic invention?

A: It is certainly Catholic, but in no way an invention. Yet, some Protestants call purgatory a Catholic money maker. At the beginning of the Reformation, there was still some hesitation, especially on Luther's part, if this doctrine should be retained, but as the breach widened, the denial of purgatory by the Reformers became universal. Modern Protestants, while they avoid the name purgatory, now often speak of "the middle state." Orthodox Christians speak in terms of a "theosis," a journey of transformation.

Yet, we find indications of purgatory in both the Old and New Testament. One of the strongest lines can be found in Matthew 5:25-26, when Jesus ends one of His parables with the following statement: "you be put in prison; truly, I say to you, you will never get out till you have paid the last penny."

We find also indications of purgatory very early in Christianity. St. Augustine's mother asked her son to remember her soul in his Masses. Graffiti in the catacombs of the first three centuries recorded prayers for the dead. Some of the earliest Christian writings also refer to the Christian practice of praying for the dead. St. Ambrose said about the deceased, "We have loved them during life; let us not abandon them until we have conducted them by our prayers into the house of the Lord." Such prayers would make no sense if these early Christians thought the souls of the dead were already in hell or in heaven, for they could no longer benefit from prayers. Besides, the Bible speaks of "the limbo of the Fathers," where the just who had died before the redemption by Jesus were waiting for Heaven to be opened to them. Doesn't that come close to a purgatory...?

Q: Back to the original sin: It doesn't explain where *physical* evil comes from.

A: Indeed, physical evil appears to be a completely different, rather stubborn issue. Physical *pain* is perhaps the easiest case – a warning sign that the body is in trouble. We need not look at it as evil. But what about physical *suffering*, you might ask.

The Book of Genesis seems to suggest that suffering is a consequence of the Fall too, when God says to the serpent "upon your belly you shall go," and to Eve "I will greatly multiply your pain in childbearing; in pain you shall bring forth children" (Gen.

3:14-16). This makes one wonder if there was a physical change in the world as a result of the Fall. Were there "thistles and thorns" *before* the Fall? St. Thomas Aquinas makes a very astute remark here: "Some say that the animals, which are wild now and kill other animals, were not that way [in paradise ...]. But this is entirely unreasonable. The nature of animals was not changed by the sin of man."

And yet, since the Fall, there is not only *mental* suffering (grief, hatred, frustration, heartbreak, guilt, humiliation, anxiety, loneliness, misery, self-pity) but also *physical* suffering (pain, illness, disability, hunger, poverty, death). We discussed earlier that Aquinas keeps stressing that "If all evil would be banned, the universe would lack much good. If it couldn't kill animals, the lion would not be able to live." Is that a sufficient explanation for physical evil? Perhaps it is, perhaps it is not.

First of all, we should also consider the fact that nature is bound to follow its God-given laws of nature; well, the laws of nature must operate as they do, if intelligent and free agents are to exist. We must distinguish between what God wills and what He allows. God doesn't will earthquakes, but He allows them when they are a consequence of the laws of nature – in the same way as God doesn't will wars but allows them when humans use their freedom to start them. God wills perfection but allows imperfection.

But I think there is a much more important, often overlooked, consideration. When speaking of physical *evil*, we find ourselves already in a mental, spiritual, even moral context. By asserting "evil exists," we use already ethical, moral standards. When speaking of "evil," we are asserting somehow that it "should" not exist. We are evaluating physical suffering as wrong or bad – something no animal would be able to do.

If there were no humans, there wouldn't be any evil. Animals, on their part, do not have any ethical values, so they follow whatever pops up in their brains. They have no moral considerations. Hence, the relationship between predator and prey has nothing to do with morality or evil; if predators really had a conscience guided by morality, their lives would be pretty tough. The prey doesn't consider the predator "evil" – perhaps painful, but not evil. The world of humans, on the other hand, is very different!

Q: I can accept the idea that animals never cause moral evil, but what about physical evil?

A: Indeed, animals never do awful things out of meanness or cruelty, for the simple reason that they have no morality – and thus no cruelty or meanness, and no evil. Humans, in contrast, certainly do have the capacity of performing real atrocities. If animals do seem to do awful things, it is only because *we* consider their actions "awful" and "evil" according to *our* standards of morality.

Something similar holds for physical evil. In the animal world, there's no physical evil, because the word *evil* implies already human evaluation. As a consequence, physical events only become evil when we assess them as evil and dub them as evil. So the "thorns and thistles" may have always been there, but since the Fall and because of the newly fallen consciousness of human beings, they were felt not only as painful but also as distressing, as physical *evil*. Animals may experience pain but not evil when giving birth. Humans, on the other hand, do! Hence, the cause of physical evil is ultimately sin. Without sin, physical evils wouldn't rankle or embitter us.

Only humans take diseases and catastrophes as something that shouldn't be, as something that seems to be acting against them personally. Animals may "dislike" these things, but they do not question them in terms of "Why me?" Only humans know of God, so they ask the question "Is something wrong between God and me?" or "Why do bad things happen to good people?" Since animals do not know about good and bad, they cannot ask why bad things happen to good animals. Only humans can – and they can find the answer to their questions at the beginning of the Book of Genesis: "of the tree of the knowledge of good and evil you shall not eat, for in the day that you eat of it you shall die" (Gen. 2:17).

That tree in Genesis is part of human life; it symbolizes that "Man is dependent on his Creator and subject to the laws of creation and to the moral norms that govern the use of freedom" (CCC 396). So sin – and with it comes evil – is basically lack of trust in God's goodness. The harmony in which Adam and Eve had found themselves is now destroyed, and harmony with creation is broken (CCC 400). Had there not been sin, physical evils wouldn't affect us.

Q: That's quite an unexpected turn!

A: It's not that astonishing. C. S. Lewis said basically something similar in his book *Mere Christianity*, "My argument against God was that the universe seemed so cruel and unjust. But how had I got this idea of just and unjust? A man does not call a line crooked unless he has some idea of a straight line. What was I comparing this universe with when I called it unjust? [...] Of course I could have given up my idea of justice by saying it was nothing but a private idea of my own. But if I did that, then my argument against God collapsed too – for the argument depended on saying the world was really unjust, not simply that it did not happen to please my fancies."

Lewis is stating here that calling the universe cruel (physical evil) and unjust (moral evil) must already assume that we have a moral and spiritual standard deriving from Heaven – and that is the place where God resides. Asserting "evil exists" (both physical and moral) would imply an ethical standard against which to define good and evil; and such a standard implies the existence of God. Without God, we couldn't even speak of evil. Thanks to God, we know what the world "should" be like. We know of "evil" because we have an idea of "good" and of what things should be like, if everything were "good."

Q: I know of Christians who keep maintaining that evil and suffering come directly from God's hand.

A: Some indeed do, and they usually refer to certain passages in the Bible, such as "I form light and create darkness, I make weal and create woe, I am the LORD, who do all these things" (Is. 45:7), or "He sent darkness, and made the land dark; for they rebelled against his words" (Ps. 105:28), or "Is it not from the mouth of the Most High that good and evil come?" (Lamentations 3:38), or "Does evil befall a city, unless the LORD has done it?" (Amos 3:6).

The common message seems to be: Evil suffered is evil deserved. In this view, evil is not only something that God allows but even wills. However, there are many other Biblical passages telling us that God does NOT cause evil and suffering, but that WE caused them. We discussed earlier that God did not *create* evil, but He may *use* it when we ourselves caused it. No wonder, the Bible keeps struggling with the problem of evil. Who doesn't? It is at the core of any religion. I always remember St. Augustine's exclamation in his autobiography: "I sought where evil comes from, and there was no solution."

Q: Doesn't the Book of Job offer many answers, though, to our problem of evil?

A: True, the Book of Job is one of the pivotal books in the Scriptures with respect to suffering – apart from the Gospels. But do not let this book fool you. It is one of those cases where taking one sentence out of its context can easily and completely deceive you.

Who is Job? He is a man stripped of everything, including his health, and almost his faith too. His friends come to comfort him with all the "comforting" answers religious and pious people tend to come up with:

- When bad things happen to good people, they must have sinned (Job 2). Be good so you can do well.

- When God strikes, He has reason to do so (Job 4). You must have asked for it!

- We deserve what we get and we get what we deserve (Job 4). God does pay back!

- Can a man be more pure than his Maker (4:17). God has reasons we do not know.

- Blessed is the man whom God corrects (5:17). It's the old rule of "No pain, no gain."

- God's justice is beyond our understanding (36:5). What God ordains is right.

- He is the best teacher (36:22). So listen up!

Q: Haven't we all been bombarded with explanations like these?

A: Yes, "the pious" often use such lines to hit people who were diagnosed with cancer or lost a child. But according to Job, they are actually "blasphemous" statements about God. Job didn't accept even one of them. He keeps repeating that a God who hits back is not the God he knows. And the entire Bible stands behind him: Evil and suffering *do* exist but *shouldn't* exist; they may be part of *life* but not of *creation*. Job's "comforters," who have all the answers, turn out to be in fact his "adversaries," who provide cover-ups for all the suffering in the world – thereby changing God into an enemy. St. James makes a very strong case: "Let no one say when he is tempted, 'I am tempted by God'; for God cannot be tempted with evil and he himself tempts no one" (Jas. 1:13). It is the devil who tempts.

Job, for his part, is very firm in his stand: the God I know would never do what you are telling me. Evil or suffering is too serious and too devastating to blame God for it. Therefore, Job keeps asking for *God*'s personal answer instead: Is something wrong between God and me? Job hasn't lost God at all when he exclaims those eternal words well known from Handel's *Messiah*: "I know that my Redeemer liveth" (19:25) – which means "I know…" that God is God-*with*-us (*Emmanuel*), not God-*against*-us. He confirms his belief in God, in spite of the fact that "God can sometimes seem to be absent and incapable of stopping evil" (CCC 272).

Q: Well, did Job receive an answer from God?

A: Perhaps not on first sight. At the end of the book, God seems to bombard Job with a cascade of questions: Where were you, Job, when I did this? Where were you when I did that? It is like reversing Job's repeated question "Where were you, God, when I was stricken by misery?"

However, do not read God's torrent of questions the wrong way. It is not anticipating an answer like "you were nowhere and nothing." God's answer is not meant in a demeaning way. Instead it is asking Job: Don't you remember how I shut up the sea, a menace to life (38:8), how I created light in the darkness (38:12) to light your path, and how I use my arm to protect people like you (40:9)? In other words, it is *I*, a caring God, who created all of this – a home furnished with TLC. Have you forgotten that, Job?

At last, Job gets it; he gets the answer in its fullness: "I had heard of thee by the hearing of the ear, but now my eye sees thee" (42:5). He is saying something like this: Now I understand You; now I can see Your passion and obsession with your creatures, because You allowed me to read Your heart.

Did Job receive an answer? Yes and no. He was not given a settlement of his questions, but he was set free from his questions. He received the confirmation that there's nothing wrong between God and him. If you want to say that Job was "put to the test" by God, you need to stress also that the test was not meant to prove that God can do whatever He desires, but that God desires to do whatever He can for Job and any other human being. Even when Abraham was put to the test, as the Book of Genesis (22:1) puts it, God was not trying to prove He can do whatever He wants – for instance, something as radical as asking the sacrifice of Abrahams only son – but God expressed His desire to do whatever He could for Abraham.

Q: Yet the Bible keeps using explanations that appear to me as betraying the seriousness of evil and suffering.

A: You might be surprised that the Bible itself is often very critical of such "cheap" explanations.

- The simple slogan of "Evil suffered is evil deserved" is challenged, for instance, by the prophet Jeremiah: "Why does the way of the wicked prosper?" (12:1).

- The idea that people have to pay for the sins of their ancestors is also being contested: "Our fathers sinned, and are no more; and we bear their iniquities" (Lam. 5:7). Even prophets protested against such simple views by assuring their audience that the son is not punished for his father's iniquities (Ezekiel 18; Jeremiah 31:29; John 9:3).

- The book Ecclesiastes questions the idea that the misery of good people will soon turn for the good: "there is a righteous man who perishes in his righteousness, and there is a wicked man who prolongs his life in his evil-doing" (7:15). Think of it this way: Some people do return to God because of a tragedy, but that doesn't mean God would ever *send* them tragedies to *force* their conversion.

Q: Why did it take the Bible so long to come to terms with evil and suffering?

A: Indeed, the people of the Old Testament had to learn the hard way that there is no instant repayment for our actions, and that we certainly cannot demand instant rewards for our behavior. Israel had to learn that the idea of *instant* repayment calls for better alternatives! God's revelation has been a gradual process until it came to its fullness in Jesus Christ. The Catechism puts it as follows: "God has revealed himself to man by gradually communicating his own mystery in deeds and in words" (69).

Some of those old answers may look "cheap" in hindsight, but they are only "cheap" in the sense that they do not go to the root of the problem – sin. Somehow, the Old Testament hadn't reached yet the summit of God's revelation in Jesus the Messiah, who went to the full depth of sin and suffering by identifying Himself with our suffering in order to eradicate the effects of sin. The Good News of Jesus Christ is actually the "reverse side" of the doctrine of original sin (cf. CCC 389).

In the meantime, the Bible moans and groans under the pain of suffering. The best I can do at this point is repeating what the Catechism says: "God is infinitely good and all his works are good. Yet no one can escape the experience of suffering or the evils in nature which seem to be linked to the limitations proper to creatures; and above all to the question of moral evil" (CCC 385).

Q: I still think we are left with more questions than answers.

A: At least we have got one vital answer: God did not create or cause evil and suffering. We saw that the Book of Job is actually one long protracted charge against the misconception that afflictions are meant to *punish* us, to *test* us, to *discipline* us, to *correct* us, to *purify* us, or to *teach* us a lesson. All we can say is that God may *use* those afflictions that way, but He did not *produce* them for that reason. God doesn't strike us with afflictions, but whenever evil strikes, God may use it for a better purpose. He may use it but didn't cause it. He uses, not what *He* did wrong, but what *we* did wrong. He may give a divine twist to our wrong human decisions. God can write straight even on the crooked lines of our history.

Pope Benedict XVI acknowledges in his book Jesus of Nazareth (Part II, 31) that "God grants to evil and to evildoers a large measure of freedom – too large, we might think. Even so, history does not slip through his fingers." In everything that happens, we can discern God's "hand" – not a hand that *causes* all the good and bad things that we read about in the newspapers, but a hand that *holds* all these things together by saving them for a better purpose and destination.

We do not know all God's reasons, we do not know all the answers, but we do know that God is with us, by our side. God's ultimate answer to Job's quest is actually not an answer at all but God-self. God came down to Job Himself – as He came down to all of us at the fullness of time in Jesus Christ. In other words, the Bible may not give answers that settle all our questions, but it has the right Address for us to go to with our questions.

Q: Nevertheless, many Christians still think it is God who bestows evil and suffering on us.

A: You are right. They often quote "The Lord has given, the Lord has taken" – meaning that evil and suffering happen when God takes the good away that He has given. Those Christians isolate this quote from its context – the Book of Job (1:21) – and choose to forget about all the other things the Bible has to say about evil and suffering. That is how we got those awful insurance policy clauses in terms of "Acts of God," as if accidents come from a God who takes away what He has given.

However, God is never the source of evil and suffering. Jesus testifies to this: He cured blindness but never caused it. God doesn't *punish* us, but allows us to punish ourselves and each other. God doesn't *inflict* suffering on us, but He does allow us to bring suffering upon ourselves and each other. God isn't the Creator of evil, but He is the Creator of free human beings who have the potential, the choice, to cause evil. God created good things, not evil things – for evil is not a thing. God hates evil and suffering. That is why the *Our Father* has us pray "Deliver us from evil." That is why Jesus heals the blind, the deaf, and the lame – especially on the Day of the Lord.

Sickness is a sign of the action of evil in this world; that is why Jesus shows us in his healings that the Kingdom of God, God Himself, is near. As Pope Benedict put it in his Angelus Address of 2/5/12, "Jesus Christ came to conquer evil at its root, and the healings are an anticipation of his victory, obtained by his death and resurrection." Similar to the way St. Thomas Aquinas stressed that evil is not a "thing" that God would create or cause, Jesus conveys the same message. Jesus, the human face of God on earth, was never seen to *cause* anyone to be blind, to be lame, to become a leper, but He would rather *cure* people from blindness and leprosy, as such afflictions show the *absence* of something *good* that should have been.

Q: How can God deliver us from something He didn't create?

A: When praying "Deliver us from evil," we are not asking God to take something, a thing, away, for we saw that evil is not a "thing." Unfortunately, our current translation of this sentence is not explicit enough. When Matthew (6:13) cites how Jesus prayed the *Our Father*, he uses the word evil (*poneros*) in a way that can be neuter or masculine, but according to New Testament parallels, should be taken as masculine: the *Evil One* – which makes even more sense in connection with the previous line that says "And lead us not into temptation" where Matthew is not speaking of God tempting us (for "God [...] himself tests no one" according to James 1:13) but of the final ordeal of this world (*peirasmos*). This last word is also used when Jesus tells his followers on His last night "Pray that you may be spared the test" (Mk. 14:37, Mt. 26:41,

Lk. 22:4, all use the word *peirasmos*). Jesus is speaking here of the temptation led by Satan that comes with the final ordeal.

In life, we may be confronted and surrounded by all kinds of evils (notice the plural) – physical evils as well as moral evils – but we may still learn from them because they can be used for a greater good. However, what can really destroy us is evil in its singular version, the force that is out to separate us from God. This kind of evil is connected with the Evil One. The source of all evils is not to be found in God, but in His enemy – Satan or evil itself. Again, do not take God and Satan as two eternal principles locked in permanent conflict (like in Dualism and Manichaeism, CCC 285), for Satan and other demons are fallen Angels that were created good by God (CCC 391). The source of all evil is not God but Satan. As St. James tells us: "Let no one say when he is tempted, 'I am tempted by God'; for God cannot be tempted with evil and he himself tempts no one" (Jas. 1:13). It is the devil who tempts. When Jesus was led into the wilderness by the Spirit, he was tempted by the devil (Mt. 4:1).

Q: I am glad you are finally mentioning a force coming from beyond our physical world that can cause evil.

A: I did so already when I spoke of the evil force deceiving Adam and Eve in paradise. The serpent (or snake, or dragon in Rev. 12:9; 20:2) is typically identified with God's antagonist and adversary – the satanic one (Satan), the diabolic one (the devil, the demon, the divider). The Book of Wisdom says, "through the devil's envy death entered the world" (2:24).

The serpent is the smooth voice of the big lie, "a seductive voice, opposed to God, [...] a fallen angel" (CCC 391). It is the voice of God's enemy, saying that you can only be yourself by leading your own life, by being number one rather than number two, by making God look like our biggest rival, by stealing the fruit from the Owner's tree of life and death. Satan is the "father of all lies."

Well, Adam and Eve did fall into the trap, were tricked, and even bedeviled. They wanted to be "like God" in the sense of "next to God," but not "under God"; they wanted to be independent *creators*, ruling their own lives, instead of being dependent *creatures*; they wanted to be their own commanders-in-chief instead of being under His command. But they ended up under Satan's command; they were deceived by lies and sold their souls.

Q: Is the serpent of Genesis really Satan?

A: Let me explain why the Church thinks so. The Bible is in a constant battle with "idols." We found out, in the previous chapter, that an idol in itself can do nothing; left alone, it will deteriorate, rust, rot, or chip. Scripture calls idols literally "nothings" when it says "all the gods of the peoples are idols; but the LORD made the heavens" (Ps. 96:5). So where does their power come from then? Well, the idol itself is nothing, but every idol has a demon associated with it. Demons are the spiritual agents acting in all idolatry. St. Thomas speaks of "demons, who offered themselves to be worshiped by men, by giving answers in the idols, and doing things which to men seemed marvelous."

We can find these demons all over the Bible: "They sacrificed their sons and their daughters to the demons" (Ps. 106:37) and "They sacrificed to demons which were no gods" (Deut. 32:17). These and other passages identify idols with demons that energize their worship, and they describe demonism as the dynamic of idolatry, inspiring the perverted worship. The serpent of Paradise was also one of those idols – a "nothing" energized by demons. Apparently, demons were around as early as the very beginning of mankind. So perhaps Adam and Eve's first sin was idolatry. If we would really believe that the Lord is God, we would never sin. So sin is actually proof of idolatry – a denial of God.

And those demons are still around, for Satan keeps speaking from his vipers nest, even right now. He speaks from his den in Hell – a place of fire (for us to burn), a place of coldness (far away from God's Love), and a place of darkness (far away from the Eternal Light) – and that all of these together. Mark Twain said he didn't believe in Hell but was afraid he would go there. I can see why... But keep remembering there is another Voice calling us, "Where are you?" (Gen. 3:9). This is the voice coming from God, who never lets us down – and that is why there is still hope, no matter how bad things have gotten. The Bible starts in Genesis with the old Adam and the old Eve, but it ends in Revelation with the new Adam, Jesus our Savior, and the new Eve, personified in our Blessed Mother and her Church.

Q: This satanic source of evil seems to be pretty powerful.

A: It certainly is. Evil is part of a much larger picture – a cosmic warfare, that is, between Good and Evil, between God and Satan (not as two eternal principles locked in permanent conflict, for Satan and other demons are fallen Angels made by God as good Angels). It is God's aim for each one of us to attain Heaven after death, whereas Satan's aim is to ensure that as many people as possible miss that eternal goal. It is only the religious "eye" that sees all of history as a cosmic and constant warfare between God and Satan, waged everywhere and daily – "24/7." It "sees" how the power of evil, the darkness of Satan, enabled men such as Hitler, Stalin, and Mao to spellbind and enslave the minds and spirits of millions, creating hell ahead of time, right here on earth.

Only religious people are able to see this dimension in history that historians usually miss – a broken world that needs to be restored. Keep in mind that our history is also His-story. This underlying process explains how some people have sold their souls by following "orders" that stem from sources far beyond their own resources. They feel empowered from "on high."

Q: Sounds nice, but I still feel abandoned each time I fall victim to evil and suffering. At those moments, I cannot help yelling: Where are You, God?

A: I take it you are not questioning God's existence anymore – like atheists do – but you are questioning God's faithfulness as to how He can abandon you when evil strikes you – like abandoned spouses want to interrogate those who have dumped them. I take it that your questioning is no longer coming from a skeptical mind but rather from a broken heart. I take it that you have reached a point where the problem of evil is no longer an intellectual problem but an existential one. And rightly so! Why?

To humanists, Marxists, and Buddhists, suffering is as painful as it is to Jews and Christians, but the former are not haunted with this piercing question, "Why does God abandon *me*?" Believing in a God of *love* and in a *good* creation causes the pain of suffering to penetrate to a deeper level – to the level of "Is something wrong between God and me?" In response, the Gospel of John tells us, "God sent the Son into the world, not to condemn the world, but that the world might be saved through him" (3:17).

Both the good and the bad – everything – is being held together in God's hands. In time, God's love will be superior to all the cruelties and absurdities of this world, as it has been superior to the Cross of Jesus. So even when things do not go well, they will end well, for God is so much as capable to use even the worst for the best. In other words, all that we do today will be used by God to build tomorrow's Kingdom. We may not know what the future holds, but we do know that God holds the future. We are born, not to be part of the ending (as in atheism), but part of the beginning (so says Christianity).

Q: Sounds nice, but I still feel abandoned each time I fall victim to evil and suffering.

A: At least, you do not ask anymore if there *is* a God, but you have come to doubt whether He is there for *you*. Yet your question "Where are You, God?" is still very ambiguous. If I ask myself why evil strikes ME, I could ask myself as well why evil would NOT strike me. Realizing suffering is everywhere may help us de-center from our own suffering. Or consider the example of an infection. We tend to be surprised each time we get an infection, but we should be surprised that we usually do *not* get an infection. The real wonder comes from our beautifully designed immunity system – another wonderful piece of creation, but perhaps not perfect.

The same is true of the tantalizing question as to why bad things happen to *good* people. We could as well ask why good things happen to *bad* people. Who is to say we are good people? Aren't we all bad due to the original sin? Asking things this way gives us a completely different perspective on evil and suffering: We are no longer "good" people who suffer "bad" things; we are "bad" people who enjoy so many "good" things. As Jesus once said, "No one is good but God alone." And besides, who is to say suffering is all bad, or bad forever? We said earlier that God is certainly able to use suffering for a better purpose, for something good. So never turn misery into self-pity.

Q: Are you telling me suffering is not all that bad?

A: No, suffering is indeed bad, but God may use evil and suffering, which befell us or were caused by us, for a better good – for a better purpose (to discipline us, to purify us, to correct us, to test and teach us). But there is a much more important goal: suffering can be used for our *redemption*. Redemption is actually a culmination point in the Bible. We find it already in the Old Testament when some take upon themselves the sins and burdens of others so that all will be free of the consequences of sin.

This counter-intuitive, revolutionary view turns things really upside down. Whenever anyone suffers and even dies so that others may live, that is when redemption occurs. The Prophet Isaiah summarized it when he said: "by his knowledge shall the righteous one, my servant, make many to be accounted righteous; and he shall bear their iniquities" (53:11). This kind of suffering forebodes the ultimate redemptive sacrifice that takes place in the New Testament: the crucifixion of Jesus as a sacrifice for *all* of us and for *all* our sins. In terms of "instant repayment," Jesus' life and message would have been refuted, with the Cross being the final blow to His credentials – but God could even use His Son's death for a greater good. As Pope Benedict XVI puts it in his book *Jesus of Nazareth* (Part II, 231), "the filth of the world is truly absorbed, wiped out, and transformed in the pain of infinite love."

Cardinal Stanislaw Dziwisz said about his ailing friend Blessed Pope John Paul II, "Today there is a cult of beauty and strength, of youth, but he showed that suffering has a redemptive value to humans and also for society." Indeed, the Pope wanted to suffer for the Church and for humanity, as all the saints have done. Pope Benedict said something similar in his Angelus Address on 2/5/12, "As Jesus confronted the evil one with the force of love that came to him from the Father, so we too can confront and win out in the trial of sickness, keeping our hearts immersed in God's love."

Q: Yet, many people tend to abandon *God* when they feel God has abandoned *them*.

A: Yes, that happens all the time. Confronted with evil and suffering, people become either bitter or better. Some do turn away from God, but they can never turn away from suffering – and ultimately, they cannot get away from God. Yet, turning away from God happens again and again – on a small scale and on a large scale. On a small scale, people easily turn angry or disappointed in life. Some people even end up losing all their faith and hope. They just cannot deal with this latest loss, this latest disaster, this latest disease. They may always have considered God as an intervening God – that is, intervening on their request. However, a religion that promises immediate answers to prayer and instant awards for good behavior is merely a commercialized version of religion, promoted by some TV ministers. Prayer is not giving God a to-do list; it is not meant to change *God*'s mind, but *ours*.

Indeed, it is so easy and so human to get angry at God, when we feel left alone. C.S. Lewis was even angry at God while still an atheist: "I was also very angry with him for not existing. I was also angry with him for having created the world." Ultimately, Lewis found God back, because God wanted to be found. Suffering is, like freedom, a two-way street: Some drift farther away, others feel drawn closer to Him. The choice is up to us. Since evil came forth from rebellion against God, it shouldn't surprise us that it can also further strengthen rebellion against God.

Q: What did you mean when you said some people abandon God on a large scale?

A: The Holocaust (*Shoa*) is perhaps the best example. In the Bible, God declares the Jews a chosen people. After the Holocaust, many Jews felt their being chosen by God was the cause of near extinction by the Nazis, so they decided they would choose to un-choose God. They no longer wanted to keep their part of the Covenant, for they felt abandoned by God as a people. Hence, they asked for a "divorce."

Those who did so actually enforced what Hitler couldn't have done better – separating them from God. They had lost the reason as to why they had been chosen – the reason being to be the people that God needs to be His witness in this world. They decide to be no longer trustees of God's covenant with the world; they no longer understand the divine purpose for which God had chosen them; they no longer know for whom they have survived the suffering of the Holocaust. That is actually a very sad outcome.

Something similar may happen to Christians as well: They make up for 75% of all persecutions today. I hope and pray this doesn't cause another abandonment of God on a large scale.

Q: You spoke about this redemptive power that comes from suffering. Tell me more about it.

A: More than other Judeo-Christian traditions, it is Catholicism in particular that emphasizes suffering as a source of redemption. Just think of the Catholic crucifix with its naked corpse, in contrast to the Protestant cross with its vacant wood or the Orthodox icon with its gold. This Catholic conception is not born from stoicism, which is the mere tolerance of suffering, but it invites us to transform suffering into a source of redemption.

Trust and surrender – that is a Catholic motto. The coming of Jesus was like D-Day, the day of invasion into enemy territory. But ultimately, there will be V-Day, the day of victory. But this will take redemptive suffering. Jesus came, not to abolish, but to sanctify suffering with His presence. Jesus did not save us *from* the cross, but instead He saved us *by* the cross. Even in suffering – or particularly in suffering – we can find the Glory of God, for Jesus is the human face of God – and a human face comes with tears.

The message of Golgotha is that God is love – and love wants to share. God's love wants to share everything with us, even our sufferings. Our God-in-charge is also a God-in-pain. We can meet God everywhere, even on Golgotha of all places. When we ask Jesus how much He loves us, He will tell us "This much…" Then He spread His arms and died for us. Through Jesus' death, we were redeemed, so we can meet our Maker after death "face to face."

Q: Are you saying that Jesus is the final answer to our problem of evil and suffering?

A: I would certainly say so. The final answer doesn't come from *words* but from a *person* called Jesus – a divine person. Jesus has given us quite a reversal of perspective on evil and suffering! Each new cross in this world is another way of crucifying God. God is a crucified, afflicted God.

At the time of Jesus, many who strictly followed the Law of Moses thought they could claim their goods in return. Sickness and poverty, suffering and evil, were seen in a rather straightforward way – something like this: Evil suffered is evil deserved. But things have dramatically changed since Jesus, or at least they were seen in a much clearer light: The ones who followed Him learned they had to take up their cross. Like spouses once promised each other to be faithful "in good and in bad days," Christians have promised God to follow Jesus by being faithful "in good and in bad days."

Through Jesus, we have a God who knows what suffering is. From now on, whatever used to be considered a seal of God's blessing – such as wealth and health – may as well be a hindrance to His blessings. Even suffering can at times become a blessing… This was well put by Pope Benedict XVI in his book *Jesus of Nazareth* (Part II, 232): "God himself 'drinks the cup' of every horror to the dregs and thereby restores justice through the greatness of his love, which, through suffering, transforms the darkness."

Q: How can we tap into this redemptive power of suffering as an opening for God?

A: Jesus is our role model. God's "solution" to the problem of evil is his Son Jesus Christ – not an intellectual but existential "solution." The Father's love sent his Son to die for us in order to defeat the power of evil in human nature: That is the heart of the Christian story.

The Boston College philosopher Peter Kreeft rephrases this as follows: "How do we get God off the hook for allowing evil? God is not *off* the hook; God *is* the hook. That's the point of a crucifix. That's why the doctrine of the Divinity of Christ is crucial: If that is not God there on the cross but only a good man, then God is not on the hook, on the cross, in our suffering. And if God is not on the hook, then God is not off the hook. How could he sit there in heaven and ignore our tears?"

In other words, Golgotha has become a "meeting place" for all those who suffer. From now on, in the words of the Catechism, "Suffering, a consequence of original sin, acquires a new meaning; it becomes a participation in the saving work of Jesus." (1521). In Him, we "offer up" our sufferings, for we are participants and co-workers in His creation. Where else would we go if not to Jesus? More than intellectual understanding, we need personal acceptance.

Q: The Catechism calls suffering a consequence of original sin. So we are back at the issue of the *original sin*.

A: Yes, we are. The consequence of original sin has been unending misery, a pit from which no one can escape by their own efforts. Only God can provide a way for human beings to return to their original status from before the Fall. Until this salvation appears on earth, suffering remains the endemic state of humanity. The hopeful side of this doctrine is that with the coming of God's Son, who alone can remove the original sin, it will be possible for a redeemed humanity to live in an ideal world free from suffering – which is the Kingdom of Heaven, a broken world restored.

Let me quote Peter Kreeft one more time: "He didn't give us a placebo or a pill or good advice. He gave us himself. He came. He entered space and time and suffering. He came, like a lover. Love seeks above all intimacy, presence, togetherness. He came. […] He did the most important thing and he gave the most important gift: himself. Out of our cry, 'My God, my God, why hast Thou forsaken me?' he came, all the way, right into that cry." Pope Benedict summarized this during his *Urbi et Orbi* blessing on Christmas Day 2011 with one single sentence: "Jesus Christ is the proof that God has heard our cry."

When Blessed Mother Teresa of Calcutta was asked how she could face all those dying people around her, she referred to each one of them as "Jesus in that distressing disguise." Behold the Lamb!

Q: Do you really think you have found a solution to the problem of evil and suffering?

A: As I said before, God's solution to the problem of evil is not a *theoretical* but an *existential* response. The answer is not some-thing but some-one – His Son Jesus Christ. The Father's love sent his Son who died for us to defeat the power of evil in human nature – which is the heart of the Christian story, and it has become the center of human history. Jesus is the human face of God – and a human face comes with tears. Our tears are His tears, for God is not a God of evil but a God of love. "As one whom his mother comforts, so I will comfort you" (Is. 66:13) or "Can a woman forget her sucking child, that she should have no compassion on the son of her womb? Even these may forget, yet I will not forget you." (Is. 49:15).

When the Son of God came into our world, He came also into our suffering. He walks with us not only in our sufferings but even in our sins. He does not turn His face from us, even if we repeatedly turn our face away from Him. He endures all our failings, transgressions, offenses, wrongdoings, crimes, and felonies – just to be with us. Do we let Him?

Q: Aren't you about to glorify suffering?

A: We live in a world that runs away from suffering. Since the time of our youth, we have been conditioned to view suffering as an impediment to happiness. We look for ways to end the pain rather than ways to embrace it. Even a simple headache can send us hurrying to the medicine cabinet for a speedy cure. This worldview, which is so embedded in our culture, tells us that the less we suffer, the happier we will be.

Yet, in the writings of the Saints, we find an entirely different reality, telling us that it is precisely suffering that strengthens us, humbles us, and forges us into saints, so we become like St. Paul: "I have been crucified with Christ; it is no longer I who live, but Christ who lives in me; and the life I now live in the flesh I live by faith in the Son of God, who loved me and gave himself for me" (Gal. 2:20). Ironically, it is in the midst of our suffering that most of our growth and maturation takes place.

When we ask God "Why me?" we may actually hear Jesus whisper in response "Why Me?" And we know the answer. Some people said to Mother Teresa, they wouldn't do her work for a million dollars. She quipped she wouldn't either, but she would do it for God. No matter how bad things get, there is Someone carrying us through. God's love carries us through. To whom else can we bring all our pain if not to God?

Q: It must be a privilege of Saints to have discovered this mystery of redemption!

A: Yes, it is a privilege of the Saints among us, as you can gather from the following testimonies:

- Thomas A. Kempis: "No one so deeply feels what Christ endured as one who has had to suffer as He did."

- St. Faustina; "Sufferings, adversities, humiliations, failures and suspicions that have come my way are splinters that keep alive the fire of my love for You, O Jesus."

- St. Padre Pio: "even in the midst of so much suffering, I am happy because it seems as if my heart is beating with Jesus' heart."

- St. Padre Pio again: "Yes, I love the cross, the cross alone. I love it because I always see it behind Jesus' shoulders."

- St. Teresa of Avila: "We always find that those who walked closest to Christ were those who had to bear the greatest trials."

- St. Rosa of Lima: "Apart from the cross, there is no other ladder by which we may get to Heaven."

This list could go on and on. But it is not only the Saints who say this – we could and should join them ourselves. That is not to say we need to go out of our way to seek suffering, for we all have our fair share of distress without looking for more. Yet, do not feel bashful to join the company of these "happy few," because we live in a broken world, so there will always be suffering in life.

Never forget that the question "How real is evil?" runs parallel with the question "How real is Satan?" The Catholic Church doesn't want us to forget that Satan is a real force to reckon with. If there is no Satan, then the Cross is a hoax; if there is no Satan, then the whole economy of salvation is up for grabs. No wonder Christianity sees the history of humanity as a perpetual, cosmic warfare between God and Lucifer, between good and evil, between the Light of God and the darkness of evil, between God calling us to be like His image and Satan enticing us to be our own image. Not only does this cosmic warfare occur on the large scale of history, it also rages on the small scale of our inner self where decisions are being made *for* or *against* God. Those tiny, personal decisions shape history as well. Behind this visible and natural world there is an invisible and supernatural world. Human beings actually live in *two* worlds. They need to look beyond the natural to see the supernatural, beyond the present to see the eternal, beyond what can be seen to that which cannot be seen.

Q: At the end of this chapter, I need a brief answer to the question that you placed in its header: How evil is suffering?

A: My answer would be as follows. Suffering is an evil – one of those evils (plural) that came forth from evil (singular), from Satan who lured Adam and Eve into making the wrong choices and who keeps luring you and me to make wrong choices as well. Because of this, we experience suffering as being evil, but it is through the eyes of Jesus that we can see suffering also as a source of redemption. Thanks to Jesus, suffering has become a redemptive power, so we can "offer it up" for the salvation of souls – in the same way as Jesus' suffering and death achieved for us the salvation of *all* those souls who believe and trust in Him. Golgotha has become a "meeting place" for all of us who suffer; our tears have become His tears.

Suffering is a two-way street: When you look with the eyes of Satan, it is pure evil that takes us away from God, but seen through the eyes of God, it may turn into salvation and redemption that brings us back closer to Him. Thus, suffering has this mysterious potential of redeeming us, transforming us, transfiguring us. You might think the less we suffer, the closer to God we will be – but it might actually be the opposite. Let me quote Saint Rosa of Lima one more time: "Apart from the cross, there is no other ladder by which we may get to Heaven." And isn't Heaven the final destination we should all be striving for on our journey from the seen to the unseen? Life-saving answers to our life-size questions come only from God. When God is absent, nothing is good!

There is probably no better way of summarizing and concluding this book than using the following listing of statements about who we are as Catholics:

- Our family has spanned the centuries... and the globe.
- With God's grace, we started hospitals to care for the sick.
- We establish orphanages, and help the poor.
- We are the largest charitable organization on the planet, bringing relief and comfort to those in need.
- We educate more children than any other scholarly or religious institution.
- We developed the scientific method.... and laws of evidence.
- We founded the college system.
- We defend the dignity of all human life, and uphold marriage and family.
- Cities were named after our revered saints, who navigated a sacred path before us. [...]
- We are...... the Catholic Church... with over one billion in our family sharing in the sacraments and fullness of Christian faith.

www.catholicscomehome.org

Suggestions for Further Reading

Bochenski, Joseph M., O.P. (1996), *The Road to Understanding.* Genesis Publishing.

Chesterton, G.K. (2012), *Orthodoxy.* Simon and Brown.

Donohue, William (2012), *Why Catholicism Matters.* Image.

Feser, Edward (2009), *Aquinas: A Beginner's Guide.* Oneworld Publications.

George, Francis Cardinal (2011), *God in Action.* Image.

Groeschel, Benedict (2009), *Tears of God.* Ignatius Press.

John Paul II (2002), *Restoring Faith in Reason.* SCM Press.

Kreeft, Peter (1999), *A Refutation of Moral Relativism.* Ignatius Press

Kreeft, Peter (2008), *Because God is Real.* Ignatius Press.

Kreeft, Peter and Ronald Tacelli SJ (2009), *Handbook of Catholic Apologetics. Reasoned Answers to Questions of Faith.* Ignatius Press.

Lewis, C.S (1952), *Mere Christianity.* Westwood.

Madrid, Patrick (2006), *A Pocket Guide to Catholic Apologetics.* Our Sunday Visitor

Madrid, Patrick (2010), *The Godless Delusion.* Our Sunday Visitor

Ratzinger, Joseph Cardinal (1995), *"In the Beginning."* Eerdmans Publishing Company.

Schönborn, Christoph Cardinal (2011), *Man, the Image of God.* Ignatius Press.

Schönborn, Christoph Cardinal (2007), *Chance or Purpose?* Ignatius Press.

Spitzer SJ, Robert (2010), *New Proofs for the Existence of God: Contributions of Contemporary Physics and Philosophy.* Eerdmans Publishing

Spitzer SJ, Robert (2011), *Ten Universal Principles.* Ignatius Press.

About the Author

Dr. Gerard M. Verschuuren writes on the interface of Faith and Reason in the Catholic Church. He is a human geneticist who also earned a doctorate in the philosophy of science.

He studied and worked at universities in Europe and the United States.

His most recent books are:

- *God and Evolution? – Science Meets Faith* (2012, Pauline Books and Media)

- *What Makes You Tick – A New Paradigm for Neuroscience* (2012, Solas Press)

- *Darwin's Philosophical Legacy – The Good and the Not-So-Good* (2012, Lexington Books).

He also gives talks and leads conferences on faith and reason, science and religion, creation and evolution – in the context of evangelization.

He can be contacted at www.where-do-we-come-from.com

Endorsements

"This lively and accessible work should awaken or reawaken many Catholics to the glories of their Church as a beacon of faith and reason. It's a real contribution to the New Evangelization."

Mary Ann Glendon
Professor of Law, Harvard University,
Former US Ambassador to the Holy See

"After a lifetime in the academy, I am convinced that the highest priority in the New Evangelization is intellectual evangelization, and specifically, apologetics – answering the major questions which so deeply concern our young people: Does God exist? Are we mere matter? Is there a conflict between the bible and science? Does evolution have to be rejected? What is happiness? Are we really free? How can suffering be reconciled with a loving God? This book does all of this in an incredibly accessible, engaging, and intelligent way – which paves the way into the mind and heart of the living God.

Fr. Robert Spitzer, S.J.
President of the *Magis Center of Reason and Faith*,
Former President Gonzaga University

I find this book concise, coherent, courageous, challenging, and very Catholic. It will offer food for thought and fuel for discussions."

Fr. Marcel Chappin, S.J.
Professor at the Theology Department
Pontifical Gregorian University in Rome

"If you constantly find yourself in conversation about the Catholic Faith with skeptics, doubters and seekers, this is the book for you. Dr. Verschuuren does not leave anything out. Every argument or question that anyone has ever heard about the relationships between faith and reason, and religion and science is addressed in this book. If you've ever questioned evolution or creationism; if you've ever wondered whether faith can be rational or whether morality can be rational; if you are a scientist, a philosopher, seeker of truth, this book is definitely for you! Read it, share it, discuss it, use it in small group sessions or for large seminars, as part of your catechism or RCIA, in your science or religion classroom or for your new evangelisation strategy. It is probably the most complete Catholic/Science apologetics book that has ever been written."

Deacon Pedro Guevara-Mann
Producer *Salt + Light* TV, Canada

"With a trained scientist's attention to detail and precision, Gerard Verschuuren answers with aplomb, clarity, and conviction a variety of scientific and philosophical questions about God, science, and Christianity. Taking into account the riches of Sacred Scripture, the wisdom of the Church Fathers and popes, and the perennial philosophy of St. Thomas Aquinas, this book provides an impressive array of lucid and compelling answers to many of today's most-asked Big Questions."

Patrick Madrid
Author and radio host (patrickmadrid.com)
Adjunct professor of Theology at Franciscan University of Steubenville

271